"Brilliant...I'm amazed there hasn't been a book like this until now."
Steven Bernstein ASC, BSC, Director of Photography, Monster

*"**ON THE SET** should be required reading for all film
production courses. It's a must-read for anyone truly
interested in the behind the scenes of movie making!"*
Los Angeles Film Teachers' Association

"A wonderfully practical guide to the real world of filmmaking."
Mick Garris, Director, The Stand and The Shining Miniseries

*"Salamoff blazes a well-marked trail on his anecdotal
journey through the Hollywood jungle...truly capturing
the town's unique tribal customs. Keep it close at hand."*
American Cinematographer Magazine

*"If you want to learn what it's really like on a movie set,
stop reading this quote and get on with the book."*
Stephen Susco, Screenwriter, The Grudge 1 & 2

*"Not since Machiavelli's **The Prince** has the social contract between
humans been so thoroughly examined."*
Jeff Goldsmith, The Q&A with Jeff Goldsmith

*"Thanks to Mr. Salamoff, I don't have to pretend
that I know what goes on, on-set anymore"*
Peter Schwerin, Producer, Scary Movie 1 & 2

*"Good things come in small packages. Gives you the complete scope
of movie-making. Everyone from fan to professional will enjoy this
wonderful book. I have two copies in my office!"*
Robert Holguin, President, The Saturn Awards

ON THE SET:

THE HIDDEN RULES OF MOVIE MAKING ETIQUETTE

3rd Edition

Paul J. Salamoff

T
TAVIN
PRESS

ON THE SET:
THE HIDDEN RULES OF MOVIE MAKING ETIQUETTE
Paul J. Salamoff

3rd Edition

Published in Los Angeles in 2012 by
TAVIN PRESS
2418 N. Keystone St.
Burbank, CA 91504

Original Edition
MOVIE SETS 101: THE DEFINITIVE SURVIVOR'S GUIDE
Published in Los Angeles in 2005

© TAVIN PRESS 2009, 2012

ISBN13 978-0-9772911-4-4

Library of Congress Control Number: 2012934837

This book was Designed and Produced by
TAVIN PRESS

Illustrations by
Bill Zahn & Jacob Hair

Edited by
Jeff Bond & Sharon Komola Secora

CONTENTS

<u>ACKNOWLEDGEMENTS</u>

Many people contributed their vast knowledge and wisdom to this book. I would like to personally thank the following:

Steven Berstein, ASC, BSC	Colin Matthews
Boylee	Eric Miller
Steve Demko	Karri O'Reilly
Pen Densham	Mary Beth Ramsey
Tony Gardner	Peter Schwerin
Chris Gore	Alex Simon
Vance Hartwell	Joel Whist
Scott Maginnis	Douglas White
Darryl Marko	David E. Williams

I also want to thank my incredible team of transcribers who, without their help, I would have never made my deadline:

Viviana Zarragoitia
Sharon Komola Secora
Thom Stitt
Jennifer Canepa Lackey
Lucy Webb

And finally my support group of family and friends:

Noel & Iris Clarke
Marla Dennis
Kailey Marsh
Juli Nunn & Richard Porter
Adam & Barbara Salamoff
Stephen Susco
Jeff Bond & Brooke Vimtrup
Bill Zahn

Mom and Dad

Melissa, Samantha & Ethan

INTRODUCTION

As I began working on this newly revised and expanded 3rd edition of ON THE SET one of the things that kept hitting me was that everyone had a fascinating story to tell about how they started working in the industry. If it were possible for a book like this to have a theme this one's would be *"Everyone has a story."*

So, considering that I have worked in the industry for over 22 years and have worn many hats in that time, it felt natural to share mine.

How exactly does a nobody from a small town in Massachusetts with absolutely zero industry contacts go from being a make-up FX artist to a Writer/Producer and eventually to an Executive?

It was quite simple...Well, not really.

When I was 5 years old my parents took my brother and I to see a double-feature of STAR WARS and LOGAN'S RUN at a drive-in and, as they recount, my eyes completely bugged from my head. I was hooked.

Fortunately my parents were very supportive of my interests and together we would watch "THE TWILIGHT ZONE", "THE OUTER LIMITS", "STAR TREK" and "SPACE: 1999". Though my all-time favorite was the BBC's "DOCTOR WHO", which I have been obsessed with my entire life.

I grew up in Natick, MA and when I was 13 years old my father took me to a horror convention in Boston. One of the guests was Make-Up FX Goremeister, Tom Savini. His name was synonymous with the blood and guts films of the 1980's. Famous for DAWN OF THE DEAD, FRIDAY THE 13TH PARTS 1 & 4 and CREEPSHOW among others.

Savini did a presentation in one of the main halls and brought a table full of his props and creations. It was just amazing. A moment in time etched into my brain.

This guy was paid to make monsters for a living!

MONSTERS!

I made up my mind right then and there that I would follow in his footsteps.

As you would expect, I first experimented with my new craft during Halloween making elaborate costumes. While in high school, I worked at a movie theater and a video store and both places allowed me to make displays and costumes for upcoming horror releases.

When looking at colleges there was no question that I wanted to attend a school in Los Angeles. I was lucky enough to get into my first choice, USC. I didn't immediately get into the Film School but that didn't stop me from filling out my schedule with as many film classes as they would allow.

One of the most frequent sayings in the industry is *"It's who you know."* Well that couldn't be truer and going to USC introduced me to a great number of fellow students who have gone on to greatness. That's why it's so important to treat everyone with respect and consideration. The person you treated nicely might be in a position to help you out one day and conversely, the person you treated poorly could be the one that keeps you from getting that dream job.

After working on a number of student films, I was introduced by one of the Directors to his friend Taylor White (of the website *CreatureFeatures.com*) who was working as the coordinator for Tony Gardner's Alterian Studios, one of the bigger make-up FX shops. Taylor got me an interview with Tony and I impressed him enough that he hired me as the shop runner.

When I was not out running errands, I got to work on the movies including THE ADDAMS FAMILY, The "SWAMP THING" TV series and MOM & DAD SAVE THE WORLD. I never imagined that I would get to work on movies at such a young age (I was only 19 at the time). I decided to jump in headfirst and worked in FX pretty much solid for 14 years, working at over 25 different FX shops, on over 40 Films and 10 TV series, not to mention more commercials than I can remember.

I never thought I would be fortunate enough to work on so many great projects so early in my career. I decided that even though I enjoyed doing FX, I wanted to look for other avenues to explore in the industry.

I loved writing and set my sights on becoming a Screenwriter. I taught myself the craft while I was still early in my FX career and just kept writing, getting better and more confident at it with each script I wrote. My first 3 scripts were crap, but I kept on working at it until people started to take notice of my abilities.

Because of the connections I made at school and on the job, I was able to get my scripts read and eventually produced. With these produced credits as well as a collection of unproduced spec scripts, I was more desirable to Literary Managers and Agents. Keep in mind, a lot of the *"industry game"* is about perception. If you are perceived to be an up-and-comer then people are going to want to hitch their wagon to you.

I got my Manager first, and with his guidance, I was able to secure more jobs as well as get my first Agent and Entertainment Lawyer. Mind you this took some time, but I now had a team behind me.

Because of the organizational skills I learned working in special FX, I realized I had abilities as a Producer and I started getting asked to produce short films and videos for people I had worked for in the past. As I filled out my resume even more, I then started producing DVD special feature content and soon feature films.

Then out of left field, my friend Garrick Dion, who was working as a Development Executive for David Lancaster Productions, called me up and said they were looking for a new V.P. of Production to take over from the one who was leaving. The thought of being an executive had never crossed my mind. Furthermore I had zero experience. Garrick was extremely persuasive and told me that my years working on set and my organizational skills made me a perfect candidate. So I met with David Lancaster and we hit it off. The next thing you know I was an Executive working on such films as Wes Craven's THE BREED and HOLLOW MAN 2.

As luck would have it, less than a year into that gig, Lancaster got tapped to become the new Co-President of BOLD Films and he brought Garrick and I into the deal. So now we were BOLD's Director of Development and V.P. of Production respectively.

My first responsibility was to finish delivering four of their films. Up till that point I was completely unaware of what delivering a movie entailed, but I threw myself into it and soon became an expert at it.

I stayed at BOLD for a while working on the Golden Globe nominated BOBBY and MIDDLE OF NOWHERE, but left after STARSHIP TROOPERS: MARAUDER in order to refocus my efforts on writing because that is where my heart was.

I got a new Agent and hit the ground running. To supplement my income, I would work as a Producer overseeing trailers and marketing videos for upcoming video games at gNET Media. I was also being wooed by another production company called Rat Bastard Productions. After holding them at bay for a few months, I decided to join them as their President of Production when they made me an offer I couldn't refuse.

Always looking for new avenues to explore, I then fell into writing comic books and graphic novels as well as short stories, novels and non-fiction books.

After almost a quarter century, I'm still going strong with no plans of stopping. I've learned a lot over the years especially from working on this book. Like I said, everyone has a story and boy there are some captivating ones within these pages. I hope you read each and every one of them and learn from them as much as I did and still do.

I'll see you ON THE SET!

Paul J. Salamoff
September 2012

MOVIE SETS:
A BRIEF OVERVIEW

There is nothing in the world that can prepare you for what it is actually like on the set of a motion picture. The experience is truly like something out of a movie itself.

If you think I'm joking, just consider the fact that an average film costs in excess of $80 million dollars, with many upwards of $200 million. Studios spend a great deal of time and effort into making sure that they see a return on their investment, sometimes even matching the budget of the movie with an equally expensive marketing campaign. Not only are jobs at stake but also the studios themselves.

This fear of public and financial failure trickles down all the way to the set where the films are being shot. Studios watch over Executives, Executives watch over Producers, Producers watch over Directors, and on and on down the chain.

Now this isn't to say that working on a set can't be a fun and rewarding experience, it's just important to be prepared for the type of environment it is. Even down to the most miniscule student film, you have to remember that somebody's dime and/or reputation is on the line.

A good movie set becomes like an extended family where people work together for the well being of the group and a common good (i.e. completing the film on time and on budget). There will be squabbles and disagreements, but the end result is people pulling together.

On the other hand, a bad movie set can become a war of attrition where people are constantly fighting and working against each other, which culminates in an overall feeling of oppression and dissatisfaction.

Let's face facts. Movie sets are primarily made up of artists, and most artists are known for their egos and stubbornness. Learning how to deal with people and be easy to deal with yourself is just as important as doing your job competently.

Be Prepared!

Now, that being said, lets begin at the beginning. It all starts with the written word: The screenplay. A studio or production company decides, for better or for worse, that it has faith in a story and would like to develop, produce, and then distribute it in the theaters.

They will next attach Producers and a Director to oversee the project. During pre-production the script is turned into a workable shooting script and a budget and schedule are figured out for the film. Key personnel are then hired to head the different departments, locations are scouted and casting begins. Also during this period, which could take from two months to a year (or even longer), a Production Designer creates the look and feel of the film. Stages are rented and the construction of the sets is put in motion.

Once this process is complete, production can begin. Unfortunately these days, pre-production time is usually shorter rather than longer and as they say, *"If you fail to plan, then you plan to fail."* The less prepared a production is, the more that the unforeseen problems (like inclement weather) will wreak havoc on the schedule. It is possible for productions to spiral out of control. In the worst cases, a completion bond company will take over the film and finish it with regard only for the money, not the creative expression.

An average film can be shot in six to ten weeks, but movies requiring a lot of stunts, special effects, or exotic locales can take considerably longer. Some films are years in the making.

A shooting day can average between ten to twelve hours long. Believe me, some days can be even longer. Most productions like to keep their days at a comfortable length to avoid forced calls (which equate to more money), otherwise they have to start at a later time the next day. By the end of the week they might have to come in too late to adequately shoot exterior shots. Also, most productions shoot a five-day week, but if they're behind as the end of the schedule nears, they can shoot six and seven days a week if necessary.

During the actual shooting, most productions have a first unit team which consists of all the major key personnel and lead Actors as well as a second unit team which is usually more condensed and shoots the footage that first unit was unable to get or that doesn't require the main Actors and typically doesn't require a lot of creative decisions. The Second Unit Director is usually a Producer, Director of Photography or Stunt Coordinator. Though with that said, bigger budget films can have quite large second units that are more complimentary to the first unit and utilize principal performers. It is not uncommon to have more than two units going at the same time, especially these days with shorter production times and grander subjects.

After first unit wraps, the second unit usually continues to shoot or a new reduced unit will finish. This reduced unit may or may not involve the film's original Director, and is a mix of both first and second units. When they are done, production is wrapped...but not necessarily over.

As post-production begins, editing is usually already underway. As the raw elements come together, holes in the film may appear where needed footage doesn't exist, or the existing footage just doesn't cut it. At this point, production will start up again for reshoots and pickups. This can happen almost immediately or even a month before the film is scheduled to come out in theaters. Trust me, this happens more times than you would believe, especially with test screenings becoming so important.

During post-production, the film is edited and the real bulk of the visual and sound effects begin. These days, the typical way of gauging a film's potential is by test screening it. They hire an outside company to recruit members of the general public (people who work in the industry are barred from these screenings) and show them a rough cut of the film. The audience fills out cards that rate different elements of the movie. The tallied information gives the studio a sense of what the reaction is...in theory. Trust me, this is a shoddy process at best and many decent films have been butchered because of this method, but *"that's the way the cookie crumbles."*

Once the film is locked, which means that the studio, Producers and Director are satisfied with the version of the film, the final sound mix is completed. A Music Composer writes and records the score for the film and songs are added if necessary.

Once all the elements are completed, an answer print will be struck. This is the first print of the film received from the laboratory that has been color and light corrected with the soundtrack synchronized to the image.

However, these days with the advent of digital projection, a major motion picture will rely heavily on digital cinema. For this, a DCP (Digital Camera Package) is created. The DCP, in essence, is the new "release print." Essentially it is a digital file contained on a portable hard drive. Specialized projectors at the theaters download the DCP and then project the image digitally. The end result is a higher quality image and a less expensive means of distribution. It is also more secure than a film print because the DCP is encrypted and can only play on the projector it is assigned to for a specifically set period of time.

At this point, release prints and/or DCP's can be made. Now I say "can", because *it ain't over till the fat lady sings.*" Like I said before, eleventh-hour changes have been made at this point. If a studio is nervous about a movie, it would rather tinker with it until the last minute than take the risk of releasing a potential bomb.

Once the studio has signed off and all the "t's" have been crossed and the "i's" have been dotted, the release prints and/or DCP's will be manufactured and shipped to a theater near you.

So there you have it folks, from conception to birth. The film's future now rests in the hands of the fickle general public. A real bomb may not even last a week in the theaters while a real winner will not only turn a profit but also leave a lasting impression for generations to come.

Movies can be magic and what goes on behind the scenes can be just as fascinating as what rolls on the screen. If you are or want to be a part of the madness, remember that celluloid is forever and as you toil the long hard days on set, don't lose the love or enthusiasm that got you there in the first place.

CHAPTER ONE

"Who asked for the Martini?"

THE
PRODUCTION
DEPARTMENT

A BRIEF OVERVIEW

The Production Department is the core of a movie set. Without these individuals, chaos would surely ensue. Obviously, the Director is the key element of a set, the proverbial *"Captain of the ship,"* and it is his/her vision that drives the entire production. Everyone is supposedly on set to support this ideal and see it to fruition.

The vision begins with the screenplay, which is the blueprint for the movie. The Screenwriter has spent time crafting a story on paper that must now be translated on film. Sometimes things that look good when written don't translate well visually. A good Director will recognize these problems and endeavor to work with the Writer to fix them before shooting begins. But, as with many films (especially these days), they are rewritten on the set or sometimes even in post-production.

If the Director is captain, then the Studio is the *"Commander-in-Chief"* and the Producers are the *"Generals."* These entities are in charge of the monetary aspects of a production. Not only do they provide the boatloads of cash necessary to make a film, but they control it to make sure that it is spent properly.

It's typically the Producer's head on the chopping block if the movie goes too far over time or over budget. Needless to say, the job is quite stressful and most Producers are not known for their people skills.

Assisting the Director on the set is a staff of individuals whose responsibility it is to make sure that the schedule is adhered to and that everyone is where they are supposed to be at all times. They are called A.D.'s and what they do is quite a daunting task. The chain of command is very important. Each A.D. has a specific job ranging from completely overseeing the set to running around and doing odd jobs.

What usually ensues is controlled chaos, though a skilled staff is prepared for all types of curveballs and will always deliver a finished film.

THE PLAYERS

Director: Translates the written screenplay visually by guiding the Actors and crew. The Captain of the ship.

Screenwriter: Author of the screenplay.

Executive Producer: Individual who adds their influence and business skills to helping the movie get cast, financed and produced but does not usually take the daily responsibility.

Producer: Helps to turn the screenplay into a shootable script. Assembles the creative team to bring the story to the screen.

Line Producer: Deals with the day-to-day production of the film and is responsible for making sure the movie is completed on time and on budget.

Unit Production Manager (UPM): Oversees the hiring of the crew, the rental of equipment and its return at the end of production. Also helps to determine the budget of the film and that the production adheres to it.

1st Assistant Director (1st A.D.): Responsible for all activity on a movie set. It is their job to ensure that everything stays on schedule and on budget.

2nd Assistant Director (2nd A.D.): In charge of all the Actors on a set. Makes the call sheet and makes sure that script revisions get to the appropriate people.

2nd 2nd Assistant Director (2nd 2nd A.D.): a.k.a. 3rd A.D. Makes sure the cast is where they are supposed to be. Schedules pick-ups and drop-offs and tracks the crew's in and out times.

Production Assistant (P.A.): Carries out any and all tasks instructed by the A.D.'s. The set *"Gopher."*

Script Supervisor: Meticulously oversees continuity as well as details script and dialogue changes during filming.

TERMS YOU SHOULD KNOW

Abby Singer

Term used to identify the next-to-last shot of the day. It is derived from stories about the Director Abby Singer, who was notorious for claiming a shot was the last of the day and then doing another.

"Action"

Called by the Director or the 1st A.D. after the cameras are rolling to indicate to the Actors that the scene should begin.

call sheet

Single two-sided document that contains all the necessary information about that particular shooting day.

"Camera reloads"

Signals that it is necessary to change out the film canister on the camera with a new magazine or, in digital filmmaking, to load another data storage unit.

circled takes

The Script Supervisor keeps track of particular "takes" that the Director likes by circling the take number on the camera report. The lab will then know what footage to develop and what to discard.

continuity

Copious notes kept in order to ensure that the shots blend together seamlessly.

coverage

The various other camera angles that the Director might use to help stylize the finished scene when it's edited.

cover set

An alternative shooting location to keep the movie on budget and not falling behind schedule when the planned location is unusable. Film productions generally shoot all their exteriors first and use the interior scenes as cover in case of bad weather.

crew call

The time when the crew must arrive on set ready to work. Found on the daily call sheet.

"Cut"

Called by the Director or the 1st A.D. when the take has concluded. It signals the Camera Operator to stop rolling film.

dailies

a.k.a. rushes. Unedited footage from prior days shown to the Director to ensure that it is usable. Usually screened with the Director and key crew members at lunch or after the following shoot day.

martini shot

Term used for the last shot of the day. It is derived from the practice of having martinis at the wrap of the day.

"On a bell" / "Lock it up"

Yelled by the A.D. to alert the crew that a filmed scene is about to commence and that the stage is closed.

"Rolling"

Lets the crew know that the camera has been activated and film or digital media is being exposed.

Second Unit

A second, smaller film crew that frequently is used to capture stunt sequences, chases etc. often using Stunt Doubles of the main Actors. Second unit has a separate Director, A.D., etc.. and this shooting often happens parallel to the main shoot, thus keeping the pace of production economical.

take

Term used to describe the time between when the camera begins rolling and when the Director yells "Cut."

wigwag

Electrical device that has a bell and a red light. When the red light is on and the bell rings once, it signifies that filming is in progress and access to the set is prohibited.

THE RULES OF SETIQUETTE

• When the wigwag (red light) is on, never enter the set. A scene is in progress.

• One sound of the warning bell means that the camera is rolling. Two chimes means that the shot is over and it is safe to enter the set.

• Turn off your walkie and/or cell phone (or set it to vibrate only) before the camera starts rolling.

• Never offer suggestions about how the film should be made unless you are asked. There are some Directors who do solicit the crew for suggestions from time to time (especially on comedies), but there is a reason why the Director is the Director. Respect that.

• Until they yell *"Cut"* don't start talking or moving about, even if you think the shot is over. Some Directors keep the camera rolling in hopes of getting a magic moment. The last thing they need is for it to be unusable because you decided they were done.

• Guests are not allowed on set unless they are given permission by the Producers. Movies have become increasingly top secret for reasons of marketing and promotion. The last thing a studio needs is their secret ending revealed on the Internet by an unauthorized visitor before they even finish shooting.

• Try not to pester the A.D. staff with unnecessary questions. Almost all the information you need for the day can be found on the call sheet.

• Respect the A.D. chain of command. Know precisely what each person deals with so you don't bother the 1st A.D. with something a P.A. should handle.

• If you are a key personnel member, always alert an A.D. if you are stepping off set. It's their job to know where you are and it can cause delays if you can't be found.

ADVICE FROM THE EXPERTS

Bryan Singer
Director / Producer
(JACK THE GIANT KILLER, VALKYRIE, THE USUAL SUSPECTS)

REALLY Super 8

When I was about 11 years old, a friend took me out to take pictures with a 35mm SLR camera and the whole idea of taking photographs, doing time exposures and really being able to play with film really intrigued me. So I convinced my parents to buy me a 35mm camera, Pentax K-1000 and I took a lot of pictures with it. I never did my own developing, but eventually I got a darkroom and did my own printing. I really enjoyed it and used my dark room quite heavily.

When I was about 13, I was visiting a friend in Atlanta and we made a little movie called THE STAR TREK MURDERS using his wind-up 8mm camera. When we got back to my home in New Jersey, I borrowed a friend's 8mm camera to make some more films primarily war and horror. Eventually, I graduated to working with super 8.

Everything changed when I saw the movie E.T. I was very moved by it. The TV news show 20/20 did a profile on Steven Spielberg's life and I recognized the fact that he was this Jewish, nerdy kid with a drawer full of 8mm movies, much like myself and I thought, *"Wow, I would like to do that for a living. I'd like to be that person and one day, make something as incredible and moving as E.T."* So that night I decided from that moment on I would be a filmmaker...or at least try to be.

Into The Lion's Den

I went to the School of Visual Arts in New York City and studied film there, which was mostly vocational training. I then took a semester off to earn money and later transferred to USC. Ultimately I was accepted into USC's Critical Studies program where I studied film criticism and theory. Because I had already made a lot of films and had vocational training, in my senior year I set out to make a 16mm film. One of the kids from my neighborhood that I had made 8mm films with was Ethan Hawke. At this point in his career he had finished shooting DEAD POETS SOCIETY and was in LA making a movie called DAD with Ted Danson, Jack Lemmon and Kevin Spacey.

While Ethan was doing that movie, we went out to dinner and discussed making a 16mm film about our lives. So I quickly wrote a script about five friends who meet in a diner after their first semester out of high school and realize that they've grown apart. Ethan played one of the roles and he got Dylan Kussman, who was also in DEAD POETS SOCIETY, as well as a few other Actors including myself (I'm quite terrible) and we made this DINER-like film, called LION'S DEN.

After it was made, the goal was to get it seen by as many people as possible. I solicited two other filmmakers of short films to partner with for a screening at the DGA. We rented the facility and took out an ad in Variety and the Hollywood Reporter then sent out 2,000 invitations using the Hollywood Creative Directory to create our invitation list. I knew Sam Raimi's brother Ted and asked him to see if Sam would be up for hosting the screening. Luckily Sam agreed provided that we made the event in conjunction with a charity. I happily chose the Sierra Club, which is my mom's favorite charity. So Sam hosted the sold-out event and it was a wonderful evening for everyone involved.

The Gray Zone

I've always believed that a film is written three times. Once on the page, a second time on the set and the third time in the cutting room. And these are three separate rewrites, meaning that when you're on the set, you'll discover that things aren't exactly how you saw them in your head: The actors aren't what you thought, the set's a bit different, you don't have the equipment that you thought you would have, etc. So when you're filming the movie, you have to make the best of what the script's intention was. In the cutting room, when faced with all the footage, you then craft a movie that is inspired by the script, but may not exactly be the script. You should never be anchored by anything. You should always be flexible. A big thing I do is have a solid idea of what 50% of the movie should look like and keep the other 50% gray in my mind for what I'm going to discover along the way.

I'm More Flexible Than I Look

Whenever problems arise, I put myself in the position of the other person. *What does the other person really want? Where's the other person coming from?* Being flexible if very important because if there's an obstacle or a note (particularly if somebody is willing to pay for it), you can't just hyper-react. You need to say to yourself, *"Okay, let me find out the essence of what they want and figure out a way to make it work for the movie."*

During X2: X-MEN UNITED, Tom Roth, the Chairman of FOX, had an issue with the end of the movie (which at the time was a stand-off with the President in the White House). Tom said, *"You know, by the time this movie comes out, the United States is going to be in war in Iraq, and I just think there needs to be something uplifting at the end and here's my thoughts."*

He pitched an idea that I did not totally respond to. But instead of saying, *"Screw it!"* I said, *"Okay, maybe not the scene you pitched, but how about this scene."* And I pitched him what ultimately became the film's ending. Tom was perfectly happy because I covered the beats that he was concerned about and I got something out of it too - I got to show that Xavier's school was back up and running (which I didn't have before) and it became one of my favorite moments in the movie.

"Sadly, there is the division between the set world and the development world, which is rather unfortunate because everybody should be working together."

Sig Libowitz, Production Executive

Wes Craven
Director / Producer / Screenwriter
(RED EYE, SCREAM QUADRILOGY, A NIGHTMARE ON ELM ST.)

You've Entered Another Dimension...

To make a good movie, I need to be able to see it in my head and to get it through the camera. It sounds simplistic, but at times it's difficult to stay focused on that concept, especially when there is so much going on around you. Everybody else on the set is interested in their little area of concern and it's easy to get swept up in all those different aspects.

The Old Man And The Sea

The first thing I do when I arrive on the set is pass out the day's shot-list to all the department heads. This way they can literally see where we are in the course of the day and can plan ahead. It also lets them know that the *"old man"* knows what he's doing by instilling a sense that the Captain is at the wheel and that things will be okay. I've had so many crew members come up to me and tell me that I wouldn't believe how many Directors come on set without knowing what they're going to shoot that day. That's astonishing to me.

Mother May I?

The Script Supervisor is your mother figure, your unofficial helper. They are typically a personal and sympathetic person on the set that sits next to you and watches over you in a maternal way. Because they write everything down, they tend to know what you're doing and because they are not perceived as a power figure it allows you the opportunity to cultivate that relationship.

On Being A Director

Your creativity and all of your smarts are never quite in play as they are when you are on a set directing. It's like being given a wonderful ship to pilot with the best crew in the world. If you have a really good script, you are well prepared and you know what you're doing, nothing I can conceive of can compare. It is such a unique position that literally when you are back in the real world, you have to make a major adjustment.

The Director's Diet

One thing that most people don't realize is that directing a movie is incredibly physically demanding. Most of the time you are working on little sleep (a good night for me is about 4 hours). Spread that out over 50 to 60 shooting days combined with the enormous amount of pressure and stress, you're under and it can really take its toll. I literally go into training before I step on a set. I watch what I eat and what I drink and I try to lay off the craft service table as much as possible.

"As a Producer, it's not necessary to create problems just so you can solve them."

Gale Anne Hurd, Producer

Ron Underwood
Director
(MIGHTY JOE YOUNG, CITY SLICKERS, TREMORS)

On Being A Director

It's important to be a leader that people can follow and to, at the very least, give a sense of knowing what you want. You don't have to bluff your way through not knowing things, but everyone on the set is looking to you for guidance and they need to feel like there is some sort of structure to the madness. If you are unable to be decisive or assertive of what you are going for, it can lead to mass chaos. I can't say that I always know what I want, but you have to allow a process of discovery and exploration to be within the bounds of moving toward a specific goal as opposed to being all over the place.

A "Short" Story

I wanted to make films throughout my life. At age 10, I got a hold of my grandfather's 8mm camera and started making films about the neighborhood kids coming over. We would do stunts and blow up things. We did whatever we could do to entertain ourselves and make a cool movie. I then made some films that I entered into the Kodak Film Festival. I won some awards but never really thought about doing it as a career until I was in college. At that point film had become so important to me in terms of watching movies and understanding the world more through movies than real life. In college I also started seeing movies that I had never seen before: Older films, like CITIZEN KANE, opened my eyes to why these films are so important. I then decided to transfer to the USC film school, and that's where I finished my education. When I was there, I made a short student film about these hang gliding guys who jumped off of cliffs. It turned out to be the first film made on this subject and Paramount bought it and released it. It wound up doing pretty good. It also introduced me to this whole market of short films (that no longer exists) and after I finished with school I dove into making these shorts full time.

The Dewy-Decimal Education

I soon became interested in getting into features and worked in those doing production kind of stuff such as being a P.A. or Location Manager, but it wasn't satisfying because I was yearning to make my own films. I then went to work for a company who made educational films and got to make lots of films over a period of years. It afforded me the opportunity and freedom to try new things because nobody was really paying attention. In retrospect, it was really good experience and training because of the ability to experiment with technique and story telling. At that point, I knew I wanted to get into dramatic film so I started making these films that focused more on story and characters. For instance, I had to make a film about the reference section in the library. So I did a film about a little boy who gets locked into the reference section and the books come alive and bully him into learning about what we needed to show. These kinds of films really taught me a lot about what was entertainment, because they were really such dry subjects and you had to find something to make them palatable and entertain people along the way.

I, Robot

One of my other assignments was to create a story about writing a term paper. One of the guys I was working with was Steve Wilson (a.k.a. S.S. Wilson). We came up with the idea of this teenage girl who doesn't want to write her term paper, so she tries to trick her robot to write it for her. The robot proves to be smarter and in turn tricks the girl into writing it herself. Steve wrote the script and also did the animation of the robot. Steve realized how wonderful the idea of the robot was and thought that it might make a great character for a feature. So, we started working on the script and developing it. Ultimately it became the script SHORT CIRCUIT. You never know what's going to lead to what.

Right Under My Feet

I was originally going to direct SHORT CIRCUIT, but it became a very hot script and it was obvious that my involvement in it was only hurting the project, so we sold that and Steve, Brent Maddox and I started brainstorming on what could be done on a low-budget that a first-time filmmaker would be able to get off the ground. We started going through ideas and we remembered this idea that Steve had. He had got the idea while sitting on a rock in the desert just wondering what would happen if there was a monster and he couldn't get off the rock. If you haven't guessed by now, that idea was TREMORS. It seemed like a great vehicle because it was a monster movie, which would be possible for a first-time Director to handle, and also the monster wasn't seen a lot, because it was underground. It made it a lot less expensive.

We started working on a treatment but when we pitched it, we were faced with these open-mouthed stares like we were absolutely nuts talking about underground 30-foot worms. Nobody really got it, so it became a lengthy process to get TREMORS off the ground. Once they did get the screenplay together, it came together very quickly. Within hours Universal green-lit it. Our Agent felt like we really needed somebody with credibility to back us and make it work and recommended Gale Anne Hurd. She was a perfect choice. Once we got into production it was very different than what I thought it would be like. Having been on films before, I thought there would be a lot more time and more of everything, but it seemed very similar to those few thousand dollar movies I used to do. The process is the same but so are the problems. You are always thrown when they hit, so the more experience you get, the more prepared you'll be when the problems arise. Just always remember, anything can happen.

Daddy's Girl

I got my daughter a job as a P.A. on MIGHTY JOE YOUNG. It was the first time she ever worked on a film set. Thinking that she should look professional on her first day, she came to the set wearing high heels and dressy shorts. Needless to say, the crew had a field day with this and they all called her *"Princess"* all day long. She also had to deal with the fact that she was running around for hours in the most impractical footwear. She came home in tears and I did my best to console her. The next day she was in jeans and tennis shoes and eventually she gained their respect, but that came with time and some hard work on her part.

"When you're interviewing your department heads, the goal is to find people not just for this movie, but people you're going to be possibly working with for the rest of your life."

Bryan Singer, Director/Producer

Pen Densham
Producer / Screenwriter / Director
(CO-CHAIRMAN, TRILOGY ENTERTAINMENT GROUP)

General Pen Densham

A wise Producer is somebody who pulls all of the constructive elements together of a film so they work cohesively. Films are always a large, mechanical warfare item. There's an enormous army of people being used to pull together a single image and so the coordination of these things is really important. Making a film is solving a million problems and each movie is a process of elements that have never been put together before.

It's an experiment in creativity - you have a script, you have the Actors, you have the technical crew and none of these people have ever done this particular movie before, but they're all professionals and the key is to give them the inspiration to solve the problems so the movie can get accomplished. It's always amazing how many things do get accomplished despite weather issues or temperament or just the logistics of things not working when you expect them to.

A Cast Of Thousands

One of the things that I've always said about producing is it's not just finding a cast for your movie, but it's also casting your crew. This means that you should understand exactly what they do, because you are really looking for people that will collaborate at the level of your budget and not go over budget. You're looking for people who are going to bring strength to your Director and make him or her a strong advocate and ally. You need problem solvers.

Oh, Canada...

Ever since I was a small child, my parents made short films and sold them to the movie theaters in England. I actually saw my own folks producing and directing movies. So I knew it was possible to follow in their footsteps. When I left school and started trying to make movies, I ended up in Canada, where making films was putting pieces of the problem together; getting a piece of money here, borrowing a piece of equipment there, getting a lab to give you credit here, until you put the movie together. And I did all that business side of it so that I could try and put my dreams on a screen not realizing that what I was actually doing was producing. To me it was just everything that was necessary to do to in order to get a movie made.

The Advocate

I advocate Writers and Directors trying to produce their own material because it gives you more control of how the money is spent and it brings you closer to trying to see your own vision facilitated. When you allow someone else to take total control of the way the funding is spent, there is a chance (and it's not always negative) that you might be asked to do things that aren't the way you anticipated. My mentor was Norman Jewison and he produced as a Director. He always knew how he was spending his money, where he was allocating his time and resources, and he was able to make movies that won Oscars with major film stars in them. He never lost the ability to have the bigger vision of making sure that a film was put together in a way that he, as a Director, wanted to shoot it on the set.

And For My Next Trick...

I did a film for TNT called HOUDINI and one of the things that they had asked me to do was to spend a very small amount of money in relationship to the cost of a film. It was somewhere around $8,000,000 dollars, and I was making a nearly 95-minute period drama filled with stunts and crowd scenes. So what I did was I hired a Line Producer who had never spent more than $4,000,000 dollars on a movie. I was sure that that person was used to problem solving at that kind of budget level. I was scared of hiring somebody who was used to making movies in the $20-30 million dollars because those film solutions wouldn't apply to the kinds of goals and problems that we were facing in trying to make a period movie at that scale for that kind of money. That particular experience paid off immensely and made it possible to shoot a very large-looking film at a very economical budget in a short period of time.

"The first time I was on a movie set I faked my way through it. I acted as though I knew what I was doing and it all seemed to work out."

James Gunn, Screenwriter

Dustin Lance Black
Academy Award™ Winning Screenwriter / Producer
("8", J. EDGAR, MILK, "BIG LOVE")

Sometimes I Have To Go Number 2

I started as a Writer in television and as a Writer in television, you're running the show and you're hiring the Directors, casting the episodes, working with the Art Department and the Camera Department. The Actors are coming to you for questions because you, unlike the Directors, have the insight into their character's true motivations and where this story is ultimately going.

It's a very different culture than when I made the transition into features, where the Director rules. Often times, the Writer isn't asked to participate or even invited to be on set. But in my experience most Directors liked having me participating, especially when it was a true-life story. There's a lot of texture that sometimes doesn't make it onto the page that is useful information. So in that way, there's a way to collaborate with your Director that ultimately helps the film.

Now that said, you kind of have to accept the fact that you're the #2 guy on a feature set, and it's more about suggesting than demanding. That's the difference between being a Writer on a TV set, where you are sort of the dictator, and on a feature set, where you're supposed to be there to sort of aid in the Director's vision of the work that you brought to him.

The Best Job In The World

Being a Writer is one of the few jobs where you get to spend all day mentally masturbating in coffee shops. That aside, it's also one of the few ways into the film business that has no overhead because as luck would have it most people don't actually read ink and paper scripts anymore.

The real value of your work is what's coming out of your mind and your heart and when I first got out of UCLA Film School, that's all I had. I didn't have any money, and pretty much no one is going to throw money at a young, recently graduated film student to go make your dream projects, nor should they, because you probably need a little schooling in the real world first.

Writing became the thing that I could do while still being true to my creative spirit. I never thought I was going to be a Writer, for me it was just a way in but it soon developed into this career. Initially I was writing spec scripts, then one of those turned into a TV movie, and the TV movie turned into a role as a Writer on "BIG LOVE." At that point, I'd fallen in love with writing and then three seasons in, I found myself as a Co-Producer. The rest is history.

The Truth Is Out There

I am a huge fan of doing true stories partly because you get studios that will finance research trips. I get sent on these adventures to meet my heroes as well as the great villains of history and to hear their stories. I get to meet and interact with people and things that have fascinated me for so long. I literally get paid to touch history.

I believe there's potency to a true story especially if you find a piece of history that is talking about today even though it occurred 30, 50, 100 or 3,000 years ago. That's what fascinates me about biopics. There is a tangible power to lessons learned from the past. Whenever I come across one of those, like MILK or J. EDGAR or like my next two projects: THE BAREFOOT BANDIT and UNDER THE BANNER OF HEAVEN, and I can honestly answer the question *"This story from the past needs to be told now because of..."* then I think it's a true story worth telling.

MILK Does The Body Good

The whole experience of making MILK felt like a fairytale. When we made the movie we didn't even think we'd get good distribution, much less all of the Oscar love. I certainly never thought I would be up there and have that opportunity. I mean, when I was writing the film, trying to get it put together, my big fear was that there was this competing project, that's all I was focused on - making sure mine got done first and best.

So that moment when you actually win an Oscar is unbelievable and there's just a lot of shock when you hear your name. Thankfully, Sean Penn had prepped me for that. He described for me what it feels like to hear your name. You want to pass out, but you can't, because the whole world is watching and so you just get up there and try not to screw it up and remember everyone's names.

The Suit Makes The Man

I've had the opportunity to work very closely with wonderful Costumers on my films. They are collaborators with the Actors to help build character and tell a story through what they're wearing. Oftentimes, it's in those fittings that I get to interact with the

Costumer and the Actor and we start talking about character. We discuss who this person is and who this person was. Ultimately a lot of really good factual and emotional information comes out of that process.

What people wear is so telling of who they are and what their character is like. When Sean Penn first put on his second-hand suit to portray Harvey Milk, Costumer Danny Glicker and I talked a lot with him about what the suit looked like, what kind it was, where he got it from and how old it was down to the holes in the bottom of the shoes. When he walked out onto the set that day several of Harvey's real friends were there and were amazed because he was so authentic. I know that's Sean and his abilities, but I also feel it's something about slipping on the exact right pair of shoes because when you get it right, it's transformative.

"Don't assume that if you approach someone wearing a headset that they are listening to you. Sometimes you might think they are listening when in fact they are speaking to someone else on their walkie."

Rachel Flackett, Production Assistant

Philip Segal
Writer / Producer
(PRESIDENT, ORIGINAL PRODUCTIONS)

The "Keys" To Success
The best advice is to really get to know the department keys on a film set. Really know who's working on that set and have them not only learn to respect you, but to appreciate why you're there and what

you're there to do. I always found that my sets are happier and we get a lot more accomplished when everyone feels like they're part of the team. It doesn't matter whether you are craft service or the D.P. or anything in between, I treat everybody the same. Respect everybody and then everybody creates a happier environment and, for me, it has always generated more positive results.

From Page To Screen

My mother introduced me to reading at a very early age. She was, and still is, a voracious reader. So I, at an early age, began reading the classics. She gave me PAPILLON to read, so when I discovered that it had been turned into a motion picture, I had to see it. The experience of seeing this narrative form turned into this visual experience gave me this incredible passion to want to tell stories. I just love to tell stories to the broadest audience I can find, so it just all came together for me at a very early age. Telling stories is all I've ever really wanted to do and producing is the greatest form of being able to do that.

The Outsider

I didn't have any friends or relatives in the business, so I was an outsider. I didn't know what or how I was going to break into this business, but I was so sort of enamored with the studios. This was the early 80's, so it was still relatively a docile place in terms of getting on to these lots and they didn't have the kind of problems and security issues they have today, so in other words, it was a lot easier to sneak onto a studio lot.

And that's what I did. I climbed over the fence of FOX and found myself standing in the parking place of a Casting Director by the name of Mike Fenton. He cast most of the major movies like THE GODFATHER, E.T., and RAIDERS OF THE LOST ARK. I was standing in his space when he pulled in and he asked if he could help me, basically he was saying, *"Get out of my parking space."* I said, *"I need a job."* He said, *"Well, I don't really have a job, but if you come in and talk to my assistant, we do take interns."* And that day, she hired me as an intern. To cut a long story short, his Assistant became pregnant, and when she left, he hired me as his Assistant and that's how I broke into the business.

The Producers

The best Producers know their craft inside and out. The ones who are on because they had money or knew someone or controlled a piece of material, I really don't consider Producers at all. The ones who really have gotten their hands dirty and understand their craft and have actually gone out and physically made something are the ones that I really have a lot of respect for.

So I realized that I would have to learn every craft in order to be a good Producer, whether it was casting, physical production or post-production. I made it my goal to expand my knowledge base and to gather information from all facets of the business. So that's what I did as my career sort of tumbled forward. I've worked for studios and I've worked for networks and found myself stepping into different positions to where I was able to build up my resume and really get some great job opportunities.

The Reality Of Reality

The difference between reality and scripted television is nuanced by the kind of production that you are involved in. Some reality shows are heavily scripted while others are sort of tossing pebbles in a pond to watch what happens. The fundamental divergence between reality television and scripted television is that sense of *"in the moment"*, stolen images, as it were. It's that triumph of instantly examining something through a lens and voyeuristically experiencing it. I find that's the lens of reality TV. Narrative television still is, and will always be compelling characters in great storytelling.

"Most departments on a movie set have the tendency to think that what they're doing is the only important thing. But after working in many different departments, I have come to realize that the ultimate vision comes from the Director."

Patrick Tatopoulos, Production Designer

David Grossman
Executive Producer / Director
("DESPERATE HOUSEWIVES", "CSI: MIAMI", "BUFFY", "ANGEL")

The Storyteller

I started as an A.D. on a number of variety and live TV shows but soon found myself gravitating towards storytelling. I liked the idea in scripted TV of using visuals to enhance the story as opposed to music or variety TV, where you're generally using the cameras to capture the moment. This desire ultimately led me to pursue jobs in scripted material. Ironically, I found that things I had learned shooting live music and comedy such as its rhythms and sounds, translated not only into scripted comedy, but into drama and action as well.

Pigeon Feed

Because it's human nature for people to want a safe bet, there's a certain amount of pigeon-holing in this industry. I've been aware that I've been pigeon-holed at times, but it didn't bother me because I might get stuck (for lack of a better word) doing a show like "BUFFY, THE VAMPIRE SLAYER" for a number of episodes which is fantasy/horror, but that opened the door to doing episodes for "ALLEY MCBEAL" which was more suit and tie. That show soon led to a run of CSI, CSI:NY and CSI:MIAMI. My resume became very eclectic and thankfully people started to recognize that if you had range as a Director that was a good thing. With that said, you should know your limits. I know that there are certain genres I wouldn't be good at because there are aspects of them that honestly don't interest me. So, if I don't have an interest in it, there's no sense in me doing it because it would show in the final product.

Old Sparky

As a Director you have to know your material to the point where you don't have your head in the book but your eyes and ears on the set. You have to be open to ideas that may spark in rehearsal, spark in the middle of shooting or spark because the trucks are parked in the wrong spot and you can't shoot the way you planned. The Director sets the tone on the set. You're not there to make friends and not everything is smooth sailing. You may bump heads or may not bump heads. It's part of the creative process. I like to set the tone on my sets where the Actor can feel free to fail, and once they have that safety net, then great things can happen.

15 Minutes Of Fame

All the problems and challenges that a Director faces are the same up and down the line whether it be a $100 million epic or a low budget student film. It's all relative to what you're doing because on a basic level you're facing the same problems. All that matters is whether the scene works. Because, whether it took you 15 minutes or 15 hours to get that incredible camera shot, once you're in the editing bay, if it doesn't work you have to throw it out. The audience doesn't care what you went through to get that shot. They only care about the finished product they see on the screen.

"The most important thing to do when stepping onto a set is to clue yourself into the mood of the set and adjust yourself to it because it's never about you and your mood."

Marianne Maddelena, Producer

James Gunn
Screenwriter / Director
(SUPER, SLITHER, DAWN OF THE DEAD, SCOOBY-DOO)

Brave New World

A movie set is its own little culture with its own language and its own way of going about things. There are certain things there that are socially acceptable and things there that are not socially acceptable or different from regular society. You have to be accustomed to that culture. Obviously there are books you can read and people you can ask for help. But none of that is going to tell you everything. You have to experience it first hand.

Lego My Ego

Writing a movie is a lot different from writing a novel because it's a community effort and that means that there are a lot of egos to deal with. A lot of people think Hollywood is all about egos, but in fact most of the successful people in the industry are the ones who absolutely let go of their egos 100%. If you do that, you can then concentrate foremost on the quality of the vision that you're creating.

Friends Forever

Every movie that I've been on, my best friends on set have been the Actors. They are the people I like dealing with the most. The biggest joy for me is actually seeing them perform the words I wrote. Because I come from an acting background, my scripts are generally pretty Actor friendly. A lot of the humor comes solely out of the performance of the Actor. My scripts aren't necessarily about looking beautiful or anything like that, they're about acting. If the Actors are good, usually the scene works, if they aren't, well, you get something else.

Setting A Course For Adventure

As a Screenwriter, it's important to be on good terms with the Director. The reason is very simple: when the ship sails you're either on his boat or not on the boat at all. I love making movies and I love being involved with the actual production of the film. With TROMEO & JULIET I was there for every single second of the Production. I even directed the Actors in many scenes. For THE SPECIALS, I was also an Actor, so I was there for most of the filming and with SCOOBY DOO, I went down to Australia to be on location while they shot. That isn't always the case for Writers. Quite often, Writers aren't wanted around.

"I genuinely believe that a lot of the Directors who are stepping into their own right now are inspired by the things that we were inspired by."

Greg Nicotero, Make-Up FX Artist

Marianne Maddelena
Producer
(SCREAM QUADRILOGY, RED EYE, THE HILLS HAVE EYES)

Shiny Happy People

Wes Craven and I make sure we hire people we like and who have positive attitudes. We have a rule that once we figure out that someone is a *"bad egg"* we get rid of them or don't ask them back. We once fired a Production Designer for using foul language and being misogynistic and also got rid of a Set Dresser who spent most of his time picking up on the Extras. We frequently won't bring back people who have bad attitudes or throw temper tantrums. There is no room on a set for moody people. Keep your problems at home.

On Being A Producer

My greatest responsibility is to create the tone for the set by being a positive influence as much as possible. If there is a problem or if people are not communicating well with each other, I need to figure out what I can do to help in the most judicious way. I also help keep strain off the Director by dealing with the various crewmembers and visitors that shouldn't be monopolizing his time.

Interior Design

A large part of the way I work is to have a hand in the set dressing, the wardrobe and the hair and make-up. For me to do my job effectively, I need to have good communication with those departments because they matter so much to the look of the film. I've been known to literally re-dress the set an hour before it's to be shot. It might seem crazy, but once it's on film you have to live with it.

"Aside from Directing, my other responsibility on a daily basis is to give as many answers to the New York Times crossword puzzle as possible. I'm the resident expert."

Wes Craven, Writer/Producer/Director

Sig Libowitz
Production Executive
(LOVELY & AMAZING, IN THE BEDROOM, THE ICE STORM)

Who Are The People In Your Neighborhood?

It's of the utmost importance to know what's going on around you before you step on a movie set. Get to know the crew, know what their responsibilities are and a little bit about their background and experience. At the very least, know what you're supposed to be doing and what you are there for.

Attitude Is Key

Whether I'm on set on the development side or there to oversee something for the Producers or Production Company, it's my responsibility to check that things are running smoothly. I make sure that we're staying on schedule and budget and getting a reasonable amount of set-ups for that day. I'm also there to check out if there is a good attitude on set because things can break down in a lot of strange ways and it's imperative to nip those problems in the bud to keep things from falling apart. Sometimes the crew is just not getting along and there is no way to salvage the experience as a positive one in terms of attitude. If this is the case then all you can do is recognize that it's a difficult situation while still maintaining that the work gets done on time, on budget and in a professional manner.

Are You Ready For The Summer...

Sets can literally be like camp. Especially if you shoot on location, which allows the crew to bond in a very different manner than they would if they were commuting to the studio every day. It's still hard work, but when everybody gets along you feel like you're all working towards that common goal together and it can be a fun time. Of course, not everybody has fond memories of camp and it can also be horrible, where you feel like, *"Man, I can't wait to get out of here. Who are these people and who raised them?"*

Opposites Attract?

On the flip side of the importance of attitude, I've been on the best sets where everybody is loving each other and it's sad when the last day arrives but the film ultimately just doesn't turn out all that well. And then I've been on sets where people can't wait to get away from each other and everyday is a battle and you get the most beautiful movies. I honestly don't know if the conflict on set adds to the drama in the movies or if it's just some odd coincidence, but it's very curious that sometimes the happiest set will not necessarily produce the best movie and vice versa.

"Being a Producer means you're dealing with people both artistically and financially and in a sense you're a coach, you're a pathfinder and many times you're a security blanket."

Pen Densham, Writer/Producer

Terry Morse
Producer / 1st Assistant Director
(IN THE HEAT OF THE NIGHT, THE LIST OF ADRIAN MESSENGER, TO KILL A MOCKINGBIRD)

King Of The Monsters
My dad, Terry O. Morse, was an Editor at Warner Brothers starting (as sound came in) in the late '20's. In the late '40's, at the end of his tenure, he started directing "B" movies. The movies were always about 45-50 minutes long and he ended up directing 17 of them, including SMASHING THE MONEY RING, starring Ronald Reagan and Myrna Loy.

But the one that really hit it was GODZILLA. Now GODZILLA was a completely Japanese made film when it came over to Hollywood. It was all in Japanese. There were no subtitles. My dad took that film and got it translated then hired and directed Raymond Burr for about six or seven days. He also supervised the looping of the English dialogue and did the entire cutting. It became a big hit and you'll see on the posters of GODZILLA that it's *"Directed by I. Honda and Terry Morse."* I'm very proud of my dad for that.

Remember The Alamo

When I got out of the Navy, I initially found work at Lockheed and Safeway stores. But wanting to follow in the footsteps of my father, I became an apprentice Editor and worked on a religious series called "ONCE IN YOUR LIFE." This led to becoming a Sound Effects Cutter on "THE UNTOUCHABLES" at Desilu. And then from that to working on John Wayne's ALAMO as one of the four Sound Effects Editors. This body of work helped me acquire a position as a 2nd A.D. and that eventually got me into the Director's Guild. From there I worked my way up to 1st A.D., Production Manager, Associate Producer, Producer, and then ending my career as a Vice President of a completion bond company. So it was quite a journey.

You Like Me, You Really Like me!

The crew has to like the 1st A.D. They'll bust their ass for them if they like them. But you can be liked and not do a great job like not being on top of things or not making sure that the Actors are there when the Director needs them. You're thinking all the time and fighting the sun constantly. It's hard work.

I trained under a really good 1st A.D. named Tommy Shaw. Tommy worked a lot with Richard Brooks and John Huston and I followed Tommy around. He was very loud on the set, and rough, and I tried not to be. I wanted to be loud, because that's the only way you can get things done.

A Real Class Act

I was working on BANDOLERO! which starred Jimmy Stewart, Dean Martin and Raquel Welch. We were shooting a scene in a jail all day long and were supposed to finish it that night because we had something to do the next day, and Jimmy Stewart wasn't going to work the next day. There were two close-ups of Dean Martin but behind him was a window and it was getting too dark to shoot.

The Director decided to call it the day and shoot the remaining two shots the next day. Jimmy Stewart wasn't in the shot so Dean said, *"You don't have to come out, Jimmy, I'll do my lines with the script girl, don't worry about it."* Well, the next morning Jimmy was there.

He came out, and not only that, he put on his complete wardrobe, to read offstage lines for Dean Martin. After that Jimmy Stewart would appear on the Dean Martin show every once in a while because they became terrific friends based on their mutual respect for each other.

"I highly recommend that before you shoot a scene to reread it very carefully, no matter how familiar you think you are with it, because there are inevitably little details that you might have forgotten about."

Stuart Gordon, Director/Writer

Rachel Flackett
Production Assistant
(AMERICAN DREAMZ, FRAILTY, SCARY MOVIE 2, LITTLE NICKY)

Secret Agent

I like to think that the Set P.A.'s are like the nerdy know-it-all kids in elementary school who are always helping the teacher pass out papers or admonishing the other kids for being disruptive. I tattle on everybody. I'm there to disseminate information and to help with the cohesiveness by making sure that everyone is on the same page in the schedule. I'm also a kind of a spy. I'll keep track if an Actor goes off in one direction and have to surreptitiously follow them and report on their movements so if they're needed on set I can grab them easily and not waste time.

Top Ten Requests

Craft Service is the best department to have on your side, especially if you want to have food that you like eating on set. I deal with a lot of Actors that like particular food items that are not common at the craft service table. It's great to have someone, especially when you're in the middle of nowhere, who is willing to accommodate the odd requests of the Actors. Otherwise you'll find yourself getting chewed out for not having a can of caffeine-free diet Dr. Pepper in their hands two seconds after they've asked for it.

Smoke 'Em If You've Got 'Em

I was working on a drug-related comedy and one of the things I was asked, which I found to be quite absurd, was to keep the two stars of the movie from getting too stoned. The first day of shooting, I walked into the Lead Actor's trailer just as he was about to light up a blunt. Without a moment to spare, I demanded that he stop and put it away. It wasn't until later that I realized that I probably put my life on the line. I'm sure he would have had no qualms about *"bustin' a cap in me"* for my impertinence.

All In The Family

Generally, the entertainment industry attracts a wackier brand of person. You usually have an eclectic bunch of people on the crew that understand the stresses of the job but are still able to look on the lighter side and laugh at themselves and the foibles of others. If you have a crew like that, who know what they're in for and are not going to take it too seriously, you're very lucky. You're with them for anywhere from eleven to twenty hours a day and, because you feel like you've just been through war with them, you naturally develop a familial-like bond.

TALES FROM THE SET

The worst thing that I've ever seen was on a show where the Writer/Director was completely out of line. The Executive Producers wanted a re-write on the script, which they were more than happy to pay for. They liked the concept but felt it just wasn't coming together. At the production meeting the Director walked in and told everybody to throw the revised script that they had been using for prep for the last two weeks, on the floor. He passed around a box that had the original script he had written and insisted that it was the one they were going to use for shooting. Not only was it a major blow-off of the Executive Producer's wishes but also we were set to start shooting in two days and now everyone was two weeks behind! To make matters even worse, the Director was constantly yelling at the departments when things weren't what or where they were supposed to be. And of course things were constantly going to wrong because he changed everything at the last minute. It was a nightmare.

Donald Bruce, Production Accountant

I was Liz Taylor's P.A. on a movie many, many years ago called HEATHER & LOUELLA. I was in her trailer getting her pretzels and apples as well as food for her poodles, when she arrived and announced she wasn't interested in working that day. I didn't realize the implication of what she was saying, so I just went out onto the set and told the first person I could, which happened to be the 1st A.D., who was frantically setting up the first of a ridiculous amount of set-ups on an unreasonable day. Ms. Taylor's was in every scene and I announced to him that she would not be coming out to play today.

He went ballistic on me. So I got in his face and it just got ridiculous. The net result of that was they lost an entire day of production. Ms. Taylor went home and the 1st A.D. had a complete meltdown. I didn't realize you don't walk out into the middle of a set and give the 1st A.D. this horror story. All I could do once the damage had been done was to watch the ripple effect of what I had caused. It was quite extraordinary.

Phillip Segal, Writer/Producer

It was the first day of shooting on a high budget music video for a little tin-pot dictator of a Director. We were out at 29 Palms and the call time was 4:30am so a lot of the crew drove out the night before and stayed at the hotel. At 4:00am, we hear screaming from the parking lot down below and it's the Director yelling at everyone to get into the vans and go because he decided he wanted to start a half hour earlier.

Unfortunately, the Set Dresser and her assistant were driving out from LA that morning, planning on getting to the parking lot by 4:25am. They showed up at 4:15am with nobody there. So they raced in their car, trying to catch up with the convoy. Because it was still dark, the Set Dresser couldn't see well and hit the soft shoulder on the desert and it spun her jeep across the road and flipped it. She got thrown out and broke her neck and died.

Meanwhile the Director's on the set, screaming about why the Art Department's not ready and none of these sets are dressed. The Art Department soon finds out what's happened to the Set Dresser and they all quit. An even more tragic coda to this story was she'd only been married for 2 weeks.

By the end of our third 23-24 hour day the entire crew is feeling the strain. Exhausted, I nodded off on the sidewalk in a director's chair when suddenly I feel this hand grab me by the shoulder and yank me out of the chair. A moment later one of those big Yukon trucks, reversing down the sidewalk, takes out the chair that I was just sitting in. This girl jumps out and says, *"Hey you, take that food out of the back of my truck,"* and starts to walk off. I've had it at this point and reply, *"Hey, how about go F**K yourself? You almost ran me over, how many more people are going to die on this movie before you people get your act together?"*

She stops, looks at me then reaches across the trestle table and slaps me across the face. I saw red. I literally was going to go punch her lights out. Thank God my buddy was there to hold me back. The next thing I know two sheriffs who witness the whole thing come running over and put her in cuffs. They want to know if I'm going to press charges. The Gaffer comes running up to me and goes, *"I really need this account, please don't press charges."* And the 1st AD, who's witnessed all this too is like, *"Ok, that's a wrap, my effing staff are hitting the crew, we're out of here."* That was the end of the night.

I ultimately didn't press charges like I should've done, and what do you know, but that Gaffer all of a sudden lost my number and I never got called from him again. To add insult to injury, I later found out that the girl who slapped me was the Producer's little sister. You've got to love this industry.

Anonymous Set Lighting Technician

My first job on a film set was as one of about a zillion P.A.'s working on BONFIRE OF THE VANITIES. The shoot was long, complicated and controversial. We were shooting on a bond trading floor near the World Trade Center. There were several hundred Extras, most of them real bond traders and security was a prime concern. I was positioned in front of the entrance to the floor and told in dramatic fashion by a self important P.A. that, *"NO ONE IS ALLOWED ON THE SET WITHOUT AN OFFICIAL 'BONFIRE' ID BADGE!!! NO EXCEPTIONS."* Of course, when Tom Hanks walked by in costume a while later, I knew enough not to ask for his laminated orange "Bonfire" pass. I'm dumb but I'm not that dumb. Then I told a dumpy looking guy with scraggly hair and a beard that he needed a pass to get on the set. He glowered and mumbled angrily. An A.D. grabbed my arm and said: *"You idiot, that's the Director, Brian DePalma."* Oops.

Kevin Dougherty, Production Assistant

I was working on a movie in China where I soon discovered that they have a completely different manner of working on sets. Their concept of chain of command is very different from ours and they run their sets in an extremely formal way. One day while setting up a shot, I made what I thought to be, an innocent statement to the

Director about how something could be done in a different way to make it easier on the Puppeteers and on the crew. But because I stated it in public, it was perceived as rude. The next thing I know, the Director is four inches from my face screaming and belittling me in front of the entire crew. Later that day, the Director came up to me and apologized but explained that he understood what I was asking for but, because of the way I asked, he had no choice but to berate me publicly in order to save face.

Tony Gardner, Make-Up F/X Artist

While Wes was shooting the Drew Barrymore death sequence at the beginning of SCREAM, I was in the house entertaining some people who were visiting the set. Without paying attention, our group walked out of the house giggling and laughing right at the moment Drew was trying to be dying. Wes just gave me the dirtiest look and I realized that here I am so trained in set etiquette, but yet I was the culprit of a major breach of it. I walked onto a working set that was very serious and in the process of getting to a point that was really dramatic and I almost ruined the moment.

Marianne Maddelena, Producer

I had an Actor working on a project. The Writer/Director was a first-timer and he was a bit of a dictator. He treated the Actors and crew like they were there to serve his whims. It got to the point where the crew revolted and walked off the set. He lost the trust of everyone. They had to shut down for a couple of days and they had to set the Director straight.

J.B. Roberts, Talent Manager

At the end of a shoot day, the Production Office told their Lead Actor that they would call him in the morning with the location, as it was looking like it may change. The Actor was never told the original location either. So he waited by the phone but received no call, no page...no contact. So he left for the city where he knew the shooting was taking place, 50 miles away... hoping to make up some travel time in the late schedule. He stopped half way...still no call at home...yes, roomies were there covering the phone. He had his pager on and his cell phone on in the car. Still no call from the Production Office. Hours later, in frustration, he headed home.

On his return, he finally received a call: It was the Director calling to chew him out for being a flake for not showing up to set. Furthermore, they had to shoot the back of someone else's head and compromised the whole shoot day. Unfortunately for the Lead Actor, he lost all that day's scenes in the storyline because there was no time in the schedule to reshoot them later. On top of that, during the remaining days of shooting, the rest of the cast and crew treated him like scum and talked behind his back. It finally came to light that the source of the problem was a Production Assistant who didn't follow the instructions of the Production Manager. Of course by then, the damage had been done.

Hester Schell, Casting Director

I'll be happy to admit that when I first started in the industry, I was quite possibly the worst P.A. that ever worked in this business. I was working on a show and was given the only key to the location for the next day's shoot. It was a long night and I passed out on my bed when I got home. Crew call was 7am. When I woke up and looked at my clock it was already past 11am (Mind you this was before cell phones and pagers). Realizing that my situation couldn't possibly get any worse at this point, I rolled over and went back to sleep. I finally arrived on set after 2pm and of course was fired on the spot. Not exactly one of my finest hours.

Anonymous Director

I was working on a movie out in the desert with this once big-time Director who was in desperate need of a new hit film. The D.P. was one of his closest friends and had asked the Director if his son could work on the camera crew. The Director didn't know the D.P.'s son but had no problem with it. The kid's first day on set he was incredibly nervous and over-anxious. We had just filmed this big stunt, which was the biggest action sequence of the film. The kid decided he was going to run the mag from the set to the camera truck and just as he was passing by the Director, he tripped. The film mag fell to the ground and split open. The Director watched in horror as the film unspooled entirely at his feet. It took an incredible amount of man hours plus thousands of dollars to get this shot and it was totally destroyed in the matter of a few seconds. The Director had a meltdown and screamed his head off at the D.P. for his son's incompetence. Ironically the kid wasn't fired. As far as the action sequence goes, they didn't have the money to reshoot it, so the script was rewritten to lose it entirely.

Eric Bates, Prop Master

CHAPTER TWO

"I'm an Actor, not Atmosphere!"

THE
TALENT
DEPARTMENT

A BRIEF OVERVIEW

As a film goes into production (or sometimes before), the Director, with the help of a Casting Agent, will begin auditioning Actors to fill the various key rolls in the film. Some films benefit from having a movie star as the lead, while others quite the opposite.

Unless a Director is sure of whom he/she wants, the audition process will take weeks if not months to complete. Once decisions are made, the Production makes offers to the Actors. These may consist of just money or could include other perks, such as a piece of the back end (i.e. profit made after the film is released).

"If all the world's a stage and men and women merely its players,"
I hope they all have good representation. Some movies may be great on the wallet but bad on the career, so most Actors have Agents and Managers to help negotiate their contracts and guide them into making smart career choices.

Until recently there were two major unions that protected Actors: SAG (Screen Actors Guild) and AFTRA (American Federation of Television and Radio Artists). These organizations establish rules and guidelines about pay scales, as well as how performers are treated on the set. On March 30, 2012, they merged to form one union called SAG-AFTRA.

Actors are broken into two major categories: "Above the line" and "Below the line". The former includes the movie stars and Lead Actors whose names usually appear in the opening credits of a film. They are usually afforded large trailers, assistants and/or access to amenities not given to the rest of the crew. "Below the line" performers are made up of the Day Players and Extras. Usually working for scale, they are typically given the bare bones of what is required by the unions.

But whether a major star or a bit player, an Actor is required to bring dimensional life to a written character. It's not easy and it takes not only talent, but skill and bravery - the reward being a performance that is memorable because it speaks to the audience.

THE PLAYERS

Actor/Actress: An individual who portrays a character in a motion picture.

Stand In: A person who resembles an Actor in height and build hired to take the place of the Actor while lights are being placed and other adjustments on the set are made. This allows for the Actor to rest between set ups.

Body Double: Person with the same physical characteristics of a certain Actor to be used for scenes that don't require seeing the Actor's face or scenes involving nudity.

Stunt Double: A trained Stunt Person who bears a physical resemblance to an Actor used for sequences that are deemed too dangerous for that Actor.

Atmosphere (Extra): Individuals hired to portray incidental characters with no speaking lines.

Casting Director: Chooses and negotiates contracts with the Actors in the film.

Extra Wrangler: Coordinates the Extras for given scenes. Determines amount needed and which Extras are best suited.

TERMS YOU SHOULD KNOW

Acting Coach
A Teacher who works closely with Actors, helping to develop the characters they portray in the film.

Agent
A member of a talent agency who represents the better interests of their client (i.e. an Actor). They assist in negotiating contracts as well as making sure that their client's needs are addressed before and during filming.

Assistant
Individual employed by an Actor who carries out the wishes and/or needs of the Actor. Helps to coordinate the Actor's schedule as well as perform odd jobs.

audition
An opportunity for an Actor to try out for a role in a film. Sometimes recorded on film or video and referred to as a "screen test."

back end
A negotiated percentage of profit paid to an Actor later based on the performance of the movie.

call back
A request to audition for a part a second time.

forced call
Union rules require that an Actor be given 12 hours turnaround from the time they wrap the night before to the next day of filming. If the Actor is required to arrive on set prior to that time, they receive a cash remuneration.

Hold (H)
Designates that an Actor is not needed for that day of filming.

Manager
Like an Agent, this individual is part of the Actor's team. Generally works closely in determining acting roles to take.

non-union
The film is not affiliated with a union and therefore the Actors are not protected under the guidelines of the guild.

On Call (O/C)
Designates that an Actor is possibly needed for that day of filming and should be prepared to be called in to shoot.

rehearsal
The time allotted to practice scenes from the movie. Sometimes done in advance of shooting, other times right before a scene is to be filmed.

residuals
Money paid to Actors from profits received by video, television, and other ancillary markets.

run lines
Requested by an Actor in order to rehearse dialogue for an upcoming scene.

SAG-AFTRA
A merger of the Screen Actors Guild and the America Federation of Televison and Radio Artist. A union for Actors and Stunt Performers that negotiates salaries and working conditions for its members. Represents over 150,000 Actors in film, television, industrials, commercials, music videos, video games and other new media.

sides
Script pages of scenes being shot on that day. Allows an Actor to quickly find and focus on the day's material.

Talent

Another name for principal Actors.

Trainer

Individual hired by Production to keep an Actor in proper physical condition or to instruct an Actor how to portray a particular type of physical role (i.e. boxer, fencing, etc.).

THE RULES OF SETIQUETTE

• Never take a photograph of an Actor without his/her expressed permission. This is to protect them from unguarded moments that could be exploited in the tabloids.

• Never sit in a chair designated for an Actor or the Cast. That is solely their place to relax and they shouldn't have to ask to have it vacated.

• Never enter an Actor's trailer without knocking first and/or having a good reason. Frequently Actors will use their spare time to rehearse or just plain relax. Just because they are not on the set doesn't mean they're not working.

• Atmosphere are people too, treat them as such.

• Don't pester the Actors for autographs. To ply their trade, they need to feel that they are in a safe environment and surrounded by professionals, not a bunch a fans.

• Never solicit an Actor with a script during a shoot. Not only is it unprofessional, but it puts them on the spot. There are proper channels to go through to have them see your work and if the script is as "brilliant" as you say, it will find its way into their hands.

• Unless you're the Director, don't ever give advice to an Actor or presume to know how they should play their part. If they want your input, they'll ask.

• Be considerate and respectful when talking to the Actors, especially when discussing their body of work. Try to imagine how many times they've had the same conversation about the role that made them a star.

• Don't ask an Actor, *"What have you done that I would have seen you in?"* It's an awkward and embarrassing question for them to answer. If you really must know, look it up yourself on the Internet.

ADVICE FROM THE EXPERTS

Noel Clarke
Actor / Writer / Producer / Director
(STAR TREK 2, ADULTHOOD, "DOCTOR WHO")

Those Names At The End Of A Movie

I think respecting everybody on set is immensely important, not just because you want a long career, but because all these people generally work a lot harder than you do as an Actor. They usually get on set before you, sort everything out before you get there, look after you throughout the day, and then leave after you.

A big problem I've seen with young Actors or Actors who get to success very quickly is that they tend to be disrespectful to people that they may deem beneath them on the production crew. They'll be all smiley to the Producers, but to the P.A.s it's, *"Make my tea!"* or *"Do this!"* and *"Do that!"* Everyone's job on a film set is equally important. That's the reason film credits take 5 minutes at the end of a movie. Regardless if your name's at the top, there are still hundreds of people that are also in the credits that have worked equally as hard and they should all be respected.

Captain Of The Ship

Even though as a Director you're the captain of the ship, at the end of the day it's still a team effort, and as a Director you have to realize that respect, attitude and mood comes from the top down. If you're one of those Directors who come in an angry mood, you create a tension and a vibe on set that is not always a pleasant work environment. People don't want to talk as much, which means they're less likely to suggest ideas that can help you.

I'm not saying you have to be in a good mood all the time, but if things go wrong (which they will), you need to be in a place where you can deal with it without getting stressed and getting angry and screaming at people because nobody will want to work with you. I've worked with the one of the biggest Directors in the world and the guy comes in everyday and is polite and says hello to everyone. If things are done wrong, he doesn't shout, he just explains why he wants something done the way he wants it done. That's definitely the way to be.

Perception Is EVERYTHING

It's interesting how outside people perceive success. I found that even though I was doing well as an Actor, I was consistently going up for TV jobs but not getting them simply because in their minds I was a nobody regardless of my talent. So, I'm a guy that adapts and learns pretty quickly. I made a conscious decision to do more theater. Within two years, I had won a Laurence Olivier Award and then went back to these same people who before wouldn't give me the time of day and all of a sudden I was this respected theater Actor. The truth of the matter is, I'd only done 4 or 5 plays. But because I suddenly won an award I was now "a somebody" even though as an Actor I was still the same guy they auditioned the year before.

Share The Wealth

I've gotten some very sound advice over the years but the best was: *Don't be afraid to share*. Don't always feel you have to do everything because you'll water-down your quality. I realized I don't always need to write the entire script for one of my projects. I can come up with the idea and write the first draft then give it to one of my writing team so they can get credit (and money) and as a unit, we all move forward. The irony is that even though I may only be a piece of the puzzle, it can still be perceived by the public as a *"Noel Clarke film."* So the only caveat is that if you're going to share, you have to make sure that you have quality control at all times because you ultimately may take the blame if it's a failure.

"The first thing I knew to do was to accept the fact that I knew nothing."

Steve Demko, Post-Production Supervisor

Andre Royo
Actor
(RED TAILS, "THE WIRE", "FRINGE")

Preparation A

Preparation is always key. Preparation sets you up and helps you relax, knowing that you've done all that you can do to get ready for your first day or your third day on the set. It builds confidence because you know, no matter what turn a Director or a fellow Actor may throw your way, you're prepared because you know your character. Everyone gets nervous - that's part of the thrill of being an Actor - is that nerve that you get, or that little sense of fear that you get right before the Director yells *"Action."* When you settle in and relax and know that you're prepared it makes for a more enjoyable experience all the way around.

Andre Says *"Relax"*

It's of utmost importance to know yourself and relax. You're going to be on set for 16 hours or more and you can very easily overdo it. When I first started acting on sets, I tended to arrive in the morning and right away grab a quick bite to eat and then go directly to my trailer to go over my lines for hours and hours and hours. By the time I got to shoot the scene I was exhausted and stale. I had to learn to be patient and enjoy the down time: Get some sleep, bring a book, bring some music. Do things to get the concept of filming OFF my mind for a little while. This is especially important if you're the lead character and you're pretty much in front of the camera most of the time. Enjoy your time inside the trailer.

Everything To Everyone

The first time it hit me that I wanted to be an Actor was when I was young because I loved to be the center of attention. I was an attention junkie, the class clown in school. I liked the fact that I could tell a story or re-enact a scene and have people engage in what I was doing in front of them. I was addicted to the attention. I was constantly asked by my parents, my relatives and my teachers: *"What do you want to be when you grow up?"* I always felt the pressure of not

knowing. Everything I saw on TV or in the movies looked great.
I would see an Actor one day in a movie and he'd be a cowboy and then next week my dad would show me another movie and the same Actor was now an astronaut. The next time he's a teacher. The concept was incredible to me. So an Actor was the first thing that came out of my mouth because I realized that an Actor could be EVERY-THING. He could BE a doctor. He could BE a lawyer. He could BE a teacher. Saying that I wanted to be an Actor was also the easy way out of having long conversations with my parents.

My Name Is Andre Royo…And I'm An Actor.

"I am an Actor" is somewhat a state of being. I love the craft, I want to learn the craft and perform for others, so by definition I'm an Actor just as much as Denzel Washington or Lawrence Fishburne. But the difference between being an "Actor" and a "working Actor" is a check. As a "working Actor" you come to a certain place in your career where THAT's what pays the bills and provides for you and your family.

When I first got started I went to an acting school in New York called HB Studios: A place for me to study acting and surround myself with positive energy all around me. When you surround yourself with that energy, opportunities start to happen. Luckily, there were constantly posts for auditions on the school bulletin board. That's how I got my first audition for an independent film and my first audition for a play.

I was fortunate enough to get cast in a play and a film. I did a good job on both and word got around. So invariably somebody else would then hire me for another play or for an independent film. That went on for a little while until my closet and my TV stand were full of all these independent films and I was suddenly a "working Actor."

Can You Dig It?

When I was in my mid-20's I was working the door at a club. A female friend of mine knew I was an Actor and fortunately for me was dating an established film Director who she brought to the club one night. I was the asshole who says *"you can come in!"* So, I made a big show of letting the Director in and made him feel real important. He stopped and talked to me and was like *"Hey, I heard you're an Actor. I heard you're pretty good."* And, I was like *"I am."* I was confident. But keep in mind there's a difference between confidence and cocky. I was a little bit of both which was fine but you just have to know how to balance that so you don't rub people the wrong way. You have to have the confidence to stand up and say *"Look, you give me a shot and I'll bring it."* And he gave me a shot. The Director was John Singleton and the movie was SHAFT, my first theatrical release. That led to other auditions and other opportunities, and then I ended up on "THE WIRE".

"The hardest thing about being an Actor is to know when not to speak."

Daniel Roebuck, Actor

Doug Jones
Actor
(FANTASTIC FOUR: RISE OF THE SILVER SURFER, HELLBOY, PAN'S LABYRINTH, HOCUS POCUS)

Tears Of A Clown

Growing up as an awkward child who needed to become a class clown in order to survive, I found solace at the end of each day by flipping on the TV. It was in my TV where people were working out their family issues in a half hour sit-com, or singing and dancing their way through comedy sketches in variety shows: A happy world that I wanted to be part of. Going into high school, the stage was good to me. I saw an audience responding with laughter, tears and applause to something that I was doing on that stage and it became extremely addicting.

How To Be A Monster...Without Being A Monster

I moved out to Los Angeles to be close to the Hollywood machine in 1985, not knowing anyone or anything about show business. I took a TV commercial acting class that was taught by the west coast president of the Wilhelmina Agency. After my second class session with him, he asked if I had an agent. I didn't even know what an agent was, so he gave me his card and told me to call him at the office. I screamed with joy all the way home in the car.

They sent me out on commercial auditions for about six months before I landed my first paid role as a dancing mummy for an airline. Then a few months later, I booked a campaign for McDonald's as a piano-playing crooner with a crescent moon for a head called "Mac Tonight."

Three years and twenty-seven commercials later, this campaign marked me as a tall, skinny, physically expressive type who moved well and didn't complain like a typical diva Actor. That is when the referrals started going around about me in the creature effects side of the movie/TV business, and it snowballed over the years into what my career has become today. I'm known mostly for my fantasy roles in prosthetic make-ups and monster suits.

This Contract Is Etched In...Sand?!

Tight budgets will often be the cause of stress and bad behavior from the Producers and that tends to trickle down to the other departments. More than once on film shoots, I have been approached by an Assistant to a Producer who wanted me to sign an amended contract after I have already signed a contract that they agreed on with my Agents. The first time this happened, the math looked similar, but the wording allowed them to use my above-scale salary as a way of not paying overtime. Overtime that would have been paid for in the original agreement. I signed this amended contract out of complete ignorance, and got an earful from my agent later. Lesson learned. Never sign anything unless your Agent or Manager has reviewed and approved.

This happened again on other productions that were trying to save money, and by then I knew to play dumb and tell them to take it up with my Agent. This type of trick might save the production a little money, but in the long run, they left one of their Actors feeling assaulted and unappreciated. That type of treatment can work its way on-camera in an actor's performance, so they only shoot themselves in the creative foot with such a shifty business decision.

Creature "Affects"

In a particularly horrific monster suit for a low-budget horror film, I was told by the 1st A.D. that it was time to go to set, as they were about to shoot a scene of mine. I went in, and the Director angrily asked what I was doing there. I said the 1st A.D. told me it was time. The Director then flew off the handle, telling me he didn't have a 1st A.D., and he wanted me to point out who said this. I was mortified, as his rant was loud and in front of the entire crew. I pointed out the nice fellow, and the Director screamed, *"He is not an A.D.! He is nothing!"* The entire crew stood there, silent, not knowing how to proceed.

What I took away from that day was that if you have any sort of complaint with anyone on a movie set, it's best to take it up with them in private. Blowing up like that in front of the crew only brings down morale, and makes one look like a complete jerk that no one wants to do their best work for. Not the mood I wanted to be in while wearing a seventy-five pound rubber suit.

Do your best. People know when you are giving 100% and it is all that can ever be asked of you.
                    Scott Maginnis, Prop Master

Daniel Roebuck
Actor
("Lost", The Fugitive, The River's Edge "Nash Bridges",
"Matlock", The Late Shift)

Dressed For Success

The first advice that I give to any new Actor stepping onto a set for the first time is: *"Hang up your clothes"*. Actors unfortunately have ego issues and it's easy for them to believe that they are the most important people on a set when in reality they're only a piece in a very big puzzle. If you get in the habit of hanging up your clothes, it gives you a sense that you recognize how important everybody's job is. The Costume Department doesn't have the time to gather your clothes, even if they're going to clean them. If they're hung up, they can be grabbed quickly and they can leave.

On Being An Actor

Come prepared to do the work. You better know your lines cold, know how to hit your mark, and don't hold anybody up. Also, stay out of the way. A natural curiosity is great but if you can step back and listen, you'll learn a lot about how it really works on a set.

A Spoonful Of Sugar

If you're not courteous to everybody on a set than you shouldn't be in this business in the first place. If an Actor decides that they're only going to be nice to the Producer and the Director because they can get them another job, then they are a moron. Quite frankly, the crew is working just as hard if not harder and any way you can make their lives easier is going to make yours doubly so.

I still confuse the Grips when I introduce myself. I approach and say, *"My name's Dan"*, and five times out of ten they answer with, *"I'm just the Grip."*. They're usually thinking *"Why are you talking to me? What did I do? Did I do something wrong?"* That's the reputation that Actors have, that they just cause trouble.

Mind Your P's And Q's

I see Actors who offer their opinion on issues that don't involve them. I've seen an Actor speaking to a Director about a scene and another Actor butt in and offer a suggestion. You simply don't go up to another Actor and tell them how to read a line, especially an Actor of the same or of greater stature. When another Actor does that to me I suggest they speak with the Director and address it with him first.

With Great Power Comes Great Responsibility

As an Actor, when you're fortunate enough to have a lead or starring role, the responsibility is higher because you can set the tone. How you treat the crew is how the other Actors will treat the crew. Keep the crew laughing and entertained. It keeps things moving and makes their job easier, especially for those 14 to 16 hour days. It's the right thing to do. When there is a star on a show who is miserable it's a hard day for everyone.

"A lot of times people get hired solely because they remind the Director of his ex-girlfriend and conversely, sometimes Actors don't get hired for that very same reason."
Mindy Johnson-Plate, Casting Director

Elaine Hendrix
Actress
(INSPECTOR GADGET 2, THE PARENT TRAP, ROMY & MICHELLE'S
HIGH SCHOOL REUNION)

Baby Steps

I can remember my first time stepping onto a set. I felt like I didn't want to get in anybody's way. I was a little shy and a little quiet.

I learned that the best course of action is to go there, be yourself, listen and pay attention. Feel free to ask questions. You don't have to pretend that you know what you're doing. And most importantly have fun.

On Being An Actor

Be professional first and foremost. I'm there to say my lines, hit my marks and do my job. Secondly, I'm there to have a good time and build a camaraderie with the cast & crew, to have a good relationship and collaboration with those around me. So I make sure to build a rapport with everyone from the Producers to the Craft Service. I've been very fortunate to work with people who feel the same way. I've had a lot of fun experiences that creatively were rewarding experiences.

Attitude Is Everything

It's important to maintain a positive attitude and as much as you shouldn't take your work home with you, you shouldn't take your home to work either. I was working with a Hair & Make-Up artist who seemed unable to leave her personal life at home and she brought a great deal of drama into the hair/make-up trailer and ultimately onto the set. She was constantly late and always making up excuses as to what was happening in her personal life. She would share inappropriate stories with me as well as the other Actors on the set. She was stepping over the line with what's acceptable behavior. I cared about this person but her personal drama was getting in the way of being able to work. She was filled with such negativity and drama. She ultimately got fired because she was affecting relationships on the crew and was unable to do her job properly.

The Land Of Cotton

I've seen some things on set that were in poor taste, or watched people make big boo-boos in regards to even everyday etiquette. Being from the South, manners were a prominent part of my upbringing. Nobody likes somebody throwing tantrums, or being late or someone who bosses people around. It comes down to basic courtesy.

"If an Actor asks about cutting a line, more times than naught you should lose it. Most Actors ask for more lines, so to have one suggest losing one should be looked at and taken seriously."

Stuart Gordon, Director/Writer

Rusty Schwimmer
Actress
(RUNAWAY JURY, THE PERFECT STORM, TWISTER)

Badda-Bing
The first time I was on a set, it was a film directed by Henry Winkler. Robert Pastorelli showed me around and showed me the ropes for the four days that I was on set. He told me what to do and what not to do and was constantly there for me. I think that because of the action he took, I felt compelled that I should do the same thing for others.

Call Me Crazy
There are Actors who would disagree but I believe that as the entertainer it is not only our job to hit our marks, say our lines, get into our key light and give a good performance but also to keep a set lively, fresh and happy. I'm one to have a great time on a set. I love to be on sets and I'll share that with everyone.

Say Cheese
If you can have a relationship with the camera crew where they feel safe with you and they know that they're equal in terms of creativity, they can give you suggestions that a Director may not be able to. Because I don't know the lens sizes, they can tell me what the frame is. A lot of times they'll whisper it in my ear that they're doing an extreme close up so I can adjust my performance. They're the ones who you possibly have the most intimacy with whether you like it or not, because they're right there, close up and personal.

Longtime Companions

If you take the gossip-quotient out, every Actor will say Hair, Make-Up and Costume are their most trusted allies on a set. They're with you from the beginning of the day till the end. When you are having a hard time with getting a line or an idea across, they can be a valuable resource. They're also there in those intimate moments when you're trying to find the sadness or the anger in the scene. If you have any insecurity of your image or how you are going to look on the screen, they're going to know. I have a tendency when I'm shooting and my adrenaline starts going to get cartoon sweat that looks like it's coming off of me like there's no tomorrow. A lot of times the Make-Up Artist can just calm me down by simply patting my forehead with powder, which really helps me relax.

Set A Course For Love

When I did THE PERFECT STORM, I was concerned that I was going to have to deal with a lot of big personalities and egos. But it turned out to be the best set that I ever worked on. There was not one jerky person on that entire crew. Everybody worked together and there was absolutely no ego to be had. I think it's because everybody else was in the same position I was in the sense that they just wanted to have a good time and put out a great product. I have found that the higher up people are as far as artistic success, the nicer they are. These are the people that don't have to pretend that they are important, they can just concentrate on doing their job.

"Ethan Hawke said something to me that I never forgot: 'Actors equal production value.' So if you really focus on your cast and respect and inspire them with confidence, you'll get great work from them."

Bryan Singer, Director/Producer

Mindy Johnson-Plate
Casting Director / Casting Associate
("THE ANDY DICK SHOW", "AS IF", THE REPLACEMENT KILLERS, SUICIDE KINGS)

Give Me An "A"...

When I was an intern, my boss pulled me into her office and told me the greatest thing I could do for her was to be sweet and welcoming to each and every Actor who walks through the door. Ask them if they have any questions about the sides or if there is anything I can do to help. This sets the tone so when they come into her office to read they'll be relaxed and ready to give their best work. She then gets to take them into the Producers.

It becomes a win-win situation all around. Because of this training, I'm adamant with my associates that when an Actor walks into our office, we be their cheerleader and that they know that they're in a supportive environment.

Advice For The Actors

This is a job where you need to have done your homework. You have to know your lines because if you walk onto a set without knowing your lines, you will not be hired again. It's as simple as that. The people who steadily work do their homework.

Ingredients For Success

Sometimes I go to set to witness how amazing the Actors we have cast are. Those are the days you feel like a chef who has compiled these great ingredients and they taste so good together. That's an amazing thing and I take very little credit for that. There's a magic that happens when you get a group of really talented people together who are willing to play. To watch gifted people work together and watch that give and take and the stunning improv, you just hope that there is film in the camera and other people will get to see what we've seen.

Slap On The Wrist

There are some Actors who think that, because they've been in big films or have won awards, they are also a Co-Director. I have been shocked to the deepest core of my being that some Actors try and help the Director, who has been hired because he is extremely talented. So I'm called onto set to talk with these people.

"I find that people don't actually understand that it is an emotional risk for an Actor when they put themselves out there and they put lines through their mouths that have never been said before and discover through their feelings."

Pen Densham, Writer/Producer

TALES FROM THE SET

You never know who anybody is on set so you just have to assume that everybody is important, especially when you're new to a set. There isn't anybody who isn't important and you just have to put on your really thick skin and be ready to help whoever asks. Such as this story that happened to me:

I was working as an A.D. on a P. Diddy music video and was instructed to go into his trailer to make sure he was doing okay so when they called him, he would be ready. I went into the trailer and P. Diddy had his feet up getting a foot massage. He had another girl just giving him a neck massage, and yet another girl sitting next to him.

I looked at him and obviously there's nothing's bothering him right now so I asked him sarcastically *"Hey, what's up, man? Do you need anything?"* and he goes, *"Nah, man, I'm cool."*

I'm about to leave when the girl sitting next to him, goes, *"Oh, I'll have a water?"* I glared at her and under my breath said *"I wasn't asking you."* Still, I begrudgingly got her water.

As I'm walking out, I see another one of the A.D.'s and I'm like, *"Who's that girl that's in there with P.Diddy?"* He replies, *"Oh you mean, J Lo?"*

In my defense, she was dressed down and had her sweats on but it suddenly all made sense why P. Diddy threw his head back and started laughing when I talked smack to her.

Steve Demko, Post-Production Supervisor

I worked on a film with an Academy Award™ winning Actress and a Foreign Film Star. Every single time the Director would set up the scene, the Actress would interject with: *"That's one way you could do it, but my idea is this..."* The Director would answer her with: *"You know what, that's a good idea. I'll tell you what, let's try it my way first and then we'll try it your way."* They would film it his way first and then, when it was time to do it her way, they would call *"Rolling"* and *"Action"* but never turn on the camera.

Anonymous Casting Director

I was having a general meeting with an Actor who had just been fired off a TV series the day before. For twenty minutes he ranted and raved about the jerk that got him fired off the show. Ironically, the guy who got him fired was not only the Lead Actor on the show, but he was also my boyfriend. I sat there stunned especially because there was a legitimate reason why he got fired. During the rant my partner nudged my foot with his as an effort to keep me calm. Luckily for this Actor, I didn't reveal to him my relationship, but he needs to learn that you can't just walk into an office and disparage anybody.

Mindy Johnson-Plate, Casting Director

A few years back I had a small role in a TV movie with a famous Superhero/Action Star. It was a late December afternoon in Savannah, GA and we were losing light rapidly. The Actor was to ride up fast on his horse, dismount, and argue with me, a newpaper reporter, all the way to the gate around a prison wall which had been constructed for the movie.

As we approached the gate, the Actor got a little carried away and threw me, not down on the ground as was scripted, but through the paper wall of the prison. Referring to the super hero character made famous by him, I said *"Hey, wrong movie pal."* Everyone on the set laughed except you know who. I didn't know I was not supposed to make any reference to his super hero alter-ego in front of him. They had to move the shot to cover the hole in the prison wall, and we got the scene done before the sun set in the West. For some reason, however, my scene did not make the final cut of the movie.

Wilbur Fitzgerald, Actor

I was working on a western in Austin, Texas outside in the blazing heat. A lot was going on and people were in a rush to finish. An Actor had a scene in which he is dying from a bullet wound and as he slowly dies, he has a monologue. The crew was so relieved to be almost done that they were whispering to each other and talking amongst themselves, laughing and having a good time all in his eyeline. Because the scene was not only technically challenging but also emotionally challenging, the Actor needed all the concentration he could get. Not a prima-donna type, he still had had enough. He stopped the shooting and demanded that they completely clear the set before he would continue. It cost the production time to fulfill his request and ultimately money because it put things behind schedule.

Rusty Schwimmer, Actress

I was on a set and the scene was about this Actress that I was working with, about her character. She gave a suggestion, which in the context of the situation was absolutely appropriate. Without thinking, the Director responded: *"No, that's stupid."* The Actress left the stage and he was left to go and deal with that problem. Even if her suggestion was not good, he should have had the common sense to use the correct words to illustrate his point.

Anonymous Actor

I was working on a low-budget feature and we were shooting some scenes on the Philadelphia L-Train around midnight. My fellow intern and I were crouched on the floor trying to not be in the shot and listening to a P.A. get chewed out on "channel 3". Then, the doors opened and the Lead Actor walks in looking very sullen and slinks into a seat across the aisle from the doorway we were sitting in to wait for his scene. So, we all started goofing around while waiting and I started telling a very nasty off color joke. At the end, everyone was laughing, including the Lead Actor. At first I was kind of proud of myself for dragging him out of character then the head P.A. started screaming about bothering the Talent. We had to wait another hour before he could get back into character. D'oh.

Nicole Yates, Set Intern

In the early 80's, I worked as an Assistant to the production team on a low-budget sword-and-sorcery film. To say these guys were green would be an understatement. We were filming a scene on location that involved the Lead Actors to be on a raft that has capsized in the middle of a river. The capsized raft was anchored in place and the Actors were sent out for the shot. At this point, the Director decides to begin setting up the shot. After they finally get the shot (an hour later) the furious lead Actor angrily emerged from the drink, punched the Director and told him to get the shot set-up with stand-ins first, before putting the real Actors in the water.

Christopher Gomersall, Production Assistant

On a film I was working on, the Extra was evidently a crackhead but I needed him for the scene. At six in the morning I had to go down this dirt road to pick him up in his trailer and the police were there. His name was Leroy and I needed Leroy come hell or high water. The police told me they were taking him into custody. I told them I was taking him to set and he was coming with me and they couldn't have him. They let me take him and then hung around the set while we shot the scene.

Chad Darnell, Extras Casting Director

One of the bit roles on J. EDGAR was portrayed by an older, established Actor and you figure, this guy probably knows his craft. He got this part on a big Clint Eastwood movie, it's shooting on Stage 16 on Warner Brothers and he only has about 4 lines. Well, he got to set and absolutely could not remember a single one of his lines. It was just take after take after take after take and he just couldn't get it right. To make matters worse, he kept making things up, and this is a period piece, so you can't just make things up, because all of a sudden he's slipping into contemporary jargon. Ironically, I was the one acting inappropriately because I was watching the crew on set while sitting at the monitors losing my crap laughing. At a certain point I had to be ushered out of the sound stage because I slipped into an Anderson Cooper-style giggle fit. Not one of my better days.

Dustin Lance Black, Screenwriter/Producer

At the end of her career, Barbara Stanwyck did a television anthology series called Barbara Stanwyck Theatre. It was a different story every week with different Actors, different setups. I was the 2nd A.D. and it was my responsibility to meet the Actors in the morning and make sure they got to makeup and hair so they can be on the set, ready at nine o'clock. So it's six in the morning, I'm standing in the dark waiting for Barbara Stanwyck to pull up and here comes this big black limo. Out from the limo first is her cook then her hairdresser and then her makeup man and they're opening up their special dressing room they had on the Desilu lot.

Finally out of the limo comes Barbara and I said, *"Good morning, Miss Stanwyck, I'm the second assistant director, is everything all right?"* And she said *"If everything was all right, I'd be home in bed with somebody on top of me."* And I didn't know what to say; I was just a young guy. So I said, *"I'm going to get down on the set."* Which she quickly retorted, *"I wish you'd get down on something."* That was my introduction to Barbara Stanwyck.

Terry Morse, Producer / 1st Assistant Producer

One time I was on a set and I was very frustrated at the blocking rehearsal for a scene and in my frustration I walked off the set and headed back to my trailer. I still had the mike on me that I didn't take the time to let the sound guy come and remove. On the way I bumped into another Actor and just went off on the Actor. I told him exactly how I felt about the stupid Director and that he didn't know what the hell he was doing. When I got to my trailer there was a knock on the door…and the Director came in.

He said *"Hey I heard you got issues with me."* To which I replied, *"What are you talking about?"* and he said *"you know, you still got the mic on"* and I was like *"Oh crap!"* I had to sit there and apologize. Not for my feelings but for not going up to the Director man-to-man and telling him how I felt and about my concerns. Instead he had to hear it from the sound guy.

To make matters worse, one of the Producers had his headset on when he heard me yelling about how incompetent the Director was. Because of this, the Director got reprimanded. It became a great big issue and it was all unnecessary. It was okay to be frustrated but the etiquette is if you're frustrated about a situation, you go through the proper channels and address that frustration. You don't storm off and pout like a little kid because not only is it unprofessional, but also you never know who's listening.

Andre Royo, Actor

I was Producing/Directing a low-budget feature and we had this name Actress who we had sent out a letter of intent to. We were scheduling a photo shoot with her but had still not received back the signed letter. This of course made me nervous because I didn't want to commit time and money to this woman and then have her fall out of the movie for some reason. On top of this, all my dealings with her were somewhat difficult. She certainly had an ego and would insist upon her ideas on wardrobe and make-up as opposed to what I felt was in the best interest of the film.

Because I come from an acting background, I feel that it doesn't matter how big you are (or used to be), you have to treat each role that comes to you like it's the best thing that has ever happened. Otherwise don't take the job. Ultimately, I decided she wasn't worth the hassle, so I recast the role and cut her loose and in the end, the film was better off for it.

Brandon Kleyla, Writer/Producer/Director

I got this phone call from set telling me I have to get there immediately. When I arrive I see four LAPD surrounding one of my Extras wearing a Boston Policeman uniform. He had decided on his lunch break to walk onto the Universal tour and ride the Jurassic Park ride while still in his costume, gun and all. Needless to say it made the Universal employees nervous, not to mention the fact that he shouldn't be on that ride because at the end you get wet.

Chad Darnell, Extras Casting Director

I was working as an Associate Producer on a low budget cable show and we were working with a Porn Actress in the interview segment. I happened to be working on a side project at the time, which ironically, needed a Porn Star to appear (no, it wasn't a porno). After we finished with the segment, without thinking I approached her and started to chat her up about my project to see if she would be interested. As soon as I finished, my Supervising Producer pulled me aside and chewed me out for soliciting this Actress for other work while on his set. He was 100% right. It's extremely bad etiquette to do what I did. In the future I should have contacted her after the show wrapped through the proper channels. Those being her Agent, Manager, or Pimp...Oops, did I just say that?

Anonymous Producer

CHAPTER THREE

"You didn't say flashing!"

THE
CAMERA
DEPARTMENT

A BRIEF OVERVIEW

Headed by the Director of Photography (a.k.a. the Cinematographer), this department encapsulates anything and everything that has to do with the camera and with the physical filming of the motion picture.

The camera truck, usually parked the closest to the set, houses all the camera equipment and has a built in darkroom for loading raw film into the magazines. Because the equipment is expensive and fragile, only authorized crew members are allowed on the vehicle.

The D.P. is one of the most important personnel on a movie set. Decisions he makes will shape and affect the ultimate look of the movie.

The highly trained and skilled camera team must follow the D.P.'s orders as well as maintain a meticulous record of all camera activity. Because so much is dependent on the quality of the image, it is a high-pressure profession.

Movies run the gambit from realism (i.e. DOG DAY AFTERNOON) to formalism (i.e. THE GOOD, THE BAD AND THE UGLY) and everywhere in between. The way the footage is shot is the main visual factor in determining what type of movie is being presented. Movies, however, can be shot in a realistic style and still be about the fantastic such as JAWS or ALIEN.

Over 200 film and television Directors of Photography belong to the American Society of Cinematographers. This fraternity denotes its members by the initials ASC after the D.P.'s name in the credits.

Every year an Oscar™ is given by the Motion Picture Association of America at their annual Academy Awards Ceremony for achievement in the field of Cinematography. Notable past winners include: Janusz Kaminski (SAVING PRIVATE RYAN), John Toll (BRAVEHEART), Vittorio Storaro (APOCALYPSE NOW), and Conrad Hall (BUTCH CASSIDY & THE SUNDANCE KID).

THE PLAYERS

Director of Photography (D.P.): a.k.a. The Cinematographer. Responsible for the overall style of the movie, including lighting, shot composition, camera movements, and any decisions involving the look of the movie, including the printing of the film.

Camera Operator: In charge of the actual operation of the camera. Works under the direct supervision of the D.P. and makes sure that the shot is set correctly.

1st Assistant Camera (1st A.C.): Responsible for the overall maintenance of the camera, as well as changing lenses and pulling focus during the shots.

2nd Assistant Camera (2nd A.C.): Marks the slate and "claps" it before each take. Takes focus marks and is in charge of loading the new magazines and keeping notes about the shooting. Also in charge of giving Actors their marks on the floor and hooking up and wrangling the cables to the monitors.

Loader: On sets with film cameras. Responsible for loading the film into the magazines and bringing them to set. They have to make sure the right film stock gets loaded, that it isn't damaged by light and, then once exposed, organized properly for processing. Most of his/her time is spent on the Camera Truck.

DIT (Digital Imaging Technician): On sets with digital cameras. Responsible for managing and organizing the digital media as it comes out of the camera. They also monitor the image color and exposure on immediate "dailies" that can be screened on their computer.

Still Photographer: Takes still pictures during the production of actual scenes from the movie, staged shots, and/or behind the scenes pictures. The shots are generally used for publicity, advertising and archives.

TERMS YOU SHOULD KNOW

"Barney"
aka blimp. Sound protective padding that goes over the camera.

body
The camera casing where the various components, such as the lens, film magazine (or harddrive), tripod, etc... attach.

"Check the gate"
Once a Director is satisfied with a series of shots, the gate of the camera is inspected. This area, where the lens connects to the camera body, is prone to becoming dirty. A "Hair in the gate" could potentially ruin a series of shots.

cherry picker
a.k.a. Condor. A camera crane used for high-angle shots.

ditty bag
A small leather utility bag containing important tools that is usually hung under the tripod's head.

dolly
A wheeled mobile platform that is designed to hold the camera, the Camera Operator and the 1st A.C. It allows the camera to silently glide across the floor for a moving shot.

fluid head
A camera mount that utilizes compressed liquid to gain smooth movement, especially for slow, precise panning and tilting of the camera.

friction head
This camera mount uses the friction between two metal parts, making it more suitable for lock off shots.

gate
The part of the camera where each frame of film is momentarily exposed. The gate supports the pressure plate and holds the film in the proper place for exposure.

geared head

Better than a fluid head, this mount utilizes a series of gears and cranks, allowing for the smoothest and most precise panning and tilting.

hi-hat

A board used to mount the camera for low-angle shots.

light meter

A hand-held device that uses a photoelectric cell to measure the amount of light either falling on a subject or reflected by a scene. Used to determine the proper F-Stop for exposure.

magazine

The removable light-proof container that holds the film. When attached to the camera, it feeds the film into the camera to be exposed then recollects it onto another spool in the container.

"Marker"

Shouted by the 2nd A.C. when he "claps" the slate at the beginning of a new take to assist the Editor with synching the sound with the image during post-production.

matte box

A device mounted to the front of the camera lens that allows for the easy placement of mattes and filters and/or a sunshade.

"Roll out"

Called out when the camera magazine runs out of film.

slate

a.k.a. clapper board, a.k.a. synch slate. The hinged board that is photographed between takes. Written on it is vital information used in editing the film. The "Clap" is used to synchronize the sound with the picture. In post-production, the Editor coordinates the two by utilizing the first frame of the sticks banging together with the first sound emitted on the soundtrack.

spider-hat

A three-legged camera mount that can either be used separately or attached to a tripod. It is approximately eight inches high and generally used for low angles or in places where a tripod would be inconvenient.

spreader

A "Y" or "T" shaped support device with three extended arms that attaches to the tripod legs.

steadicam

Used for smooth tracking shots, this device attaches to the Camera Operator via a vest and uses a system of springs to counterbalance the weight of the camera.

sticks

The name given to a tripod with wooden or aluminum legs.

tail slate

This marks the shot at the end of a take if it was not marked at the beginning. Usually the clapboard is held upside down when this is done.

video village

The area, typically near or on the set, where the viewing monitors are placed for the Director and other key production personnel.

THE RULES OF SETIQUETTE

• Always yell *"Flashing"* then take a beat when taking a picture on set that requires a flash. This is to warn anyone looking through the camera lens or taking a light reading. (also see The Electric Department)

• Never look through the camera eyepiece unless you have permission from the Director of Photography. A shot may be be lined up and any movement of the camera could ruin the take.

• Keep the monitors clear. They are meant for the Director and other key personnel, not for your personal movie watching experience.

• As a general rule, always cross behind the camera, especially when a shot is being lined up.

• If you must step in front of the camera lens, always yell *"Crossing"*. This is a consideration for the Camera Operator focusing on something through the eyepiece.

• The slate is not a toy, especially the electronic ones. They are designed to coordinate the sound with the image and unauthorized use can cause problems.

• Never place food or beverages on top of a camera case or cart. A spilled drink could ruin valuable equipment stored inside and cost production time and money.

• Stand out of the way of the lights, especially when the Director of Photography is taking light readings. A misinterpreted light reading will cause an incorrect camera setting.

• If you can see the lens of the camera, the camera can see you.

ADVICE FROM THE EXPERTS

Owen Roizman, ASC
Academy Award™ Nominated Director of Photography
(THE EXORCIST, THE FRENCH CONNECTION, NETWORK, TOOTSIE)

The Air Up There

As a rule, you should be as cordial as possible and respectful of everybody else's position on the set. Try to be cooperative in any way you can. It's also important to have an air of confidence without having arrogance. By exuding that kind of confidence, the crew around you will feel assured that you know what you're doing and work their best to always back you up.

Be All That You Can Be

The D.P. is second in command to the Director on a movie set. You have a tremendous amount of responsibility to run the major part of the crew and get the work done efficiently as well as artistically. You are equivalent to a General running a small army and you have to achieve your mission. Your mission being: to get on film or video whatever the day's schedule is and what is required to record the scenes.

The Honeymoon's Over

I have a theory that I refer to as *"The Seven Week Syndrome"*. Assuming that everyone got along pretty well to start out with, the first seven weeks on a movie is usually great. By the seventh week you start to find out if you're going to keep going and get along well. That is typically about the time everybody starts to get really tired because of the long hours and get a little antsy with one another. By week seven it starts to get a little sketchy and you find out people's true colors.

Set Peeves

It used to drive me crazy when someone would sit in the chair designated for me. I'm on my feet all the time walking around doing things because as the D.P. you're always moving around and jumping from the dolly to the set to take meter readings. When I'm ready to go, I want to sit down and watch the video monitor or watch the set and the Actors. I need to do that from my chair. From time to time I would find someone sitting in my chair and it would drive me nuts. When I first started in the business, I was too polite to ask them to vacate my chair, so I would sit somewhere else and seethe about it. Finally, as I got more experienced, I would cue my Key Grip or Dolly Grip, because they were usually my hit men, and they wouldn't hesitate to kick someone out of my chair and make sure it didn't happen again.

The Long And Winding Road

Unfortunately in our business our hours are unnecessarily long. You get fatigued and you don't do your best work. You also get worried about the health and safety of your crew as well as your own health and safety. These things can play on your mind. I've found that the films that I had the most fun on were the ones that didn't have extremely long hours. We always got the film done efficiently and, in fact, better because you do better work when you're not tired.

"The people in the Camera Department are like the high school jocks."

Tom DeSanto, Producer

Richard H. Kline, ASC
Academy Award™ Nominated Director of Photography
(STAR TREK: THE MOTION PICTURE, KING KONG, CAMELOT)

Drafted…Into The Film Business

I'm second generation in the movie industry. My father, Benjamin H. Kline, started as a Cinematographer right after World War I. In those days, he worked on a lot of B-films and is credited on over 350 films. He was known to be very fast and efficient and worked well with the crew. He was really one of the boys.

It was summer of 1943 during World War II when I graduated high school. Most of the men were in the service and my dad said, *"Look, I think I can get you a job as an Assistant Cameraman because there's a need for it now and you'll have a profession behind you if you have to go into the service."* So he got me the job and I went to work almost the next day at Columbia Pictures on a film called Cover Girl with Gene Kelly, Rita Hayworth and Eve Arden.

Being that they knew my father and my presence on set didn't interfere with the work, everybody was kind to me, like you would be to a new puppy or something. I got to really know the below the line people and quickly learned that there are no two people alike on the set. I also learned that it's truly a coordination of people and as long as you utilize your craft and pay attention people will treat you with respect. Ironically, I only worked that one day with my father. After that I went on to other shows as Second Camera Operator.

When God Closes A Door...

I was in Rome working on the first Pink Panther as a Camera Operator and we had about two weeks to go and I got a telegram from John Frankenheimer. The telegram read, *"Want you as my Cameraman, contact me immediately at Goldwyn Studio."* I showed it to Blake Edwards and Phil Latham and they said, *"Get to the phone right away."* I called Frankenheimer and he said, *"Look, I'm doing this film called Sundays In May and I want you as the Cinematographer. Finish Pink Panther and come back immediately."*

So two weeks later I came back to the states and reported to him. Embarrassed, he says, *"I can't pull it. Kirk Douglas is in the film and he's not willing to try a new Cinematographer, he's getting a little old, he wants to protect his image."* It was extremely very disappointing.

Then two days later, I got a phone call from Ray Johnson, MGM's head of the Camera Department, and he said, *"There's a Producer over here that would like to talk to you. I'd advise meeting with him, in fact, I've set up a meeting, could you be here today at 2 o'clock?"* I said, *"I'll be there."*

I met the Writer/Producer, William Froug, who said he just finished the pilot to a TV series called MR. NOVAK. He said, *"How'd you like to be my Cinematographer for the series?"* and I said, *"Well, wait a minute, I've just had two days of a very disappointing moment, are you in a position to make me a Cinematographer?"* He said, *"All I have to do is go to the phone,"* and I said, *"Go to the phone."* He called the Camera Department right then and there and said, *"Start Richard Kline prepping MR. NOVAK."*

Afterwards, I asked him why he selected me, considering we had never met. He said, *"I'll tell you how: I have 5 favorite Directors and none of them knew each other and I asked them who would they upgrade to Cinematographer if they had the opportunity and you were the first one for each of them. So that's why I made up my mind right away."*

So that's how I became a Cinematographer.

From Mr. Novak To Mr. Oscar

I wanted to get back into features after MR. NOVAK was cancelled, so I only took pilots for the next year to keep my options open. The last pilot I did was for HOUSE OF WAX and it didn't sell. Jack Warner liked it very much and decided to make it into a feature. So they added two weeks of shooting onto it. We came back, shot for two weeks and they changed the title to the CHAMBER OF HORRORS.

During the last few days of filming, Warner Bros. had just signed to do CAMELOT. They brought in Josh Logan to direct it. He was going into a projection room to look at some film and then my Editor happened to be screening footage of CHAMBER OF HORRORS. Josh asked the editor who the Cameraman was. So, he came down to the stage and introduced himself.

The next day we met for an hour and I was hired to shoot CAMELOT, which I was nominated for an Oscar. From that point on, I've been in feature films ever since.

The Final Frontier

I try not to do the same types of films over and over. I always go for new territory and work in different genres whenever possible and when it's offered to me, I grab it. I was in the Caribbean doing a film with Michael Winner when I got the call that Robert Wise wanted me to do STAR TREK. Now I'm not a Trekkie and I never really looked at the series too much. When I reported to do the film, it was all new to me and I learned how deeply entrenched people from the series were especially Gene Rodenberry. It really was a pleasure to work on in many ways but it also had a lot of bumps on the road. Even to get started it had a lot of bumps. A lot of people have been previously involved with the movie in early stages and it had a little bit of a black cloud over it as far as production. The script was never really completed to everyone's satisfaction. Every day there were changes. Sometimes you'd even get 2 or 3 changes for the same scene in a given day, which was unbelievable. The other thing I didn't realize was how plentiful the fans were and how avid and insane they were about STAR TREK. So at the end of the day, I really didn't know that the movie would turn out to be what it would turn out to be.

"The one person you really want to get cool with on a set is the D.P."

Andre Royo, Actor

Steve Adcock
Camera Operator
(TROPIC THUNDER, "DEADWOOD", LETHAL WEAPON 4)

Stranger In A Strange Land

I came over to the States in 1986 and after doing odd jobs for a while, I looked for something more permanent. I found a job listing in the LA Times for an Assistant at a rental company. I applied for it thinking it was for renting tools or office equipment but soon discovered that it was a prop rental company. I got the job and worked there for about half a year before I got really bored of it. I did something smart though while I was working there. I kept track of the names of all the Set Dressers that were renting from us. So when I decided to quit, I rang them up searching for a job as a Decorator because it seemed like a cool job.

I was fortunate enough to land a gig as an additional Set Dresser on the movie MIRACLE MILE. What I didn't realize is that I wouldn't be working with the main shooting crew. I would be prepping the sets before the crew arrived and then move on to the next set while they shot. This kind of bummed me out. One day we were setting up right next door to the main company. I snuck on the set and watched all the activity and realized that it was all centralized at the camera. I was hooked because it occurred to me that working with the camera is not only a technical and creative job, but you're right there in the mix of it.

The Journey Continues...
I talked to a Camera Assistant and asked him how I could work for his department. Because it was difficult to get into the union, he recommended I work at a camera rental house. I researched them and applied for jobs at all of them. Panavision was the first to respond and they offered me a position in their camera accessories department. I wound up staying with them for two years and worked my way through the different departments until I was working the prep floor. Through the contacts I made at Panavision, I was eventually offered the chance to work as a Loader and from there got into the union.

Open Mouth, Insert Truck
On a recent show, I was working with a first-time Director and it was getting late in the day and we were doing a shot with two people walking out of a diner. It was kind of dead in the background, so I turned to the D.P. and casually said that the shot would probably look better with a truck driving by in the background. The Director overheard me and immediately latched onto the idea. Needless to say, the rest of the crew was not pleased. Not only did I just add another

element they were not prepared for, but I just grinded the scene to a halt. I screwed up. I should have just whispered it to the D.P. and let him make the decision. Generally speaking, if suggestions like this come from the D.P., nobody usually gets upset about the extra work, but coming from me, I look like a troublemaker. At the end of the day, the shot was better for it but with that said, you've still got to think before you say something.

The Old West

"DEADWOOD" is a particularly challenging shoot because we are usually shooting outside in different types of weather conditions. It regularly gets to over 100 degrees outside and you constantly have to move through mud or dust. It also doesn't help that TV is a fast paced medium and a lot of times there will be a limited amount of takes or the Director changes his mind. So, on this show I have to be ready to adapt and be on my game but at the end of the day it's worth it because the show is so fantastic and looks great (if I don't say so myself).

"It is the 1st A.D. and the Director of Photography that make most sets work. Period."

Bill Butler, ASC, Cinematographer

Tommy James Lewis
1st Assistant Camera
(GHOSTS OF GIRLFRINDS PAST, "DEADWOOD", SCARY MOVIE 2)

The First Day Jitters

You have to learn to not be intimidated by your surroundings. People new to a set tend to have the feeling that everyone is watching them at all times and you need to somehow let that go and concentrate on how you know how to do your job. Because you typically know the right way to do at least certain things, but that George Orwellian feeling can make you second guess yourself if you're not careful. This can lead to mistakes and more feelings of insecurity and then it becomes a self-fulfilling prophecy.

Getting To Know You

One of the first things I do when I'm new to a set and I don't know anyone is get the call sheet and keep it in my back pocket. I fold it in a way so I can at least see the names of the people in the Camera Department. You need to know everyone's name to do your job. I found on many sets that when you introduce yourself to people on the set that they don't tell you what position they are. It's like they assume you should already know just by looking at them. I found this to be a big problem. To fight this, I introduce myself as *"Tommy Lewis, The 1st A.C."* and this usually prompts them to do the same. It's a very simple thing to do and at the end of the day, if there is bad communication on set it makes everyone's job a nightmare, including you.

The Road Less Traveled

I went to film school at San Francisco State University and my goal there was to learn the entire process of making a film from pre-production to post. I had no delusions about being a big-time Director when I graduated or that Hollywood would throw up its arms to embrace me. I was more practical about the whole experience and tried to get as much out of it as I could. Once I graduated I fell into the Camera Department. There was a USC student film shooting in town and I applied for the position by, in essence, lying about my abilities and experience. I wound up doing a great job and got other student film work because of it. I was working with the same D.P. and after I graduated he got a film in Amsterdam and asked me to continue on with him. This was a great opportunity to work abroad and I took full advantage of it. It was like an all-expenses paid vacation and I got a little spoiled from the very beginning of my career. I started as a 1st A.C. skipping the typical apprentice route starting at Panavision then as a Loader and working my way up.

Little Boy Blue

When I got back from Holland, I moved to Los Angeles knowing only one other person who worked in the camera department. He got me a job as a Loader on a low-budget feature for $25.00 a day. But at the same time, I still shopped myself around as a 1st A.C. because I knew that's what I was good at and wanted to do. I was comfortable and confident in this position because I wasn't intimidated by the responsibility.

Still to this day I'm young for a 1st A.C. Most of the individuals in my position are 10 to 20 years older than me. This, of course, makes it much more difficult for me to break into this core group, so sometimes I feel like I'm an outsider or last on the list to be called for a job. I gave myself 5 years and slowly but surely, I was able to make a living during this period which gave me the confidence to stick with it.

HD, Or Not HD, That Is The Question

The industry is definitely, without a doubt, going High-Def. But no one believes that film will ever go away because at the end of the day, they are entirely different mediums. Film is a chemical and mechanical process and HD is inherently electronic. So no matter how similar they look, there will always be a difference and some people will always prefer the look of film. As a 1st A.C. I happen to like working with HD. I find it a lot easier to deal with. There are just as many variables involved but they are ultimately easier to deal with and locked in as the same all the time. In film, the variables can change all the time.

"I always say that the relationship between the Director and the D.P. is analogous to a marriage. If the chemistry works, it can be great and if it doesn't work, it can be hell."

Owen Roizman, ASC, Director of Photography

Linda R. Chen
Still Photographer
(ENEMY OF THE STATE, THE USUAL SUSPECTS, CRIMSON TIDE, PULP FICTION)

The Invisible Girl

As a Still Photographer you have to be completely invisible and physically stay out of the way. You also have to be very nimble because many times you are in very awkward situations. If there's a love scene or nudity on the set you're usually right in the front line. You are also in harm's way for some very dangerous things like explosions, car chases or various special effects. When you have a box (i.e. the camera) in front of your face and your eye is trained on a specific area, it's sometimes hard to see what's going on all around you. You wind up developing great peripheral vision because you can't always see what's going on directly around you.

Developing In Your Future...

I went to the USC film school to become a Cinematographer. But when I graduated, I discovered how hard it was for a woman to be taken seriously in that role so I realized I had to do something else. I fortunately landed a job doing story development, which I did for four years. Unfortunately, the Writer's Guild strike in 1988 put me out of work for almost 6 months. During that period of time I turned to photography to pay the bills. It wound up catching hold and to be honest I was pretty burnt out on development and yearned to be on a film set anyway. Working in development did give me a different perspective on working on the set, though. I now had a broader sense of the importance of putting a movie together for commercial purposes and how to interface with the marketing/distribution arm of the studios.

Picture Perfect

The best Still Photographers are the ones that work well with the studios and deal well with the suits when they come down to the set. You need to anticipate what their concerns are and what they look for in a film to market it in a particular way. It's also important to have a broad global view of the needs of the domestic and international markets, as well, because they are so different.

A Picture's Worth A Thousand Words

Sound is always an issue. My still camera makes noises even inside of the sound blimp and I usually have to coordinate with the Sound Department when I can actually take a picture so I don't screw up a take. I always try to be mindful of sound issues, especially during a love scene or when two characters are whispering. Movie cameras make a steady humming noise, so even if it's a problem it's a constant sound; my cameras make either a clicking noise or a "zing" if it's one with a motor. These noises can easily be picked up by the mikes so I try to configure my lenses so the camera will make as little noise as possible.

Can You Picture That?

On a set, the union rules state that the Still Photographer is the only person legally able to take pictures. Of course almost every Department has photographic needs, whether it be for continuity issues or personal departmental reasons. In the old days it was the Still Photographer's job to take continuity photos but that became a lot more relaxed after a while and now with the advent of digital cameras it makes sense for the departments to be responsible for keeping track of their own continuity.

Every once in a while a crew member would cross the line and take pictures for personal reasons and distribute them off the set. This puts me in a difficult spot because I have to decide whether or not to alert the union. I can be held responsible for any pictures that leak from a set that I'm working. Part of the reason why studios hire Still Photographers is so that the Actors have a certain comfort level knowing that all the photographs taken on a set have to be approved first by the studios and then by the Actors themselves.

Picture This

My job carries some big responsibilities and many people aren't aware of what can happen if the wrong picture gets out there. One time I had to go to a non-union processing lab to have some photos developed for continuity reasons. It was a major A-List Actor who, in the scene, had blood splatters on him. He had recently got into trouble in the press for beating up somebody. I was terrified that one of these pictures of him with blood on him would somehow leak and be used to further the negative press. So, I hired a lab to stay open after hours and physically stayed there and watched them develop the pictures. I wanted to make sure that I left with the entire test prints or unused photos that would have been trashed.

"Your people should know what you like and the way you like to work so that the slightest nod of the head or the wave of a hand will get a light turned on or changed without a big fuss."

Bill Butler, ASC, Cinematographer

TALES FROM THE SET

I was working on a film in San Francisco with a Director who is notorious for being, let's just say *"a big personality"*. We were shooting a bullet car chase sequence and we had a camera mount on the front of a car and in the trunk was the clamshell video recorder. Everything was all set to go and we filmed the first take without a hitch. We opened up the trunk and pulled out the clamshell so the Director could review the footage. He hit play and almost immediately the screen goes blank. Evidently the inertia of the car taking off and slamming down caused the video recorder to malfunction. The Director was pissed off and started yelling at the Video Assist Operator. They finally reset the recorder in the trunk and did Take-2. Of course the exact same thing happened. Furious, the Director ripped the clamshell out of the trunk and smashed it on the ground where he then proceeded to stomp on it until it was busted into a hundred pieces. The poor Video Assist Operator did his best to collect all the parts but it was pretty futile at that point.

A month later the D.P. and me were out on a location scout with the Director in Napa Valley when his phone went dead. He asked the D.P. if he could use his phone to make a call to the Art Director. Reluctantly, the D.P. complied. As expected, the phone call became heated and the Director started screaming at the Art Director using every expletive in the book as the D.P. waited for the inevitable destruction of his phone. Just as the Director was about to throw the phone to the ground in anger, the D.P. lunged for it and tore it from his hand. Needless to say no one in the Camera Department was too keen on lending the Director any of our personal gear from that point on.

Anonymous Camera Operator

I was working on a TV series and it was a crazy pace. I was told that the next scene was going to be hand held. We had a third camera that was a lot lighter that the Camera Operator preferred. My 2nd A.C. volunteered to do it so I sent him to the Camera truck to convert the camera to hand held. As we set up the first shot I put the camera up on the Operator's shoulder and we rolled. It went well but as I pulled the camera off by the front rods, the support bracket with the matte box just slipped right off and the camera fell off the Operator's shoulder and slammed on the ground. Needless to say, everyone on the crew stopped what they were doing to see the camera lying on the grass, which is a very rare sight on a set. Fortunately, the camera was fine and we carried on. But what I learned is if you ever have your 2nd Assistant prepare the camera for you, make sure you double-check everything. In this situation, the 2nd A.C. did not entirely lock down the bracket that attaches the matte box to the camera, and that one little thing could have lost them an expensive Panavision Camera and possibly my job and reputation.

Anonymous 1st Assistant Camera

Normally there is only one Still Photographer on a set, though I once worked on a movie where the Lead Actor requested his own Photographer, as well. Unfortunately this Photographer wasn't as set savvy as he should have been. He was taking pictures behind me and wound up getting in the way of a Boom Operator in the middle of a very long and fast dolly shot. I all of a sudden heard a big crash behind me and turned to see the literal train wreck that had occurred. Needless to say, he was thrown off the set and asked to never return.

Linda R. Chen, Still Photographer

On the first feature I directed, I had given the D.P. a complete shot list for the entire film. I knew in my head how I wanted the film to cut together and exactly what coverage I would need. When it came time to shoot the movie, he just ignored it and insisted that we shoot other shots that I knew were not necessary. He wouldn't listen to me and would go ahead and shoot what he deemed was important after we'd finish my version, claiming that I'd thank him in the editing room. The only thing I thanked him for was having a whole bunch of extra footage that not only I didn't need, but had to pay for, to boot.

Brandon Kleyla, Writer/Producer/Director

Actors are very conscious of how they look and how they want to be portrayed, and we have to respect that. Whatever we shoot for continuity sake stays in the book. Without my knowledge, one of our crew was taking her own personal set shots of the Actors. In one instance my Actor had entered the trailer to ask a question and saw his picture up on the mirror. He wanted to know if that was something the Still Photographer had taken of him. When he found out that it wasn't he became very upset. He didn't like the fact that it was done without his authorization, not to mention the fact that it was up on display for all to see. What this crew person was evidently doing was following us around set and taking her own photos. We had to set her straight and let her know that her actions were highly inappropriate.

Monica Haynes, Costume Supervisor

I once had a scary incident while photographing a car chase. During the rehearsals they do it at quarter speed, then they ramp it up to half speed until finally they go full speed for the take. They had wet down the pavement so it had a nice sheen to catch the light. Because the car was rigged with all the equipment, it tended to favor one side and also had built up incredible centrifical force. In the scene the driver had to turn the corner at high speed. The camera crew (including me) was on the corner filming the action. As the car came around the corner, it spun out of control and nearly hit us. Because I could only see the action through my myopic view, I reacted a lot slower and barely avoided getting run over.

Linda R. Chen, Still Photographer

The Golden rule is that under no circumstances do you run out of film. It's of utmost importance that you keep an eye on the Production report to keep track of the film length count so you never run out while shooting. On low-budget films they typically buy a couple of rolls to start out with and go from there because no one wants to buy too much film and be stuck with it after the show wraps. Every penny counts. On an independent movie I was working on with an inexperienced Production team, we actually ran out of film during a shoot day. They had to call the day's shooting and the Production Manager was nowhere to be found to deal with the problem. We were all laughing because we got to go home early. The next day of filming was scheduled for a late call, so in theory, there was plenty of time to buy some more film stock. When the crew arrived on set the next day, they discovered that nobody bothered to buy any more film stock. Everyone was scratching their heads trying to figure out what the hell was going on. By the time the Production Manager shows up a half hour later, the entire crew is just lounging around or playing Frisbee. He wants to know why nobody's working and we tell him there's no film. He gets upset and wants to know why someone didn't buy some, not realizing that it's his job. Completely embarrassed, he proceeded to scramble to get some new film stock to the set as fast as humanly possible. The long and the short of it, the crew had some wonderful time off in the morning that really helped to recharge their batteries.

Eric Miller, Transportation Coordinator

I once saw a 2nd A.C. during a series of shots, slate a take by saying, *"Scene 9, for the 31st time."* The Actor walked off the set and the 2nd A.C. almost got fired.

Daniel Roebuck, Actor

CHAPTER FOUR

"This Take is MOS...So keep quiet!"

THE
SOUND
DEPARTMENT

A BRIEF OVERVIEW

In case you didn't realize it, the days of silent films are over. Ever since a flick known as THE JAZZ SINGER (no, not the one with Neil Diamond) opened in 1927, movies have been as much about the sound experience as the visual aspect. So before you can be impressed with the Ultra Stereo-DTS-Dolby-THX-Surround Sense-O-Vision, it has to be recorded on the set by the Sound Department.

First you must understand that the sound and the image are two separate entities. Yes, they are recorded at the same time, but it is not until post-production that they are married together. And it is vitally important that the sound being recorded on the set is as clear and accurate as possible.

The Sound Department is led by the Sound Mixer who runs the mixing board, which coordinates the recording of sound from various sources. He/she has to have a good ear and a superlative knowledge of recording equipment and of acoustics. Think about how different sound can be in a cramped room as opposed to an open field. The Mixer has a small team that consists of a Boom Operator and several other Assistants and Cable Pullers.

When filming a shot on the set, the camera and the sound are instructed to start rolling at the same time. Because it takes a couple of seconds for the sound equipment to get up to the proper recording speed, the Sound Operator will cue the Director when they're ready. They will record until the Director yells *"Cut"*.

Microphones placed on, near or above the Actors collect the sound and transfer it to the mixer, which records it digitally. A sound log is maintained which comments on the quality of each take. Sometimes the visual aspect is perfect, but if the sound if off, especially during key dialogue scenes, it may need to be reshot.

During post-production the best sound elements are mixed together with sound effects and finally the film soundtrack to hopefully give you the sensation of being immersed in the image.

THE PLAYERS

Sound Mixer: a.k.a. Sound Engineer. Responsible for recording of sound during the filming of the movie. Uses the mixing panel to coordinate incoming sound from various microphones used during a shot.

Boom Operator: Utilizes a boomed microphone held above the Actors' heads just out of frame to capture the sounds and dialogue as clearly as possible.

Cable / Utility: Wrangles the cables that connect the microphones to the mixer. Makes sure that they don't get in the way of the Actors or crew members.

Video Assist Operator: Individual responsible for video taping each take as it is filmed. Hooked up directly to the camera, when the footage is played back, it shows exactly what the camera shot.

<u>TERMS YOU SHOULD KNOW</u>

actual sound
Dialogue and ambient sound recorded during the filming of a scene.

ADR
(Automatic Dialogue Replacement) a.k.a. "Looping." In a post-production studio, Actors replace unusable production dialogue with new voice tracks synchronized to the picture.

ambient sound
"Room or Air Tone" Perceptible natural sound created by a real environment.

body mike
A microphone hidden on an Actor, usually in the wardrobe or concealed in the hair.

boom
a.k.a. fishpole. Mobile telescoping rod mounted to the microphone to position it out of frame, over the Actors' heads for better sound.

comtech
Wireless headset receiver given to the Director and other production staff in order to listen to production sound and/or dialogue that may be unhearable.

directional mike
a.k.a. Shotgun Mike. Utilized to pin point exact sounds and limit ambient noises. Especially good for dialogue.

mixer
a.k.a. mixing panel. Small, portable device used on the set to record and mix the sound from the various microphones. The mixer has controls for volume and equalization.

MOS
(Mit Out Sound) Film recorded without the optical strip for scenes that don't require any actual sound.

patch cord
Cable with a plug used for connecting sound equipment such as a microphone to the sound recorder.

RF hit
Drop out in the radio transmission due to interference that results in unusable recorded sound.

rifle/gun mike
Microphone that can be pointed in any direction to pick up a specific sound.

sound monitor
a.k.a. monitor speaker. Loudspeaker attached to the sound equipment used for monitoring the quality of the sound during recording. Headphones are used on the set to eliminate the extra noise.

sound speed
The rate of speed that the film passes through the camera to allow for proper audio playback when it is run through a projector. The Standardized speed is 24 frames per second.

"Speed"
Term shouted out by the Sound Recordist to let the Director know that the sound is functioning and operating at same speed as the camera and there is enough pre-roll for time code synchronization.

transmitter
Battery powered radio hidden on the Actor.

video assist
A video system attached to the camera that transmits the exact image seen through the camera lens. It allows for the simultaneous video taping of the filmed scene via a connected monitor.

wild lines
Lines of dialogue not recorded in synch with the camera for use in sound editing during Post-Production.

wild sound
(Nonsynchronous Sound) Sounds not recorded in synch with the camera for use in sound editing during post-production.

wild track
Blanket term used to identify any sound recorded not in synch with the camera. May include dialogue, ambient sound or sound effects.

"wire an actor"
To conceal a microphone and a radio transmitter on an Actor.

wireless mike
Radio transmitter worn by an Actor that sends sound over a short distance. Used when a boom mike or cabled mike are impractical.

yaggi
Hand-held stand mounted antenna used for better reception for radio mikes and to avoid RF hits.

zeppelin
a.k.a. Rycote. Vented screen placed over a shotgun microphone used to reduce the sound of wind.

THE RULES OF SETIQUETTE

• Be careful what you say on set. There has been many a time when an open mike picked up a conversation not meant for the general public.

• Be aware of body mikes. Adjustments made after the fact can affect the quality of the recorded sound or cause damage to the equipment.

• Don't play with or speak into microphones to amuse the crew or yourself for that matter. You must remember that there is someone on the receiving end of the mike who probably won't appreciate your annoying sense of humor.

• Avoid unexpected loud noises. These outbursts of sound can wreak havoc on the Sound Recordists' sensitive ears.

• When a scene is being filmed stay as quiet and still as humanly possible. Even insignificant body movements and loud breathing can be picked up by the sound equipment.

• As much as it seems absurd, stay quiet during a MOS shot. Even though there isn't any sound being recorded, the crew still needs quiet to concentrate.

• Be aware of sound cables. Because the microphone and sound cart are far apart, there needs to be lengths of cable connecting them, usually through heavy traffic areas. If someone is standing on a cable it can cause major problems when the Boom Operator has to move about during the shot.

• Never place food or drinks on or near the sound equipment. A spilled drink could severely damage the delicate equipment.

• Don't pester the Video Assist Operator to play back a scene for your personal amusement. The technology is there to help the Director and the Actors, not to be a private screening for you.

ADVICE FROM THE EXPERTS

J.M. Logan
Sound Designer
(Boo!, Demons at the Door, Black Mask 2: City of Masks)

The Invisible Man

The sound guys on set tend to be forgotten a lot of the time. They are not in the forefront of the action and will far more often work around everyone else than the other way around, but many fail to realize just how critical the Sound Department is to the completion of the film in post. It's important to realize during the heat of the battle that everything you do on the set has to be dealt with later and while you may not see the immediate results, it will all come back around again for a year in post-production. Sound is often sacrificed for the image during the shoot, as laying in sound in post is arguably cheaper than having to work around it on set, but the closer you can get to having very clean production sound the more work you save a whole crew of people later on down the road.

The Audience Is Listening

Whether the camera is rolling or not, the Sound Department hears everything, and the entire synchronicity of the set depends on everyone being able to hear each other when they need to. Generally it's a good idea to not interact with the Sound Mixer or the Boom Operator unless it's necessary, as many times they may be doing something or listening to something that is actually taking place on a completely different part of the set (that you may have no idea about) and all they have is their headphones to tell them what decisions they need to be making – even if they look idle. Do not be offended if they do not respond to you as they stare into space with headphones on, it is quite likely they didn't hear you. When they ask you to be quiet, be quiet.

Snakes In the Grass

As you would with power cables, always be aware of sound cables that may snake around the set. Stepping on them can damage them, and the Boom Operator often needs to move during a take. So a

Boom Operator that finds you standing on their cable when they need to silently walk 10 feet with their focus 15 feet in front of them and their arms above their head while narrowly skirting the edge of frame and negotiating an 18k during a take will most likely result in a microphone in an uncomfortable place. The sound cart is not your personal battery storage area. Contrary to popular belief, the recording of a minute of "wild room tone" is not actually just a time of personal reflection.

On Sound Mixers

Sound Mixers and Boom Operators work in coordination with camera and the A.D. to capture the live sound of the action while being as invisible and low maintenance as possible. This includes attending rehearsals, deciding where the most unobtrusive area for placing the boom and/or wireless mikes or even planted mikes might be in order to serve the action of the scene and/or the movement of the camera.

I Have A Black Belt in Sound

The Sound Department is one of the least obviously interactive departments as the Mixer generally digs into one area and once set, rarely needs to move during a set up, and the Boom Operator's whole job is to be the ninjas of film-making. Work life is usually friendly and often funny, but much time is spent talking with the boom on the talk back mic having private conversations about the Actors and listening to the wireless mic's that people forget are turned on.

"The business is always evolving. So you can either evolve with it or be left behind."
David Grossman, Executive Producer

James P. Slingluff
Sound Mixer / Boom Operator
(NIGHT SKIES, THE FALLEN ONES, "SON OF THE BEACH")

Sound Advice

My advice to anyone in the Sound Department stepping onto a movie set for the first time is to do your homework. That is to say, come prepared with some knowledge of the workings of the set, and with a good degree of understanding the operation and function of the tools of their position.

Know how a scene is set up to shoot, the step by step verbal process and the procedures that leads to the call of *"Action"* from the Director. Realize that there are many rehearsals that must be attended and performed to know what tools are necessary for that scene. Boom Operators must know that they will follow the dialogue and movement of the Actors and be aware of any obstacles overhead and in the path they must take. Through rehearsals they should always know what lens size is being used on the camera and what Actor or group of Actors are on camera in every shot so that the microphone selected is picking up the proper dialogue for that take. Communication is essential with the other crew members involved in the shot, so that everyone knows where they will be moving during the action. It all comes down to learning the language of the workplace and having a good idea of what's happening, then being prepared to learn the fine details on the fly.

On Being A Sound Mixer

I use my knowledge and experience to capture audio in the environment provided to me during filming. My tools are mostly electronic as well as some very primitive devices such as umbrellas and blocks of wood. I use a mixing panel to control the audio signal coming from the microphone directed at the Actor by the Boom Operator. I have the option of altering the signal sent to the recording device at this point. I can change the volume, the balance, left or right, the equalization of the frequencies and who gets to hear the sound on the set among many other things. I regulate this altered signal into the recording device to obtain the optimal recorded sound.

I must keep track of all the recorded takes on a log called a sound report. The sound report keeps record of each tape, disk, hard drive, flash card, etc., as to what is recorded on the media. This is for the transfer stage and then sound editing. I identify the roll number, the date, the production company, the title of the project, the recording device, the time code rate, the sample rate and the level of the reference tone. I must keep track of each recorded take. I identify the scene number, the take number and the time code number, if applicable. During the shot I write down any problems that occur during the take. For example if a plane is audible over the dialogue. This report is made in triplicate and a copy is given to the Script Supervisor. Another copy is attached to the original recorded media and I keep a copy for my files.

Loud And Clear

When I was a kid I loved watching movies and now I love making movies just as much. I've held several other positions in the film business and I can honestly say I hold them all in high esteem. There is nothing like sitting down and watching the fruits of your labor unfold on the screen in front of you, no matter what position you were at. It is truly a team event.

"Video Assist is a noble profession, but remember after all the hard work you do and all the stress you go through, nothing you do will make it into the final movie."

David Goldsmith, Video Assist Operator

Donald Vespoint
Boom Operator
(Hidden Agenda, "Son of the Beach", "Team Knight Rider")

Working Out

Though it may not seem like it, holding the boom is a very physical job. The boom with the smallest mike possible weighs over 8 pounds. If you're doing a long take it can get really tough on your arms so you just have to hanker down and just get through it. I don't ever want to be the reason that they have to do another take. In order to make it through a shoot day, I do my best to get enough rest the night before. Unfortunately with turn around times being what they are, especially on low-budget or non-union shows, that can be difficult.

I'm Being Followed By A Boom Shadow

One of the most difficult challenges is trying to keep shadows off the Actors during the scenes. Some lighting set-ups are incredibly elaborate, making it almost impossible to not cast shadows and that's when the Actors are standing still. As soon as they move, it's a whole other story. If you're having serious problems with the above lighting you can always put the microphone down at the Actor's knees pointing straight up and that will usually solve the problem.

Care To Run Some Lines?

A part of my job that a lot of people don't realize is that, technically speaking, I have to memorize the dialogue for all the characters in a given scene. The reason is because I need to have the boom in place before they start talking. If I don't do my job well then they'll have to loop the dialogue in Post and that costs time and money. For most of my career I worked on a lot of non-union and low-budget films. So, on a given day, I had to learn up to 20 pages of dialogue.

Can You Hear Me Now?

There are many different types of microphones and part of my job is knowing which one is going to be the most efficient for the scene. There are directional mikes that will pick up the sound of only what its pointing at and omni-directional mikes that will pick up every-thing in the room. For times when they're shooting with a wide lens, I'll have to use a wireless microphone. But that has its own set of problems, specifically where to place it on the Actor, especially if they're wearing a bathing suit or nothing at all.

The Phantom Menace

I was on location at a house and we were shooting in the bedroom. The Actor and Actress were walking around the room just talking. It should have been a pretty easy scene. Unfortunately, during Take 1, a buzzing sound rang out when they got near the closet door. After the scene cut, my Mixer came over the headset and asked me what that sound was. He wanted to know if I was crossing over an electric cable. But I wasn't. We did another take and it happened again. The same again on take three so the scene was constantly NG (no good) for sound. We had to stop filming while we searched out the phantom noise. The A.D. had everyone be quiet on the set while I slowly ran my mike around the trouble spot. It was like something out of CSI.

It turned out to be coming from the house itself! The sound was coming from a space in the wall 3ft from the closet door and 7ft up from the floor. There must have been some faulty wiring or something. Unfortunately there was no way to get rid of the noise through the mixer or fix the problem. We had to live with it. Ultimately, we shot some coverage away from that part of the wall so they could decide in Post whether they wanted to ADR it or not.

"A lot of crew members start as a Boom Operator because they think it's an easy job...Well, it's not!"

Henry Coccetti, Gaffer

David "Goldy" Goldsmith
Video Assist Operator
(TWILIGHT SAGA: BREAKING DAWN PARTS 1 & 2, MR. & MRS. SMITH, DODGEBALL, PIRATES OF THE CARIBBEAN)

Change Is Good

I consider myself a Video Assist Artist and I've been trying to get the title changed from Video Assist Operator or VPR guy because the role of Video Assist, especially in the feature film world, has expanded and become incredibly artistic. It's now a major part of my job description to edit sequences together throughout the day for the Director and Producers to look over as we're shooting. I'm even finding a lot of D.P.'s are relying on me to help make sure eye-lines are matching in a cut properly.

Personality Type F (For "Film")

Making a feature film is an all-consuming, all-departmental collaboration. So before you even think about working in the film industry remember that there is absolutely nothing glamorous about what we do. It consists of hours upon hours of boredom mixed up with 5 to 10 minutes of absolute terror every day. It also requires an incredible attention to detail and an unbelievable ability to be flexible. It is an incredibly rare breed that loves waking up long before the sun does and working this kind of roller-coaster of a job.

The Warm And Fuzzies

I worked on a film in Florida with a P.A. that was 51 years old. He was a bit of a character. I asked him why the hell he was a P.A. at his age. He told me that he'd been a carpenter his whole life and that in all of his professional working on construction crews, he had never before seen a level of professionalism that he saw in the film industry. When I asked him to elaborate, he said that you put 70 people together on day one that generally have never met one another and all of a sudden a symphony begins and everyone knows exactly what they should be doing. That doesn't exist anywhere else in the world.

Considering this wise observation, remember that you are on the adventure of a lifetime with a workload that is asinine to the average human being with challenges that are on par with climbing sheer walls of ice and if you like being hung upside down by your testicles in 90 mile per hour wind and getting beat across the face while getting yelled at, this job's for you.

One Of Those Lives: Part 1

I started out as an Actor as a kid. I had a lot of early success in my youth, but it didn't go very far. Suddenly the zits came, the braces then the weight problems and soon no one wanted to hire me anymore. After a couple of years of therapy I decided I didn't want to work in the entertainment business ever again because it ruined my life. I traveled the world and opened up a restaurant. I was touring with a band across the country until one day I found that the lead singer was banging my girlfriend. It took about eight minutes for me to break up with the band and with my girlfriend. After that blinding flash of hell I worked at a coffee bar in Hermosa Beach to get back on my feet.

There was a regular customer who came every day when I opened up at 5am. He was a Commercial Assistant Director. We got to be friends over the next couple of months and he consistently tried to convince me to get back in the industry. I wasn't interested. It all came to a head one day when he was in a bind and begged me to help him out on this 100-Collect commercial with Christopher Lloyd and a monkey. He needed an extra P.A. I finally relented and it wound up being the single hardest work day of my entire career to that point, but it was also one of the most fun. I wound up standing out from the rest of the P.A.'s and the Production Manager was so impressed with me that he invited me back for three other upcoming commercials.

One Of Those Lives: Part 2

After that I became an Assistant to the Director and soon became friends with his Video Assist Operator. I thought he had the coolest job. Not only did he get to sit all day, he got paid well to do it! It was also the first time I saw someone editing on set and it showed me a whole new creative dimension to a job that seemed so dull before. He took me under his wing as an Assistant and showed me the ropes. I soon started working on the low budget non-union commercials and videos and that's where I really learned the craft.

One day he asked me to turn over the day's invoice to the Producer. He handed it to me in an unsealed envelope. Now I know it wasn't the right thing to do, but my curiosity got the better of me and I looked at the receipt. The one-day equipment rental was $796.22. I'll never forget that number, it's burned in my mind, because here I was thinking I was Donald Trump making $350.00 for the day and this inanimate object was earning twice as much as me.

One Of Those Lives: Part 3

About 3 weeks later I got a call to do the movie LADDER 49. They said they heard I was a great worker and wanted to hire me, but they wanted to know what kind of gear I had. I told them that I had the greatest package out there even though at the time I didn't even own so much as a video cable. They asked me to FAX over my equipment list and the rental prices. I completely made up in my mind the cart that I would build for myself and put it down on paper without even bothering to research how much it would cost. I then called around to different houses and figured out how much this type of equipment would rent for and wrote that down.

The next day the Producer called back and booked me for the job. I wound up mortgaging everything I owned and maxing out my credit cards to buy the equipment I promised and the rest is history. I now have two systems and a small crew of people who work for me…of course the weight problem is still there.

"A film set is like High School with money."

Tom DeSanto, Producer

TALES FROM THE SET

I have a strong rule on my sets that no one can raise their voice to me. It's very important because directing a film is like being a General in a military operation and it really requires respect and understanding of my authority. Privately, anybody can say anything they want, but on set, in front of people, it's very important to respect my position.

On one film, I had a Video Assist Operator who apparently was the only person in the country I was shooting in who had this particular piece of technology. We were shooting a scene and I said, *"I need playback,"* and he replied, *"I'm getting it to you,"* but I don't think I heard him. So I asked again. He suddenly snapped at me and said, *"I'm fucking doing it!"* So I said, *"You're out of here,"* and I fired him on the spot. And he said, *"Good luck finding anyone else with my rig,"* which I replied with, *"People have been making movies for nearly a hundred years without your rig, I think we'll survive."*

We continued shooting the movie and everything was fine, and then a month or so later, he wrote me an apology letter. He said he'd developed a bit of an ego because of the system that he had and he was wrong. So I hired him back on the 2nd Unit and he did a great job. I'm not a grudge holder. Everyone makes mistakes, and if you're willing to cop to it and offer the respect of an apology, who am I to not accept that? I admire people who can do that and I try to do it myself when I make mistakes.

Bryan Singer, Director/Producer

Sometimes sound doesn't come through clearly when filming on set and the proper etiquette for that is to wait it out and deal with it. At the end of the take you tell the A.D. that it was N.G.(Not Good) for sound. When I was working on this low-budget horror/comedy, the Sound Mixer for some reason would take matters into his own hands. Every time there was a minor sound glitch or slight noise, he would call *"Cut"* instead of the Director and they would have to stop rolling. Big mistake. Eventually that guy got fired.

James Gunn, Screenwriter

We were doing a master shot of this family eating around a table. Because it was so wide I had to use a lavaliere mike placed in a lamp on the table to record the sound. Everything went fine with the shot. Later in the day, in the same scene the lamp catches on fire. We're filming the shot with the flaming lamp when it occurs to me that I never removed the microphone. I turned to my Boom Operator and asked him if he removed it and he shook his head. He assumed I had removed it after the master shot. We just sat and watched as the lamp continued to burn and prayed for the best.

D.J. Ritchie, Sound Mixer

It was my first day on a set as a P.A. and the Key Grip ran up to me and told me to get him a half-apple and a pancake ASAP. So I immediately ran to the Caterer and asked for the single pancake. The Caterer looked at me like I was crazy and told me that they weren't serving right now. I told him I didn't care and demanded what I asked for. Finally, he made me the pancake. I then ran to Craft Service, found an apple, cut it in half and shoved it on the plate with the pancake. I remember running back to the set like my very life depended on it. The A.D. wanted to know where the hell I had gotten off to. I showed him the plate and told him of the Key Grip's request. It took only a minute for the entire crew to laugh at me as I stood there not getting the joke.

David Goldsmith, Video Assist Operator

There are walkie talkies everywhere on a set and you have to be very careful what you say over them because you never know who's going to be listening. Every department has its own channel. Sometimes the talk on the Transportation channel gets a little ribald to put it mildly. My Drivers would usually leave their walkies wide open on the dashboard of their cars while they are driving. We were working on a film with Ann-Margret and Angie Dickinson and, even though they are older women, they are hot! Everyone in my Department young and old agreed about this fact and weren't too shy to share it amongst the Transportation Department.

One day Angie Dickinson had been working and we wrapped her and sent her off with one of our Drivers. A few minutes later, one of my crew comes over the walkie and using rather colorful language that I won't repeat says, *"Did you guys check out Ann-Margret? She is so hot. I'd love to bang her! She's hotter than any other woman I've seen this week!"* My heart literally sunk in my chest. I immediately grabbed my walkie and in the most relaxed way said, *"Good evening ladies and gentlemen, this is the Transportation Coordinator and I'd like to remind you that there are other walkies on the set, so please be respectful and mindful of what you say."* I hear dead silence on the channel. Nobody responds. Eventually, the Driver arrives back at the set and knowing exactly what's happened, I hoof it over to him. I'm expecting the worse, only to discover that the Driver has a big smirk on his face. I ask him what happened and he told me that we really dodged the bullet. The walkie was on and she had heard the comment but she said, *"First off, I'm Angie Dickinson, not Ann-Margret, but thank you for the compliment because it would be a good day when I can be as beautiful and hot as Ann Margret. Thank all the Transpo guys for their love."* She never said a word about it after that. This woman is a class act in my book.

Anonymous Transportation Coordinator

The Call Sheet for the first day of the show gave the address for the set but not for the parking at a downtown Los Angeles location. It gave general cross streets only. I arrived at the parking location and proceeded to the nearest Catering Truck I saw across the street for breakfast. The movie I was on was a relatively low-budget, but this menu was quite extent. I stepped up to the window and ordered the vegetarian eggs benedict. The Cook looked at me and asked who I was. I said that I was Jim the Sound Mixer. He said *'Are you new?"* I said *"Yeah, this is my first day."* I ate a breakfast that couldn't be beat then looked for the Camera Truck where my sound gear was. It didn't take me too long to realize that I was on the wrong movie set. I quickly walked away and proceeded to the proper set where everyone was eating a fast food breakfast.

James P. Slingluff, Sound Mixer

It was this P.A.'s first day on set and he was given a walkie and told to participate in this safety meeting. That day they were going to be shooting with wolves and the Animal Trainer let everyone know that even though they were trained, these wolves are wild animals. He went on to explain that they have electrified wire cages surrounding the wolves to protect the crew. As you'd expect, during lunch the electric wire went down and all the wolves escaped into the woods. The A.D. called the crew together and told everyone with a walkie to spread out to search for them. The Trainer reiterated that they should under no circumstances approach the wolves. Just get on the walkie and alert the Trainers. 25 minutes later they had recaptured all the wolves except for one which happened to be the most fierce of the bunch.

All of a sudden the new P.A. comes over the walkie. He's found the wolf. The Trainer got on the walkie and asked the P.A. where he was. He told him very slowly that he was right next to the wolf. The Trainer tried to keep him calm and then asked (trying to ascertain the P.A.'s location) where the wolf was. The P.A. started to blubber that the wolf was right in front of him looking straight at him. Still not helping, the Trainer kept on re-asking the question in as many ways as possible. This went on for ten minutes until finally somebody spotted the poor kid who had climbed up a tree to save himself.

David Goldsmith, Video Assist Operator

CHAPTER FIVE

"Next time, ask for a stinger!"

THE
ELECTRIC
DEPARTMENT

A BRIEF OVERVIEW

Unless you're shooting entirely outdoors in the middle of the day or relying totally on ambient light for your interiors, you're going to need electricity. This is where this department shines (pun intended!).

The electrical team is lead by the Gaffer (The Chief Lighting Technician) who is in charge of everything that has to do with lighting the set: from the power source to the extension cords used for plugging the lights in. He is responsible for assembling a lighting package that has everything that could ever be needed to adequately light each set up.

Because being caught with your pants down is not an option, it takes considerable planning and know-how to put a successful light package together. A movie that takes place solely in one room has a tremendously different package than one filmed entirely on-location in the darkest depths of Africa.

Enormous trucks house the equipment on set and a good-sized crew is enlisted to help maintain it. Being a Set Lighting Technician is not an easy job. Consider how many lights are required to light even a simple scene. It can appear at times to be a thankless profession.

Every scene has its own unique lighting arrangement, so after every set up, lights have to be adjusted, added or removed. Most of the workday is used up due to the time it takes to relight between set ups. Copious notes are maintained by various departments in order to keep the lighting consistent within the multiple shots needed for each scene.

To really get a sense of how important lighting is, try to imagine watching a horror movie like THE EXORCIST lit with harsh bright light or a romantic comedy like WHEN HARRY MET SALLY filled with darkness and shadows. They wouldn't work, because it would change the mood of each film. The style of lighting helps in determining what type of movie is being presented.

THE PLAYERS

Gaffer: a.k.a. Chief Lighting Technician. The head Set Lighting Technician working under the supervision of the Director of Photography. The Gaffer is responsible for supplying the lights as well as the power source.

Best Boy Electric: a.k.a. Assistant Chief Lighting Technician. The main Assistant to the Gaffer.

Set Lighting Technician / Lamp Operator: Electric Department crew members that assist the Gaffer by placing, operating, and maintaining all the lights on the set.

Dimmer Operator: Set Lighting Technician in charge of operating the dimmer during shooting.

TERMS YOU SHOULD KNOW

ambient light
Environmental light or general non-directional light that naturally illuminates an Actor or a scene.

ammeter
A device used by Set Lighting Technicians to measure the amount of amperage supplied by an electric current.

arc lamp
Employed when a strong luminosity is required, the slightly noisy high-intensity lamps are the preferred type of light on most movie sets. They don't have a long life but do produce an intense white light from a single source.

baby
A small 1,000 watt spotlight typically used for close-ups, angle shots, or as a kick light.

barn doors
Attached to the front of a light. Two or four hinged doors that can be adjusted and rotated to regulate the amount of light allowed to shine on the scene.

broad
Used as fill light, this rectangular floodlight projects a wide beam creating a soft and flat illumination.

brute
A large and extremely powerful (225 amps) arc spotlight used to simulate daylight when shooting interiors.

dimmer
A device that regulates the power supply to a light, allowing for it to be increased or decreased variably.

eye light

A small directional light, usually near the camera, that lights an Actor's eyes but won't affect the camera exposure.

fill light

A soft, diffused light used to counteract the harsh shadows created by the key light. Typically placed by the camera it doesn't cause shadows or affect the exposure.

follow spot

Capable of projecting a clear, circular light over a long distance, it is used to keep light on a moving actor or object. This spotlight is typically mounted on a stand which allows for smooth movement and operation by a Set Lighting Technician.

Fresnel lens

A light weight positional lens with stepped-down concentric circles that is placed in front of the bulb and allows for either a wide or concise illumination.

"Genny"

a.k.a The Generator. This is the main power source for the lighting when on location. It can also be used as an additional power source on a set. It is motor driven but relatively silent so as not to interfere with the recorded sound.

hot box

Connected to either the house power or the generator, this device is what the lighting cables plug into.

house lights

The normal built in stage lights as opposed to the ones used for lighting the set.

inky

A small 100-watt incandescent spotlight.

key light

Set first when lighting, it is main source of light on a scene and it determines the exposure setting. The higher it is placed, the less severe the shadows will be.

midget

A 200-watt spotlight with a four-inch Fresnel lens.

mini

A 200-watt spotlight with a three-inch Fresnel lens.

obie

Typically placed on or close to the camera, this small rectangular 250-watt spotlight is used to reduce the amount of shadows on an Actor's face.

peewee

A small 50-watt incandescent spotlight.

stinger

Term used for an extension cord.

tweenie

A 600-watt spotlight.

Two K

A large 2-kilowatt light that is either open-faced or equipped with a Fresnel lens.

work light

A light employed solely for illuminating a part of the set for rigging or construction while filming is not going on.

yoke

The "Y" or "U" shaped bracket attached to a light allowing it to be affixed to a stand, arm or hung from the ciling. Clamps on each side allow for easy adjustment of the light's angle.

THE RULES OF SETIQUETTE

• Never plug anything into a hot box without consulting a Set Lighting Technician first. It may be set to a different current than the device you're plugging in is rated for.

• Never move a light unless you are directly instructed by a Set Lighting Technician. You can set production back if they need to relight.

• If you accidently bump a light, notify an A.D. or the Gaffer immediately. If it is not rectified before filming continues, a scene may have to be reshot later.

• When taking flash photography on set, shouting out *"Flashing"* lets the Set Lighting Technicians know that the burst of light is from a camera flash, not a bulb burning out.

• If you notice a light burn out or a bulb that has already expired, inform the Gaffer or a Set Lighting Technician. Sometimes in all the confusion, it may go unnoticed.

• Never place anything on top of a light or resting against it. Some of the lights, especially the arc lamps, get extremely hot and can burn or cause a fire.

• Don't touch the lens or bulb of a lamp even when they are off. The oils from your fingers can boil and damage the equipment or blow a bulb.

• If you need a work light or a stinger ask a Set Lighting Technician. Do not, under any circumstances, presume to get it yourself from their set kit or from their truck. The Gaffer is responsible for any lost items from the lighting package.

ADVICE FROM THE EXPERTS

Henry Coccetti
Gaffer
(CRANK, THE HILLSIDE STRANGLER, LOVELY & AMAZING)

My "Current" Position

I didn't go to film school but I did take some TV production courses and that became the springboard to getting involved because I started to meet people and work on their projects. This invariably led to meeting other people and doing projects with them. It's all about networking. I eventually got hooked up with a low-budget direct-to-video company that did a number of films every year. It was a good way to learn because it forced me to figure out stuff on my own and hone my craft. There's definitely a learning curve that begins with actually learning the equipment and how to operate it. This information is vital in order to move up through the ranks and eventually become a Gaffer.

A lot of crew members are products of film school. I know they learn a lot of theory and history but most are not taught the practical knowledge of working on a set. The broad classroom education is a reasonably good base, but the specific application and day to day job can only be taught by jumping in and doing it.

Taking It Slow

I don't like to rush into things. I took my time learning the trade before I supervised my first show. A lot of newcomers want to rush into it and then hope for the best and that typically doesn't go over too well. The last thing you want to do is waste time and money due to your incompetence.

Arts & Crafts

The Art Department is very important to my department. When they do their job well, it makes my job that much easier. There's a big difference between trying to light a room with four white walls and one that has a lot of color and texture. The latter will look better especially if the room is darker. Also, sometimes I need to hide equipment within the frame and they can make that possible or if I need to motivate a light source they can help by providing practicals in the design.

"Learning Electric is an oral tradition especially in the low-budget and non-union world. People have to want to do this for the love of it because generally the money and the hours are terrible, but the atmosphere can be very challenging and very inspiring."

Christopher Buchakjian, Set Electrician

Trish Herremans
Best Boy
(THOR, THE MIDNIGHT MEAT TRAIN, CRANK, DROP DEAD SEXY)

Best Girl

I would be lying if I said I didn't get a certain thrill about being a girl in a predominantly male department. It makes me feel special especially when they realize that I know my stuff and can more than keep up with them. It does have a negative side though. When I first started out I was working on a crew with two other guys in Michigan. About six months into working on shows with them, I discovered that they were getting paid more for doing the same job. I immediately confronted my supervisor about it and his exact words were *"You don't lift the heavy stuff."* I just wanted to scream because I bust my hump out there. I work twice as hard, not just to prove myself, but because the work has to get done and that's my job. Many people over the years have told me that I even make the guys in the department look bad because of it.

Am I Going To Be Tested On This?

There's a lot of homework when you're a Best Boy. Sometimes you don't have enough time on set to prepare for the next day. So when I get home at night, I'll go over my notes, the call sheet and the one-line so I have a grasp of what's specifically needed for the next day and what I should anticipate being asked for.

Mrs. Fix-It

Stuff constantly breaks down, so I typically have to repair lights after we wrap. Being able to repair equipment is a big deal, because things break down constantly, especially in my department. On the bigger shows you can usually swap out the broken part, but on the smaller shows, being able to fix the equipment, makes you invaluable to the department and to the production. Keep in mind that when you return stuff you're usually down with that item for the day. If it's essential to a scene, well, I don't need to explain how bad that could be. If you can repair it, you can save the day.

Surfing The Web

I do a lot of research on my own because there are always new lights and gear or new techniques cropping up that I want to be aware of. I like to be in *"the know"* and ultimately, it makes me more of an asset to my Department. I'll generally spend hours on Google just looking for stuff to learn about.

I Have The Power!

I like playing with power. It's something you work with that can actually kill you and I kind of like that. Don't get me wrong, you have to respect the juice. This is a dangerous job and I've had my share of electrocutions over the years. But there's one thing about electricity that you can always count on: It will always do the same thing every time. So when something goes wrong, there are only so many reasons why and we have a mental checklist of possible problems that we use to solve the problems.

Urban Legends

There are a number of different stories where the term Best Boy comes from. The first one I was ever told was that a Best Boy was the code name for the Gaffer's most expendable person on their crew. The Gaffer would always have that person do the tie-in to the house electricity. If something went wrong (like the person was electrocuted) the crew wasn't losing a valuable person. I don't know if that's the truth, but I wouldn't be surprised.

"If you haven't been electrocuted, you're probably not an electrician."

Old Electrician Saying

J.A. Shane Buttle
Set Lighting Technician
(MISSION IMPOSSIBLE III, MR. & MRS. SMITH, LEMONY SNICKET)

My Way Or The Highway

There's a hundred ways to skin a cat. And on the set, there's two ways to do something: The right way and the boss's way…and they're both the same thing. The hardest thing that new guys learn is that just because on the last show they *"did it this way"* and their last boss said, *"That's the only way to do it,"* it doesn't mean that's how it's going to fly on the new show. You can always tell a newbie. They're the one who says *"Well, on the last show…"* When you've been doing this for over 15 years you'll have done the same task a million different ways and trust me, we all think we know a better way to do it, but it's not the boss's way. So just shut up and do it his way if you want to get called back. That's a very valuable lesson.

The Good, The Bad And The Set Lighting Technician

When I was 5 years old, my dad let me stay up on a Wednesday night, a school night, to watch THE GOOD, THE BAD AND THE UGLY. The movie started at 9 o'clock and ended after midnight. That opening shot of the three guys coming to kill Tuco that used these great big close-ups was my first experience of the magic of movies. The next morning I was wrecked, but said right there and then that I wanted to go to Hollywood and make movies. I soon became a big fan of Jan de Bont's work as a Cinematographer in movies like FLATLINERS and THE HUNT FOR RED OCTOBER. He crafted these stunning images using beautiful color palettes. I was blown away by the mood that could be created just by how much or little light was used. But I soon discovered that I wasn't much of an artist, I was more of a technical person. I couldn't paint a picture myself, but I knew how to get the means for painting a pretty picture. That was a tough lesson but it's important to know where you stand and it ultimately laid the groundwork for me to become a successful Lighting Technician.

I Am The Egg Man

I started out working for Sequoia Illumination, a lighting warehouse out in the valley co-owned by Clint Eastwood and Tom Stern. My job was to prep the order for Gaffers looking to light a movie. After a couple of months working there, I learned the different names for the lights and all the different distribution packages that they had for the electric. I was also gradually meeting people as they came in to rent the gear. I decided to take some initiative and had business cards made up with my name and phone number and at the bottom in tiny letters was written, *"Mr. Nice Guy and All-Around Good Egg."* The first guy that ever stopped and read that asked me if I wanted a job on the set. We have remained friends ever since.

"Social" Networking

Having longevity in this business is all about networking because you do a show and you wind up working with say 7 guys who are the core group that are lighting the set and then there are another 7 guys who are rigging behind the camera. Each of those guys knows 7 guys who know 7 more guys. It was like Facebook before Facebook. So you try to click with at least 2 or 3 of them. You kiss ass a little bit: Buy drinks, a couple of dime bags and some 6-packs on the truck. Hopefully, the next time there's a show, they remember you and call you in. Of course the flip side is that if somebody gets offended because you come onto the set with an attitude like, *"On the last show, this is how we did it,"* they're going to think you're an asshole who doesn't take instructions very well and you're not going to get called back on the next one.

We work in an industry of broken, desperate spirits. They say that Actors are insecure but the people who are behind the camera are just as bad. It's all a big popularity contest and a very dog-eat-dog, Darwinian industry. There's a great Hunter S. Thompson misquote that goes: *"Show business is a cruel and shallow money trench, a long dark plastic hallway where thieves, pimps and whores run free and most good or weak men die like dogs!"* Misquote or not, I 100% agree.

"Always carry a notebook. We all believe that our memories are perfect, but believe me, they are not. I write everything down. You should too."

Scott Maginnis, Prop Master

Sean Tanner
Set Lighting Technician
("RAISING HOPE", LITTLE CHILDREN, "CSI: NY", THE WATCHER)

On Being An Electrician
When called to set, be there, but don't be an obvious presence. Do your lighting work and don't be yelling or throwing things around. If you are going to be off-set (at staging), be listening to see if you are needed. Nothing says more about an Electrician than being prepared with proper tools. This doesn't mean overdoing the tool belt so that you can't fit through the door. Pay attention to what's going on around you, don't stage the electrical equipment in a way that is inconvenient for everybody else (doorways, stairwells, etc.), but DO put it close enough that it is accessible for set quickly. See what lighting units are used most frequently and have them prepared before the Gaffer asks for them. This is sure to get you brownie points and out of doing the crappy jobs, like wrapping up the previous location.

On Being A Gaffer

As a Gaffer, I am responsible for interpreting the D.P.'s concept for the lighting and delegating the design to the Electricians. I often will offer lighting solutions to a D.P. if I know that there is a way for my crew to achieve the same effect with the equipment we have in a more timely manner.

A Little Help From Your Friends

The Transportation Department should be your best friend, they will get your truck as close to set as possible and in return, it's proper etiquette to give them power for their battery chargers and other powered equipment. Another good ally is the Location Deptartment. You definitely want them on your side when you need to get on that roof across the street, move the condor in place 10 minutes before the time on the permit, or to go back to a location to look for missing equipment. It also doesn't hurt to have Art Deptartment on your side (esp. the swing gang), they can make sure your practicals are wired and working before you show up on set.

Pleasant Dreams

The first movie I did as an Electrician, I fell asleep on set (on the set couch, to be exact!!!) and woke up with a burning sensation on my nose, and something out of focus in my vision. When I reached up to see what it was, I found that a C-47 had been attached to my nose and that I had slept with it on for 10 minutes. Needless to say, it was funny to the crowd that had gathered to see, and that was the LAST time I ever fell asleep on set. Moral: *if you have to fall asleep, do it off set somewhere, but remember to keep your radio on.*

"If people don't even notice that the Electric Department is there than we know we're doing our job right."

Trish Herremans, Best Boy Electric

Christopher Buchakjian
Set Lighting Technician
(EAGLE EYE, INTO THE WILD, "ANGEL IN THE FAMILY")

On Film Sets

I was originally attracted to the atmosphere of working on a film set. It's exciting and fast paced as well as casual at the same time and I liked the idea of working in a very professional and technical way within this casual atmosphere. You also get to work with people who are working at the top of their game and you're not making cars or growing food, you're making art.

New York State Of Mind

I began my career in New York wanting to work in any Department they'd let me. The film community is so much smaller that everybody knows everybody. It's also easier to be fluid in the Departments. You could Grip on one show and then do Electric on the next. I ultimately fell in with a Gaffer who I had a lot of respect for. So I latched onto her in hopes that she would teach me the craft. The more I learned about using electricity and being a Set Electrician, the more interested I became in that field.

The people I learned from were real charismatic as well as being very skilled in their jobs. You got the sense that they could draw electricity from anything. They knew every trick in the book. One time we were shooting in the park and they knew how to open up a street lamp and tap into it to get power. It's a whole different style of filmmaking.

Mr. Know-It-All

I started out being the know-it-all and that really worked against me. I was trying to prove myself and always tried to have an answer for everything whether it was right or wrong. This of course, whittled away at my credibility. It caused arguments and soured some work relationships. What was so dumb about my attitude is that I would get in arguments over the stupidest things. I remember I once got in a heated argument over what the green dot meant on a duplex receptacle. I was convinced I was right. I finally realized that being like this was hurting me way more than helping and it really taught me a lesson about having a positive attitude and a willingness to learn.

On Being An Electrician

When you're working for someone, you really want to be there to support him. It's important to always be prepared to be there exactly when they need you or anticipate it ahead of time. You also need to be safe and work smart and also be efficient while you're doing it. Sometimes fast isn't necessarily the most efficient. The end goal, of course, is to get some greatness on the screen, second to that is how elegantly you do the job. In other words, did it take four people to hold a light while they got the quick shot, versus the hours it would have taken to set it properly.

TALES FROM THE SET

I did a show in Texas and we were hired as scabs and I didn't know that until I got there. The Production paid us to sit in a hotel room for days because they were anticipating that their crew was going to quit. We were ultimately brought to set and thrown into the mix with the rest of the crew after many of them had quit. It was really challenging from an emotional point of view. Ultimately, the crew accepted us into the fold, but it was really sketchy at first. If I had known why I was there, I don't think I would have let it go that far.

Anonymous Set Electrician

We were filming in a diner in downtown Los Angeles when I heard the most dreaded words you can hear on a film set: *"Fire!"* I leaped up and grabbed a fire extinguisher that luckily happened to be nearby. As I raced to the set, I discovered the crew was surrounding the generator, which was completely on fire. Nobody was doing anything even though it was escalating to the point where the set might catch on fire, as well. They had called the Fire Department but by the time they arrived it might be too late. I had to shove my way through the crowd in order to get close enough to the generator to spray it with the extinguisher. I don't exactly consider myself necessarily brave by any stretch of the imagination and in hindsight this probably wasn't the smartest thing to be doing.

For those who don't know, a generator is basically a big engine confined in a sound proofed box that's run on about 100 gallons of gasoline. In other words, this could become a huge bomb. Unbeknownst to me, the Best Boy Electric is on the opposite side of the generator with his own fire extinguisher. At the same time, we pop open the inside panels from either side of the generator and spray like crazy. Since the generator actually wasn't on fire, the only thing we accomplish is dousing each other completely with foam. So we're both standing there looking like Casper, The Friendly Ghost. To add insult to injury, the 1st A.D. then bursts into the room to bitch about why there's no power on set. It only took him a few seconds to realize why.

Eric Miller, Transportation Coordinator

I was working on a movie that was filming in a particularly religious area of Missouri and we were using this man's home as the location. Being a warm and friendly individual, the man came onto the set with hot chocolate for the crew only to discover that a hot and heavy sex scene was being filmed. The man completely flipped his lid. What we didn't know is that he was the Reverend of the local church. He threw everyone out of his house and wouldn't let them continue shooting. It took over three hours to finally talk the man into letting us continue. Needless to say, the sex scene was moved to another location.

Anonymous Set Electrician

I was working on a show that was shooting on the beach in Mexico. The Electricians were old pros in regards to laying out the electric cables safely. Unbeknownst to us, there was an earthquake off the coast of Chile that caused a rogue wave. Within 2 seconds everything 50 feet up from the shoreline is completely underwater including the electricity. One of the crew members panicked and, not wanting to get wet, leaped on top of the nearest thing, which happened to be a juncture box. Fortunately she wasn't killed, but her legs were numb and she couldn't walk for the next few days.

Anonymous Grip

I was in charge of taking care of a walk-round costume on a low-budget Children's Video and we had a girl on our crew who had never been on a set before. We were doing final touch ups on the suit, when she snapped off a picture of us right by the camera just as the D.P. was setting the shot. Needless to say, he wasn't too pleased when he got an eyeful of bright light. She immediately got yelled at by the 1st A.D. which shook her up a bit. Later that same day, we were doing repairs on the suit and asked her to get us a hair dryer. Without asking, she plugged it into the nearest hotbox. The Gaffer saw her doing this and ripped her a new one. As her eyes started to well up, I had to explain to her that there are rules that she needs to follow. I tried to spell as many of them out for her. Ultimately, I had a better Idea. So I wrote this book.

Paul J. Salamoff, Author

CHAPTER SIX

"Get your ass off my half-apple!"

THE
GRIP
DEPARTMENT

A BRIEF OVERVIEW

This is meant in the nicest possible way, but the Grips are the "grunts" of the set. If you need something, a Grip is there to get it for you. Their tireless efforts from the sidelines guarantee that the set runs as smoothly as possible.

Headed by the Key Grip and seconded by the Best Boy Grip, the department consists of a team of physically capable men and women whose job it is to lug things around and support the other departments.

Their gear consists of apple boxes, lighting stands, furniture pads, sandbags and all sorts of items designed to help rig or raise camera equipment, lights and even Actors. Most of it is stored in huge trailers and brought to the set on carts that constantly have to be packed, unpacked and moved around.

Working closely with the Director of Photography and the Gaffer, they help to determine the most efficient method of setting up the shot.

They assist the Camera Department by helping to lay the dolly track and it's a trained Grip that pushes the camera dolly when it has to move during a shot. For the Lighting Department, they provide various methods for diffusing, shielding and otherwise controlling the lights.

Five years ago the Craft Service Department was integrated into the Grip Union. Known foremost for providing snack food for the crew, they are primarily there to assist as an extra set of hands to every and all departments that need extra help. Typically they do the jobs that none of the departments wants to do.

Frequently the butt of jokes, the Grips, in reality, are truly the unsung heroes of a production.

THE PLAYERS

Key Grip: Works closely with the Gaffer and the Director of Photography to facilitate each shot (see Grip).

Best Boy Grip: a.k.a. Assistant Key Grip. Second in command of the entire Grip Department.

Dolly Grip: Pushes the dolly that supports the camera during tracking shots.

Grip: Responsible for a variety of tasks which include transporting and setting up equipment or scenery, laying dolly track, rigging elements and otherwise helping out the Camera and Electric Departments.

Craft Service: Provides snacks for the crew while filming and tends to odd jobs around the set.

TERMS YOU SHOULD KNOW

apple box
Wood box used to elevate Actors or objects so they are in a desirable position to be photographed.

baffle
A moveable wall covered with acoustic material and used to reduce sound reverb during filming.

bounce card
White posterboard or styrofoam sheets that are used to redirect light from lamps. Because of limited reflectance, they are typically held close to the Actor or positioned on stands.

C47
a.k.a. "bullet." Grip name for a standard clothespin. There are many theories where the name "C47" came from but none are substantiated.

cookie
a.k.a. cukaloris. An opaque flag with a design cut into it which allows light to pass through somewhat mottled or shadowed. Used to break up flat lighting or give the impression of an obscured light source.

C-stand
a.k.a. century stand. A metal three-legged moveable stand designed to hold objects such as flags or cards. It has the ability to be locked into a variety of positions and has almost limitless usefulness.

diffuser
Name given to a variety of materials that can be placed in front of a light to soften it. May include wire mesh, silk, gauze, frosted glass, gels, or spun glass.

flag
Rectangular piece of black opaque fabric held in a frame designed to be attached to a stand to shade or block light.

flex arm

An additional arm with multiple ball joints that can be attached to a C-stand and help in a variety of positions that a normal straight arm can't..

"furnie" pad

a.k.a. furniture pad. Large rectangular quilted blanket used for a variety of purposes including protecting set pieces, moving furniture, and padding the ground.

gaffer grip

a.k.a. gator grip. Large clamp used to secure lights to a part of a set or to a rig.

gaffer's tape

Adhesive tape that comes in a variety of colors and versions (cloth and paper) used to secure cables, stands, lights, etc. It's also used to designate camera and Actor marks.

gel

A clear plastic sheet that comes in a multitude of colors placed in front of a light to change its color.

gobo

A large opaque black fabric usually held in a frame that can serve many purposes including blocking or hiding a light source or being cut into patterns to cast a certain type of shadow.

half-apple

A wood box one half the thickness of an apple box.

jib arm

A long weighted extension arm attached to a dolly that can support a camera. It has the ability to move in a variety of ways as well as rotate 360°.

knuckle clamp

a.k.a. knuckle clamping disc head. Two rounded grooved discs that attach to C-stand with the ability to clamp around objects such as flags or diffusers.

net

Cloth mesh help in a metal frame with the ability to attach to a C-stand used to diffuse light.

pancake

A thin wood box used to elevate Actors or objects.

quarter-apple

A wood box one quarter the thickness of an apple box.

reflector board

Large foil covered board used to redirect the sun or a powerful light source. The surface of these types of boards can range from being mirror-like for a sharp clear light to having a texture for a more diffused light.

sandbag

Canvas bags divided into two pockets with a handle in-between that come in a variety of weights. Used to secure and weigh down C-stands, reflectors and scenery.

scrim

A large piece of stretched gauze or mesh that can be placed on a set or over windows to soften a background or give the impression of fog or haze.

silk

A diffuser made of a translucent white material held in a metal frame that can be placed in front of a light to lessen the illuminations overall intensity.

THE RULES OF SETIQUETTE

• Apple boxes are useful tools, they are not chairs.

• Be polite when dealing with the Grips. If you need something say *"Please"* and *"Thank you."* Just because movie sets are stressful and high pressure, doesn't mean that manners are out the window.

• If you knock or bump into a C-stand, let a Grip know right away. Accidents happen, especially in such cramped spaces. The stand may need to be reset before shooting can continue and it's better that it's discovered before they waste film on a shot they can't use.

• Don't move or touch Grip equipment unless you have permission. It's nice to be helpful, but they are trained individuals who are on set to do their job.

• Don't rely on the Grip Department for their expendables (especially tape). If it falls under their duty, they will be happy to oblige, but if it's your responsibility, try to be better prepared.

• Furniture pads are designed for a multitude of purposes, being a make-shift bed is not one of them.

• Always ask a Grip to assist you for items off the grip carts, especially apple boxes, furniture pads, and sand bags. These items are part of the grip package and if they get misplaced or lost, they are responsible.

• If you do borrow something from the Grips, be mindful to take care of it and, by all means, make sure it is returned when you are finished.

• Don't rifle through the Craft Service drawers looking for food unless you have authorization. The Craft Service professionals know where everything is and are there to assist you.

• Don't make Grip jokes on set if you know what's good for you.

ADVICE FROM THE EXPERTS

Frank Frimara
Key Grip (Retired)
("THE HOGAN FAMILY", WALKING TALL, "MCHALE'S NAVY")

Do You Want To Get "High?"

Hunger inspired me to become a Grip. In 1963, I was working at an aircraft plant making $2.80 an hour and I was at the top of my scale. A buddy of mine told me I could get a job at the studios pulling nails from lumber for $3.90 an hour. I went down to the union and the first question they ask me is if I work "High." I had no idea what he was asking me. He told me either I do work "High" or I don't work "High." I figured if I didn't, I wouldn't get the job. So I told the guy I would work high, but 45 stories was the maximum because any higher and I start getting shaky. He looked at me like I was crazy. Evidently, the highest they go is 100 feet off the floor. Needless to say, I got the job.

Moving On Up

In those days everyone started on the Construction Gang. You worked your way from the bottom up and that's how you learned the business. I did that for four years then I started on shows as an extra "Hammer," which is what they called an extra man in those days. I had a lot of old pros to teach me how the business worked and how to learn quickly on the set. I found if I paid attention and kept my mouth shut, it was easier to learn.

In The Driver's Seat

Most accidents are caused by poor judgment or the fear of losing your job. I once had an incident while shooting with an insert car. This can sometimes be dangerous if the vehicle is going too fast. I was telling the driver to take it easy, but the Director kept on demanding that the car should be going faster. Having had enough, I told them to stop the car and instructed my Grip to get off the vehicle. Of course, the Director went ballistic. I very calmly let him know that if he wanted to continue, to be my guest, but he would do it without the assistance of the Grip Department.

Full Throttle

I was on this TV show where a plane had to take off from a runway after the Actors jumped onboard. Because it was a sweltering hot day, they wanted to keep the plane engine running so it wouldn't stall during the shot. The pilot was instructed to keep the engine going while staying out of the frame. As we started to film, I noticed that the aircraft was slowly moving toward us. I got especially concerned when it went beyond its intended mark.

The plane kept moving forward and nobody seemed to be concerned. I decided to get the hell out of there and I grabbed the Camera Operator by the neck and yanked him off the camera. Just as we cleared, the plane overtook the dolly and the camera and smashed them to pieces. Luckily nobody was hurt except for some minor injuries. The propeller was destroyed along with the camera and dolly. Evidently the pilot, who was down on the cockpit floor trying to keep the engine going, didn't notice that the plane was moving. He thought the vibrations were just the engine straining to keep going.

"There's nothing more frustrating than not having a Grip Crew on your side."
Tommy James Lewis, 1st Assistant Camera

J. David Ahuna
Key Grip
("LOST", "MAGNUM P.I.", "JAKE AND THE FAT MAN", "HAWAII 5-0")

Aloha

In Hawaii you start in the Mechanics Local. So you could be a Grip one day, Electric tomorrow, and work Camera the next day. I worked on a lot of different shows in a lot of different Departments. When asked what I wanted to specialize in, I decided I wanted to be a Grip. The reason being that Grips always worked and I liked that fact that

I had to be not only creative, but quick on my feet. It was sink or swim all the way.

I've Been Working On The Railroad

I did another show where we had to build this elaborate dolly track across a ravine. It was 50 feet across and we had to build a railroad bridge across the expanse then lay the track and make sure that it was safe. When all was said and done and a lot of time was spent, the Director only went about two feet over the ravine with the dolly to achieve the shot.

Lost And Found

The toughest show was probably "LOST" not because the crew was bad (they were great), it's that the location was really challenging. Every scene was either on a mountain, in mud and rain, or down on the beach where you were working in soft sand. On top of that, the heat was pounding on you all day. But as always, every morning I would get up and thank the Lord. I look at it like, nothing can go wrong because I'm alive and I'm on top of it.

Going To The Chapel

I was on a show once where the Director wanted to lay dolly track from the inside altar of a church all the way to the outside steps. It was about 100 feet of track. The steps were pretty hazardous and cause for concern. We did the shot about ten or twelve times but the Director was still not happy with the shot. He wanted the dolly to move faster. I explained that this was unsafe and I wouldn't allow it. After a heated debate, they more or less asked me to leave. The next thing I knew, the dolly, the camera and the Operator went off the top step and people got hurt. They lost the camera and the dolly was damaged. This is why safety is always number one priority.

"We are the handymen of the set."

Frank Frimara, Grip

Richard "Dick" Babin
Key Grip / Dolly Grip (Retired)
("ENTERTAINMENT TONIGHT", "HOTEL", CLOSE ENCOUNTERS OF
THE THIRD KIND, THE POSEIDON ADVENTURE)

In The Old Days

In the early days you were first a Permit, a 3-Permit, a 2-Permit then, if there was room, you became a 1-Permit until someone died or retired. That's how you moved up and became a 1-Card. The benefit of being a 1-Card was that you were the last to go as the crew was thinned out. When I started, there were about 500 men in the union. This made advancement that much more difficult. When I finally got my 1-Card, they then introduced the 3-Card and the 2-Card. Seniority went out the door.

This was frustrating because Grips that had only been doing Gripwork for 30 days were being given 1-Card status and that wasn't right. Because you had a lot of guys who were too green to be keying shows. In my day, I worked up in the beds, setting flags and cutters. Once I had proved myself up there, I was moved down with the big guys. It is a whole new ballgame today. People are coming up too fast and not learning the way I did. We came up through the ranks and learned from the old timers.

Taking Your Life In Your Hands

When I was learning, sometimes the old timers were not so forth-coming with the information. They expected you to just sit back and watch at times or just do what they said. I was on a set and I noticed that when the Key Grip would call for a flag or double, that the older Grips would just magically appear with them. I was baffled where they were getting them so quick. I did some snooping and discovered that they would have these hidden stashes behind the walls. The next day I came in early and moved all the stashes, so when the Key Grip called for the flags, I was the one who came in with them. The other Grips were furious and wanted to know what the hell was going on. They found out later what I had done and they almost killed me. But to be honest, it was worth it, because I wanted to learn and I couldn't by watching them do it. Sometimes you have to jump in and take some initiative.

The Cycle Of Abuse

Each Key Grip works differently and you have to learn their way. When you first start out, you bounce around to different shows and meet a lot of different Keys. Eventually if you found someone you clicked with, you tried to stay with him. I was easygoing as a Key. I'm not a yeller because I got yelled at a bunch of times when I was working my way up and I didn't like it. It was embarrassing. So I resolved myself to not yell at my men. If there was a problem I'd have a talk and we'd set it straight, but it was always done in private.

You're A Mean One, Mr. Grinch

One time I had to replace the Dolly Grip on a show because he was sick. I didn't know the D.P. but I heard he was a bit of a grump so I decided to have some fun with him and break him of it. When he called for the Dolly I asked him what it looked like. He pointed to it and incredulously informed me that it was the thing with the four wheels right behind me. I walked over to it and kicked the tires a couple of times and he wanted to know what the hell I was doing. I explained that I saw the Teamsters kicking their truck tires so I figured I should do the same. For about two days I continued with this behavior but still did my job to the best of my ability. After the original Dolly Grip came back to set, he called me and asked what the hell I did to the D.P. because he was a changed man.

Set Sail For Adventure

The Poseidon Adventure was a tough film to work on because all the sets were upside down. Everything had to be built differently to accommodate the shots. Toward the end, when we were filming Shelley Winters' death scene, they used too much fire in the shot and it was really lighting that stage up. All of a sudden, the sprinkler system in the stage went off and the most rank, red water came out of those sprinklers and was raining down on the camera equipment. The D.P. was yelling out for the Grips and we're standing there like, *"Hey we're not plumbers, what the hell are we supposed to do."* The water messed up everything.

In The Water I'm A Very Skinny Lady

On another occasion on THE POSEIDON ADVENTURE, the Key Grip told me to get some parallels out of the way because they had to move in the camera really quickly. I hustled over and started pushing. To my surprise it started moving by itself. I turned and realized that Ernest Borgnine was helping me push it. I asked him what he was doing and he told me that he liked Grips and didn't mind helping. As we get it off to the side, I hear this operatic singing. I turned to Ernie and asked him what that was. He told me to keep quiet because that was Shelley Winters getting ready for her death scene.

"Craft service is my best ally on the set because they serve the coffee."
Richard H. Kline, ASC, Cinematographer

Craig Conover
Craft Service
(SORORITY BOYS, APT PUPIL, "JUST SHOOT ME", "JUDGING AMY")

The Crap Jobs...*Literally*

A lot of people on sets don't realize that Craft Service goes way beyond the serving of food. Craft Service does all the jobs that no one else wants. On "DEADWOOD" there is a Craft Service guy who cleans up after the horses. That's been a Craft Service job for over 50 years. Now that's not the same guy who makes your sandwiches, but it's still a Craft Service person who specializes in keeping the set clean.

There are members that specialize in what I call "Location Protection". They lay down the cardboard to protect the flooring, bubble wrap the banisters, and lay safety tread on stairs. Some Craft Service people work solely with the Special Effects Department. They work as an Assistant helping them with their gags and equipment. They also clean up the glass, snow, water or any other debris that some of these effects generate.

There are Craft Service professionals that work strictly at the studios that prep and strike the stages. They go in before the show arrives and clean everything from the permanents at the top of the ceiling all the way down to the pits below the stage floor. At wrap they get it ready for the next show coming in. I try to encourage new Craft Service people to do as many of these different types of jobs their first season out. It's unwise to limit yourself to just Production. Take the time to learn the rest of the job. This way you expand your abilities and make yourself more valuable to the Production as a whole.

Do Or Do Not, There Is No Try

Be prepared for everything and never, ever say *"no"* to a request. If there's something that you don't want to do or are incapable of doing, never tell them it can't be done. You tell them that you might not be able to get to that, but you can certainly find someone who can. Because at the Local, nine times out of ten, you can find someone who will.

Home Sweet Home

I recommend creating a style that's all your own and accept the fact that you can't be proficient at everything. My style is about comfort food. When you are on location, the crew is away from their home and their families. When it comes down to what people want or what they need after a 14 hour work day or at the end of a long week, it's usually pizza, meatloaf, macaroni and cheese, tomato soup, or grilled cheese. I do my best to create "home" on the stage for the crew members. Because keeping the crew happy and in the right comfort zone makes my job easier, as well.

Forward Thinking

The world of film is a sea of chaos where people change their minds at a moments notice, so I try to be very structured in my work. By being organized and planned out, everyone at least had something they can rely or depend on. I print out exactly what I am going to serve for the entire week with the times when food will be brought out and I also lay out my table the exact same way every day. It might seem trivial, but as anyone who has worked on a set knows, the more efficient you can make anything, the better.

Method To The Madness

Something I used to do that would sometimes bewilder or even upset the crew, was to have the cart with the utensils away from the craft service table so they literally had to walk a few feet away to it. The reason for this was because I didn't want people eating over the food. Another thing I do, especially when I'm on location, is to keep the craft service table away from the set, because having food on set is a bad idea. A D.P. once said to me, that there's no one on the crew with a broken leg. If they want food, they can go and get it. Besides that, he liked it because the only time he got to be off the set was when he was getting something to eat. This way he could take a nice stroll away from the chaos, clear his head and have a smoke in the time it takes to get back to the set.

Common Courtesy

If you spend enough time on set, you realize that the people around the camera have the most power, but they are the ones that very rarely get to walk away from their positions. These are the people I cater to the most. They work hard and deserve to have some refreshment along with the rest of the crew. It would always annoy me when the other Grips would walk off set to get food and not get something for the Dolly Grip. I thought it was rude and poor etiquette. So I always made sure I was there for him, as well as the others.

"In the old days, sets were a lot more relaxed. Today they've pushed the "Panic Button" and everything is so fast paced."

Richard Babin, Key Grip

TALES FROM THE SET

We had built a special device that was designed to pump cold air into these monster costumes we had built. The thing was very awkward to deal with and sensitive to any movement. In other words, a real pain in the ass. We were trying to figure something out to make it easier to deal with when a Grip came up and offered to put some wheels on the base for us. We were thrilled, so he went and got his grip kit and came back to fix our unruly machine. We got called away for a set-up and, when we returned, we realized that the way he was reconstructing our rig, it would never work properly. I had a knee-jerk reaction and told him he was building it wrong. Big mistake. He got completely bent out of shape. He immediately dropped what he was doing (including the machine, which crashed to the floor) and told us if we didn't like it we could *"F-ing do it ourselves!"* He then stormed away with his tools in a huff. The lesson here is that everyone on a set needs to be respected and especially someone from another department doing you a favor. Telling him how to do his job was probably not a good idea.

Anonymous Make-Up FX Artist

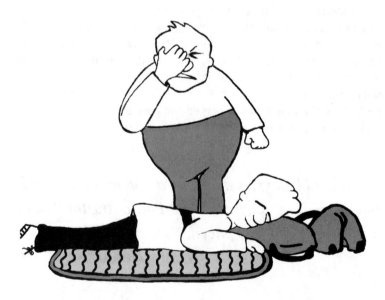

I was a P.A. on a movie back in 1992. They were shooting a scene on a dolly-crane but set it up in the wrong place. So rather than taking the crane apart (taking the camera off, removing the weights used as a counter balance), they decided to throw a Production Assistant up on the crane to keep the arm properly balanced and move the crane by pushing it. Bad call. The whole thing toppled over and the camera and P.A. fell from about 15 feet up. People rushed over to the accident. Except no one noticed the P.A., they were all bent over putting the camera back together. When they finally gave up on the shattered camera, they discovered the P.A. on the ground unconscious and got him to a hospital. His back never recovered and neither did he (He went back to investment banking and never looked back). The Grip who made the call to move the crane hasn't worked on a movie since.

Ben Odell, Production Assistant

I was working on a low-budget horror movie and the Grips had laid the electric cables along an outside concrete stairwell that lead into the set. It was brightly lit inside but there was no outside lighting so when it got dark, it was hard to see. The Physical FX Supervisor headed outside and his foot caught on the cables and he took a tumble down the stairs. He fell the whole way and was subsequently incapacitated for the next week. Anyone will tell you that losing a Department Head on a show during filming is not in anyone's best interest.

Jerry Constantine, Make-Up FX Artist

I once did something that in hindsight was poor etiquette on my part. We were doing a scene for "THE HARDY BOYS" with an Actor lying in bed watching TV. When the Director gives the signal, I'm supposed to make the move from the Actor to the TV. I was waiting patiently for the Director to give me the signal when, all of a sudden, I feel something shove into my back. I turned to the D.P. and asked him why he just did that. He told me I screwed up. I explained that I hadn't had the signal and we reset the shot. On the next take, he did the exact same thing. I told him not to do that again. Well, as you can guess, on the next take I get another boot in my back. Furious, I locked the dolly and walked off the set. I went to the grip truck and opened up a can of beer, expecting that I was going to be fired. Fifteen minutes later nothing had happened so I walked back into the stage to see what was going on. Everybody was just standing there waiting for my return. Confused, I asked them why they were waiting and they informed me that they wanted me to do the shot. They wanted to know if I was ready to continue. I told them I was as long as they moved the camera back so the Operator couldn't reach me with his foot.

Richard Babin, Key Grip

The Script Supervisor had set up a really nice stand for herself to work on. It had her script as well as notes, M&M's and her cup of coffee. Everything was ready to go for her and it was easily transportable when changing set-ups. A moment arose on set when she had to get up and address a continuity issue. When she got up to deal with the problem, one of the more notorious Grips on the set (who was always getting into some kind of trouble) decided he was going to sit in her seat. He began screwing with all her items just for the hell of it and accidentally spilled her coffee all over her script and, more importantly, her notes. Realizing he was going to get in trouble, he fled from the scene before she got back. Upon returning to her station, the Script Supervisor blew her stack. She started yelling at everyone in the vicinity. Which, if she thought about it, were probably not responsible (No one would be that stupid to hang around the scene of that crime). The lesson learned is you have to respect people's property on a set and if you do screw up, be a man and fess up to it. Don't run off like a little pansy and let others take the heat...especially if you're a Grip.

Anonymous Producer

CHAPTER SEVEN

"Did you just call me a Puff Jockey?!"

THE
HAIR & MAKE-UP
DEPARTMENT

A BRIEF OVERVIEW

Whoever said that *"Beauty is only skin deep,"* need not apply (pun intended!) to the Hair & Make-Up Departments. These two separate entities, along with The Costume Department, help to solidify the essence of a character that an Actor is portraying.

It's amazing how much a little make-up and a new hairstyle can transform an Actor, not only in look, but in personality too. Think how liberating it is wearing a costume on Halloween and you'll get the idea.

Like many of the other Departments, a Key Make-Up Artist and a Key Hairstylist work closely with the Director to create the unique vision of each character. The look might range from minimalistic (i.e. ANOTHER EARTH) to flat out over the top (i.e. THE HUNGER GAMES).

Techniques can be used to make Actors appear older while others can make them look younger. Wigs and hair extensions are utilized when necessary and facial hair, like fake mustaches and/or beards are usually provided by the Hair Department but applied by the Make-Up Artists.

Another symbiotic relationship, involves the Make-Up FX Department who provide the foam latex and/or silicone appliances that have to be applied by a union Make-Up Artist. Cuts & bruises and scars & blemishes are also applied by the Make-Up Department.

Hairstylists and Make-Up Artists arrive early to the set with the Actors. They spend this time getting them ready for the day's shoot. Depending on how elaborate the transformation is, affects how much lead time they need. During the shoot day, they each have representatives on the set to make sure that the look stays consistent and to implement the changes that are required.

Their work must be constantly documented and every minute change must be noted to maintain proper continuity.

THE PLAYERS

Key Make-Up Artist: Responsible for the look of all the Actors during the shoot. Deals with the areas above the breastbone and from the elbow to fingers.

Make-Up Assistant: Directed by the Key to apply the style of make-up and maintain it on set.

Body Make-Up Artist: Provides make-up for the areas not covered by the Make-Up Artist: below the breastbone and from the elbows up.

Key Hair Stylist: Designs the "look" of the Actor's hair based on the type of film (ie. contemporary, period piece, sci-fi, etc.).

Hair Stylist: a.k.a. Hair Dresser. Helps to create the hair styles and maintain them on the set.

Lens Technician: Specially trained individual who provides contact lenses and assists the Actor with them throughout the production.

TERMS YOU SHOULD KNOW

cape
Plastic or vinyl sheet that attaches around an Actor's neck and protects their costume while hair is trimmed or make-up is applied.

Duo
Latex based adhesive used to apply fake eyelashes

fake blood
Red liquid usually made from corn syrup with a thinning agent used to simulate real blood.

fixer spray
A liquid that is misted on top of a finished make-up that seals it and protects it from normal wear and tear.

foundation
Cream make-up that usually comes in flesh tones that is used to even out an Actor's face tone before the rest of the make-up is applied over it.

gel blood
Thick, pasty version of fake blood that can be smeared on an Actor or placed in a wound to simulate dried or crusted blood.

glycerin
Colorless syrupy liquid used as a solvent, moistener, and lubricant. It also can be used to simulate tears.

grease paint
Oil based make-up worn by Actors that comes in an almost limitless variety of colors.

hair clippers
Hand-held electric shaver used for removing or trimming hair.

hair extension
Lengths of human hair that are fused onto an Actor's real hair to simulate longer, fuller hair.

make-up call

The time that an Actor is required to show up on set to be put into hair and make-up so they are ready when it is time to shoot. Depending on how intricate the make-up and hair is, it could be anywhere from a half hour to hours before crew call.

make-up sponge

Small white triangular-shaped sponge ideal for applying all types of make-ups.

mortician's wax

Creamy flesh colored wax that can be easily blended into an Actor's skin. Helpful for creating three dimensional wounds or other skin blemishes.

mouth blood

Fake blood that is manufactured to be safe to use in an Actor's mouth.

pancake make-up

Dry make-up activated by water that is applied with a sponge or cloth and used for covering larger areas on the body.

powder puff

Round orange felt-like sponge that is used to apply powder onto an Actor. Helpful for eliminating sweat or unnatural shine.

rigid collodion

Liquid that dries with a film-like skin that is useful for creating scars and wrinkles.

Scleral lens

Hard or soft plastic contact lens that covers the white of the eye (the sclera) as well as the pupil. The hard ones tend to be uncomfortable and most Actors can only wear them for short periods of time.

spirit gum

Amber glue ideal for applying fake mustaches and beards.

spritzer

Bottle that can be filled with a variety of liquids especially water that vaporizes the liquid and mists it on an Actor. Used to simulate sweat but also useful to cool down an Actor or refresh the make-up.

tattoo ink

Specially designed ink that temporarily simulates tattoos or other body art and is removed with alcohol.

tooth stain

Paint that can be applied to teeth that can be removed easily with alcohol.

wig

A manufactured covering made from synthetic or real human hair. It allows for an Actor to have a drastically different look or hair color.

THE RULES OF SETIQUETTE

• Always knock first and wait for a response before entering the Hair or Make-Up Trailers especially when body make-up is being applied.

• Always say *"Stepping up"* when entering the Hair or Make-Up Trailers. It warns the Artist who may be working near the Actor's eyes. The Trailers tend to shift and any rocking could cause mistakes or injury.

• The Hair and Make-Up trailers are not your personal beauty salons available for you to "spruce" yourself up before, during or after the shoot day.

• Don't pester the Hairstylist about getting a haircut. They are on set to work, not provide a free hair cutting service to the crew.

• Don't bother the Hair and Make-Up staff for beauty tips. They have enough work to do as it is without being your personal stylist.

• Avoid needlessly talking to an Actor when they are getting their hair and/or make-up done. Otherwise it makes the process that much harder and can cause delays on the Actor arriving to the set on time.

• Never touch the Actor's face and/or hair during the shoot day. People took hours to get it looking just right.

• The Hair & Make-Up Department's Polaroid camera is not meant as a convenience for you to "snap off" a quick shot with an Actor. They need to constantly document the look of the Actors in every scene, especially when changes are made on the set. (also see Costume Department)

ADVICE FROM THE EXPERTS

Kenny Myers
Award Winning Make-Up Artist
(X-MEN: THE LAST STAND, WAR OF THE WORLDS, STAR TREK V & VI, BACK TO THE FUTURE II & III)

Keep Your Eyes Open

Most people that step on a set for the first time think it's a lot of people just standing around. My advice is to sit there and watch the ballet of chaos and know that everybody does a specific job. If you first watch in front of camera, then look behind the scenes, eventually you see everyone on the set approach at some point and do their job. Stand back and watch because it's fascinating to watch them do their thing.

Valuable Relationships

You are almost always working integrally with the Costumes or Special Effects Departments and they can impact what you're doing. But sometimes a Director's Assistant can be your most valuable ally. You may have a difficult Actor and the only way to keep the lines of communication open is to be able to talk to the Director and you can't always get to him because he has so many responsibilities. By talking to his Assistant, you can keep the running dialogue up. Happens quite a bit.

On Being A Make-Up Artist

If I'm a department head, my responsibilities are to both the Director and the Actor to give them both what they want as far as it functions for character and for the film. Because many times the Actors and the Director don't talk to one another, if one is happy and the other is not, I either have to get the other one happy or be the pivot for the compromise. When I'm working under someone else, my responsibilities are to them. I'm to show up and do the job by being supportive in any way possible. Or, in other words: Come in, apply the make-up, keep my mouth shut, my hands folded and take care of the Actor while he's on set.

Sometimes a Make-Up Artist will get a bad reputation because they're there to be the Actor's best friend so they can get their next job. That's not what you do when you're working for somebody. When you're the Department Head, that's your privilege. When you're a helper, that's not your job. I've seen people destroy their careers because thirty minutes after they've stepped on set, they have the Actor's home phone number. Those people don't get hired back.

"Be prepared for any event as much as possible and always have a back-up plan."
Joel Harlow, Make-Up Artist

Jacqueline Mgido
Make-Up Artist / Hair Stylist
(HOME FOR THE HOLIDAYS, "DINNER AND A MOVIE", ANOTHER WORLD: REUNION)

Deceiving Is Believing
I learned how to do make-up because my father wouldn't allow me to wear it when I was growing up. I would put it on myself and try to make it look like I wasn't wearing any, so I wouldn't get in trouble. I soon realized that I could transform myself right before his eyes without him noticing. At that point, I resolved to become a Make-Up Artist even though my parents wanted me to be a doctor. When I moved to the United States, I got a job working in cosmetics at a department store. There I learned more about doing make-up and some of the techniques. I soon realized that, if I truly wanted to pursue my dreams, I had to move to Hollywood.

On Hair And Make-Up
I like to be connected with people and transform them, whether it might be just a simple beauty make-up or an elaborate special effects application. It's the transformation aspect that I really enjoy and attracted me to become a Make-Up Artist. It truly is an art form and appeals to my creative side.

Hair is similar, but I find it more of a challenge. I hated doing it at first. One of my first jobs was doing both Hair and Make-Up for a low-budget film and I had to cut somebody's hair but I had no idea what I was doing. So I pretended I did and, much to my surprise, I actually did a good job and enjoyed doing it. After that, I decided I wanted to continue doing it, so I went to cosmetology school and got my license.

Good Vibrations

I am one of the first people the Actors see when they arrive on set and I am the first energy they feel at the start of their workday. So it is imperative to keep the Talent calm and filled with good energy. It's all about intuition because I need to read their mood accurately everyday and decide whether I should talk to them or keep my mouth shut. If the Talent is uncomfortable with you than it can be disastrous and set an odd tone for the whole day. Because first impressions are lasting impressions, I try to make my surroundings appear as sanitary as possible. Being around something clean psychologically puts people at ease. I also try to smile as much as possible and keep talking to a minimum. I especially try not to burden the Talent with a lot of questions. Most Actors will typically volunteer the information that I need.

Paging Dr. Mgido

Being the Talent's unofficial psychologist can have its negative side. When an Actor arrives on set after having his make-up done, he might react to situations unusually because of some emotional baggage that you might be privy to but the rest of the crew is not. The worst is when you are blamed for something that is privileged information between you and the Actor. You sometimes have to take the hit because the only other option is to break the trust, which would be more detrimental in the long run.

I had a situation where an Actor was drunk and high and his eyes were really bloodshot. I did my best with the make-up but he still looked awful. The Director kept on coming to me and criticizing my work, but I kept my mouth shut and got through the takes as best as I could.

A Bright Idea

Lighting is everything and I've discovered that I need to be tight with the D.P. and the Gaffer because bad lighting will make me look like I'm not doing my job properly. I was once doing an infomercial and there was a glare caused by a window that was affecting the look of an Actor. The D.P. was trying to convince me that I needed to put more make-up on the Actor but I knew for a fact that it was the lighting that was causing the problem. Unfortunately, I didn't have a relationship with the D.P. at that time, so, out of frustration, I made the mistake of telling the Director it was a lighting issue. Needless to say, the D.P. and the Gaffer got tweaked at me because I was criticizing their work.

Realizing that I crossed the line with them, I went to the Gaffer and as nicely as possible made a lighting suggestion by using my body as a shadow to demonstrate what I was talking about. He seemed to respect the fact that I knew about lighting and I was able to sell them on the change. From that point on everything was fine, but it made me realize how important it is to have a relationship with them.

God Bless Oprah

I learned a lot about lighting by watching different shows on TV and, ultimately, being on sets. I also used my own shadows when I was applying make-up on the Talent, noticing how things looked under different lighting conditions. I also learned a lot from watching Oprah...She looks fabulous! I've seen her on regular television being interviewed, then seen her show lighting and realized how incredible she and her guests looked.

"Set work is like life in general. It's got its ups and its downs. But most of the times it's just sideways."
Kenny Myers, Make-Up Artist

Linda Villalobos
Hair Department Head
(AFTER EARTH, DEATH AT A FUNERAL, SCARY MOVIE 1 & 2)

Original Recipe Or Extra Crispy

I have very curly hair and straightening it has always been a painful experience because I was constantly burning myself. I figured there had to be a better way and just playing around with it and coming up with a technique is what ultimately led me to getting into hair professionally. Talking to people, I would look at their eyes and face, then my eyes would go to their hair. It was a natural thing for me. I started out braiding cornrows, and straightening hair for money. I soon discovered how great a feeling it was creatively making someone look different. I also understood how a new look could affect someone's life in a positive way. I began to watch a lot of TV and film and study the Actor's hair. After a while I became very judgmental of what I saw and realized that I could do as good a job, if not better. So I decided to put my money where my mouth was.

A Family Affair

I am bi-coastal and would constantly travel back and forth between Los Angeles and New York. This gave me the opportunity to meet and establish relationships with people in the industry. I eventually landed my first job on "IN LIVING COLOR", It was a real cultural show which worked for me. It was really challenging, but I got to do a lot of different looks quickly, so in the end, it was the perfect job. Because I did so well on that show, I wound up bonding with the Wayans and eventually became their exclusive Hair Stylist from that point on. I soon began to learn more and more about working in film especially about the script itself, such as how to break it down and how to know each character thoroughly. It taught me more than just trying to make hair look pretty because it's not about pretty, it's about what that character needs at that moment.

Crunch Time

The thing about doing hair in the industry is it's a lot of behind-the-scenes work. There's a lot of paperwork and knowing what you are doing. When I did my first feature, I had no experience, but I was put in a position where I had to run the whole Department. Lucky for me, I am a business woman and know how to run a business. So I took what I knew from that and I applied it. You also have to be well rounded to stay afloat. You have to know your foundation and then some. You don't have to be an expert in every area, but you have to have some knowledge in everything and be well rounded so you can rise to every situation. If you do get overloaded, don't be afraid to get help. There's nothing wrong with that but, in the end, it's good to know that you can do just about everything when you're in a crunch.

Shiny Happy People

When I first meet with my crew, I tell everyone to put away their problems and that we are all going to shine. It's so important to work as a team and I welcome any of their ideas. It's also important to learn from the people you hire to help you and to learn from their expertise. Some people may specialize in a specific area and be better than you. It's okay to get their help, but it's even better to know that you know it, as well, just not to the same degree as they do. It's good to acknowledge that and share that with the people you are working with. People don't want to admit that they are not good at something, but they get hurt in the long run and you don't shine like you should. Ultimately, if your crew feels like they are an integral part of the team, they tend to have a different outlook and are more eager to do the job.

Blond Ambition

WHITE CHICKS was the first time I've worked with extensive prosthetics. My call time was usually 3am and I had to be the first one there to do stuff with hair so Special Effects could put the appliances on. The Make-Up FX crew did an amazing job with the prosthetics. It took about 5 hours to apply the prosthetics before we could put the wigs on. We then would work a 20-hour day. It became quite a challenge to hide the prosthetics under the wigs. This was one of the reasons why the hair had to be so long. It had to fall a certain way to keep the edges covered. Shawn and Marlon weren't used to having long stringy hair all over the place and it was constantly getting stuck to their lipstick. So, as soon as the Director called *"Cut!"*, I had to be there to pin it up out of their face. I literally had to stand right there and be ready to jump in, because that's how irritating it was to them after 16+ hours of this. We all worked together as a team to accomplish this affect which, ultimately, looked quite impressive.

"Make-Up artists have become the unofficial therapists of the Talent."
Jacqueline Mgido, Make-Up Artist

Brigit Cook
Hair Stylist
(Twilight, Talladega Nights, Sideways, Miss Congeniality)

Universal Fears

My family worked in the business so I was kind of attracted to it, but I kind of fell into it by accident. When I first started, I was doing hair and make-up for theater and some commercials. It was ultimately my Uncle (who was an Actor) that showed me the ropes. I eventually went to an interview at Universal Studios. 1978 was a real busy time there, especially with TV, and that's how I was able to get my foot in the door. They really needed people. I honestly didn't know what I was doing when I first started. Fortunately, there was a couple of really great old time Hair Dressers that helped me and taught me all the things I hadn't learned yet, especially about breaking down a script for a new show.

Wigging Out

If you're interested in becoming a Hair Stylist, go to cosmetology school for sure, and then maybe start by doing commercials, low-budget independent films or industrials. It's a great way to learn. At the very least, do as much as you can, before you actually start doing it for real. A story I always tell to people is that when I first started at Universal, they put me in a production meeting and I didn't have a clue what was going on. During the meeting they said they needed a stunt double wig. I figured it was a brand name. I leaned over to the

Make-Up Artist and asked where I can get the stunt double wigs and she looked at me like I was nuts!

Only Your Hairdresser Knows

Because you are physically touching someone as a Hair Stylist, you ultimately, get close to them. Actors typically tell us their life story, their problems and everything else. They tell you information that you don't necessarily even want to hear, sometimes about the night before or the goings-on, on the set. You have to be a good listener, but you also have to be diplomatic with this, especially when you are working with big Actors.

Hair And Loathing In Las Vegas

One of the hardest films I worked on was FEAR AND LOATHING IN LAS VEGAS because Johnny Depp had to be bald but also wanted to look like he had some hair on top. Unfortunately, Johnny went ahead and shaved his head and so I was stuck with trying to make him look like he had some hair. I got a toupee and cut it up into a little square and blended his own hair in with it. It was a real challenge. We did numerous film tests and the first couple didn't work out so well.

Surf's Up

While filming BLUE CRUSH, we had girls in wet suits wearing wigs. It's challenging enough working in water, let alone trying to keep wigs on in 20 feet swells. It was next to impossible to keep a watch on the wigs in those kinds of conditions. Invariable, the wigs would get pulled off by the third take. Fortunately, beforehand we came up with the idea of bungee-ing the wigs to their wetsuits so we didn't lose them in the surf.

"Try to find enjoyment in the long hours, because even though it can be kind of grueling, there's always fun during the time you spend on a show."

Ele Goudreau, Costumer

TALES FROM THE SET

I recently did a photo shoot where the Actress was two hours late. She claimed that she had been mugged on her way over to the studio. I noticed that she reeked of alcohol, but she was hysterically crying, so I tried to calm her down and get her into the make-up chair. I soon realized that she was taking a whole lot of drugs and acting psychotic. I needed to do my job, but it came clear to me that I also needed to keep my mouth shut, because she would have known if I told the Production. Ultimately, I kept on having to tell her she was beautiful in order for her to get through the shoot. Fortunately for me, nobody ever figured out the truth.

Anonymous Make-up Artist

I was once sitting in dailies of a costume and make-up test for a 20th Century Fox film. It was a small screening room that sat at most 30 people and I was there to watch an over the top character make-up I did on one of the Lead Actors. Someone walked into the room not knowing what was going on and sat down. Seconds later, he pipes in, *"Wow, he looks better than he does in real life!"* At the end of dailies, the lights come up in the theater to reveal the Lead Actor sitting right in front of the loud mouth. Needless to say, it took the guy quite some time to get his foot out of his mouth.

Anonymous Make-Up F/X Artist

I was producing an ultra low-budget horror movie and two of the Actors had to be made up as zombies for a film-within-a-film sequence. The Make-Up Artist used an old school "cotton and latex" technique to achieve the look. Everything seemed fine when we filmed the scene, but the Actors complained of some discomfort from the make-up. At the time, this seemed like the typical complaints you usually get from Actors new to wearing FX make-up. The day wrapped and the Actors went home with some moisturizer for their skin. The next morning before call, I get a panicked call from one of the Actors that his face was literally pealing off. He evidently had, what he suggested, were burns on his face. My initial thought was that he had an allergic reaction to the latex. This could probably be cleared up with some allergy medicine. That diagnosis was thrown out the window when the other Actor arrived to the set with similar (yet not as severe) symptoms. Having two Actors with the same allergic reaction to latex seemed highly unlikely. I authorized the first Actor to go to his dermatologist and gave the other Actor the offer as well (but he declined). Baffled by what could have happened, I went to the Make-Up trailer to investigate. It became apparently clear when I found the latex they had used. It was in a 5-gallon drum and it reeked of ammonia. It was obvious that they both had chemical burns caused by the caustic ammonia. To make matters worse, we had to shoot with both Actors that day and, because of the tight schedule, could not move the shots. Ultimately, the first Actor calmed down after he saw his dermatologist and came to set. He looked pretty bad and I was ready to scrap the day, but he insisted he wanted to shoot. The Make-Up Artist wound up having to use a lot of make-up to cover the burns. Luckily (with some clever shooting by the Director), we were able to shoot and make the day. By the way, did I mention that the scene we were shooting was his big sex scene?

Anonymous Producer

I was working on a low-budget independent feature and everything was being done at a really fast pace in order to keep the film on schedule and on budget. They had an Actor come in for the day and, instead of finding a double to light his shots with, they had him be

his own Stand-In. They were halfway through his make-up when they called for him to light a shot, but the make-up wasn't set or powdered. Without thinking, the Actor quickly threw on his wardrobe and rushed to set. As expected, the make-up rubbed off onto his white collar. Being that we only had this one piece of wardrobe for him, it was ruined. We did our best to get the stain out for shooting, but it was a lost cause. Ultimately, we just tucked his collar in and prayed no one noticed his really obvious tan-colored ring-around-the-collar.

Anonymous Costumer

We shot A MAN CALLED HORSE in Durango, Mexico. Dame Judith Anderson played the old Indian squaw, and she had blue eyes. So you couldn't photograph any close-ups without her wearing contact lenses. The Production Manager had bought her brown contact lenses from Sears and Roebuck and they killed her eyes. She could hardly leave them in for more than 30 seconds. Then they'd have to take them out and let her eyes rest before we could shoot again. We had this close-up scene on the side of the hill with the whole Indian village down picking berries below us. The sun's going down, and the Make-Up Artist's standing by. He says, *"Tell me when to pop 'em in, Terry."* So I say, *"Pop 'em in,"* and a moment later my second A.D. comes on the radio from down below and says, *"One of the Indian kids just threw a rock and knocked out a squaw and she's laying there."* And I said, *"Pull her behind the tent and keep the background action going. And roll the camera."* And we got the shot.

Terry Morse, Producer / 1st Assistant Producer

I was working on a film (as a Make-up FX Artist) and the scene called for the Actress to be really frantic and sweating profusely. Right before they did her close up, the Make-Up Artist walked over and instructed her to shield her eyes. She then spritzed her down with the fake sweat only to realize that she hadn't warned the Camera Operator to shield the lens. The lens was completely drenched and they had to take it all apart to clean it before they could shoot. Needless to say, the Make-Up Artist got a good chewing out from the D.P. and held up shooting for a good half hour.

Bill Zahn, Digital FX Artist

CHAPTER EIGHT

"We dress the Talent, not the crew!"

THE
COSTUME
DEPARTMENT

A BRIEF OVERVIEW

It you ask the Costume Department they'll be the first to tell you that *"Clothes do make the man...or woman."* Unless you're making a nudist film (or porno for that matter) you're going to need clothes and we're not just talking off the rack here.

As much as the way a character looks or acts, what they wear also speaks volumes. A bank executive who shows up to work in a Hawaiian shirt everyday is quite different from one who wears only hand-made Italian suits.

The Costume Designer is the key person on the production that helps to determine how each character will dress. The decisions are based on who each character is both physically and psychologically in the context of the story. As I mentioned before, clothes can inform a lot about a character without them even saying a word. Even how they wear the clothes or what accessories are added visually explains personality.

Once the Costume Designer has figured this all out, usually with a series of drawings and concepts, a team of professionals takes the vision and transforms it into reality. If the movie takes place in a contemporary setting, they will first scour stores and boutiques for existing clothing. If that fails, clothing must be manufactured from either pre-existing items or from scratch.

When dealing with a period piece or futuristic film, most Costume Departments have access to costume houses that rent out clothing ranging from 17th century dresses to up to date military uniforms. These facilities are particularly helpful for most of the characters, especially the Background Actors. Still, most lead characters have clothing designed and made specifically for them and tailored to fit precisely.

During the shoot, great pains are taken to make sure the clothing is accurate for each shot and has continuity throughout the film.

THE PLAYERS

Costume Designer: Works closely with the Director and Production Designer to determine the style of clothing for each character in the film.

Assistant Costume Designer: Assists the Costume Designer by coordinating the manufacturing of wardrobe or its renting and/or purchase.

Costume Supervisor: Oversees the Costume Department and stays on top of any and all changes made to the schedule. Handles all the paperwork and makes sure his/her crew gets paid.

Set Costumer: Responsible for the Actor's wardrobe on the set and making sure it's ready to shoot right before the cameras roll.

Costumer: Purchases or rents all the clothes and accessories necessary for the production prior to filming. During production maintains the wardrobe and assists with fittings on the Actors.

Tailor / Seamstress: a.k.a. Dressmaker. Assists in the fittings and do all the necessary alterations. Also makes the costumes to order.

TERMS YOU SHOULD KNOW

accessories
Additional items worn by a character such as: Jewelry, belts, purses, hats, etc.

aging
The process of making new clothes look old and worn.

baby wipes
Used to clean up spills and to remove dirt off clothing.

bible
Book of continuity photos.

continuity sheet
Notations of wardrobe for each character - Everything the character wears from head to toe. Includes what they're wearing, how they're wearing it and in what scenes.

costume house
Warehouse that rents costumes, storage space and office space to costumers. Items of wardrobe are organized by theme, type and period.

distress
The process of making clothes look ripped, torn and/or damaged.

Fuller's Earth
Clean dirt that comes in a variety of colors that is used to age or distress clothes.

hang tags
Manila card stock tag used to label clothes.

jockey box
Storage space located under the costume trailer designed to hold clothing and supplies.

lint roller
A drum with replaceable tape designed with the sticky side out and used to remove lint or fibers from clothing.

made to order
Making a costume from scratch for a specific Actor.

moleskin
Adhesive backed soft fabric used to protect the Actor's skin from rubbing abrasions.

multiples
More than one piece of the same costume. Sometimes referred to as doubles, triples, quadruples, etc. Especially needed for multiple takes of shots that require damage to the wardrobe.

muslin sleave
A see-through bag on a hanger designed to hold all the accessories for a specific character.

"on memo"
"Borrowing" items of clothing from a store or boutique with studio services for a period of 24hrs. to 5 days. (see studio services)

P.O.
a.k.a. purchase order. Paperwork for accounting purposes used to track individual items of wardrobe rented out during the course of a production.

schmutz
Thicker Fuller's Earth paste used to smear onto wardrobe to age or distress it.

studio services

Service provided by many major department stores and some smaller boutique stores that allows Costumers to "borrow" large amounts of clothing for a short period of time without paying. This allows for the Costumer to do fittings and have things signed off by the Director and return the unwanted clothes without hassles.

tailor's chalk

Square-shaped, waxy chalk that comes in a variety of colors used to mark changes on wardrobe during fittings.

Top-Stick

Clear hairpiece tape used for a variety of reasons such as securing items of wardrobe together or to the actors skin. Necessary when safety pins are impractical.

wardrobe rack

Large mobile box or rack on wheels used to transport costumes, accessories and the set kit to the set.

"wife beater"

Refers to a standard white tank top.

THE RULES OF SETIQUETTE

• Bring your own clothes to set. It's not the role of the Costume Department to be your personal clothing store.

• Do not harass the Costumers about having or buying wardrobe items "when the show's over." The last thing on their minds is giving away the costumes when the show wraps.

• Don't ever try on wardrobe items unless authorized by the Costumer. If anything was to happen to a piece of wardrobe, such as being misplaced or damaged, they are ultimately responsible.

• Never enter the Costume Trailer without the expressed permission of a Costumer. Actors may be in the process of a fitting and deserve the privacy they expect.

• Never remove items from a Costumer's set kit. The kit is designed for their convenience, not yours. If something they counted on being there is missing when they need it, it can reflect on their performance as well as slow down Production.

• If you are wearing a costume be mindful when you are eating and/or drinking not to spill on the clothes. There may only be that one piece, especially if you're an extra.

• The Costume Department's Polaroid camera is not meant as a convenience for you to "snap off" a quick shot with an Actor. They need to constantly document the look of the Actors in every scene, especially when changes are made on the set. (also see Hair & Make-Up Department)

• Just because you see them mending and washing clothes does not mean that the Costume Department is your personal seamstress or dry cleaner. Do not ask them to either "fix a tear" or "help get a stain out." They have enough work to do up keeping the actual wardrobe, let alone your sullied set clothes.

ADVICE FROM THE EXPERTS

Andrea Weaver
Costumer
(WALK THE LINE, SEABISCUIT, "SCARECROW AND MRS. KING",
RAGING BULL, THE STING)

Try This On For Size

In our Department the most important thing is to learn by observation from people who have done it before. Sometimes we sort of have a lack of respect from the younger people. Generally speaking, they don't want to learn by your experience. If you say to them, *"look I've done this before and this always happens so lets not go down that road, lets try plan B,"* they will inevitably think that it's not going to happen to them. They'll proceed as if you had said nothing, as if you had never had a day of experience, and they will do what they think is going to work. Ultimately, the exact same thing will happen to them. It's called learning the hard way.

Test Fitting

I started in high school doing costumes for plays and soon decided that was what I wanted to do. So I came out to California to go to the Chouinard Art School, which was one of only two art schools in Los Angeles. After I graduated I got a job working for Western Costumes, which was a great place to learn the trade. I learned from people who have been there a long time. It was on-the-job training, learning though experience. When I left Western Costume, I went out to work freelance and day checked on TV and Features. Over the years, I've worked in just about every medium there is from Live TV to TV Series to TV Movies to Film.

On The Job: Live TV

In Live TV they shoot with three cameras, so a big part of the job is learning how to stay out of the way of the cameras and not to get run over by them. It has a little bit different schedule then episodic TV. There are table readings, rehearsals, taped rehearsals and then the actual taping. People say sitcoms are easier, but I see it as the same. You're still constantly running around like crazy, you can't get the Actors for fittings when you need them and there are also a lot of last minute changes that invariably occur. Things would change even between the dress rehearsal and the shoot. So, at the end of the day, I see it very much as the same job, regardless of where I work.

On The Job: TV Series
Episodic TV is very fast paced and it's gotten faster and will continue to get more so. Sometimes it becomes about survival. When I started, we were working 10-12 hrs days and now I hear people talking about the fact that they work 70 hrs a week. Another challenge with Episodic TV is that not only do you have to prep the episode you are currently doing, you have to think about re-shoots and added scenes for the last episode as well as what's coming up for the next episode. You have to be very organized with what you are doing and concentrate and really pay attention.

On The Job: TV Movies
Mini-series and made for TV movies have their own set of challenges too. They typically hire you at the last minute and cast right before they start to shoot, so you're always running and you are always behind. Mini-series can be very challenging because it's about survival due to the amount of time you have to work on it. This is not to say that Films don't have long schedules, it's just that they're not typically working at the same pace. With a mini-series there is usually much more to shoot in the limited time.

On The Job: Films
Features have a little more of a casual approach, but still can become very difficult. Lately, a lot of features are being made for a lot less money and wind up mimicking the pace of TV. There may be a little more attention to detail in the process, but it's still done very quickly. You also don't have the time to research like you used to and you're researching on the fly, so you've got to get as much done as quickly as possible.

No Wire Hangers!

The crew that you hire is very important. The people you pick to work with you have to have experience, know what they're doing and in case you're not there, need to be able to step up and do the job without getting lost in the mix. MOMMY DEAREST contained five different periods of clothes, so from a costume point of view it was large, but we were very organized. It was well prepared and we could go into the 60's or 80's at the drop of a hat, but the personalities were very difficult to deal with. They created a problem with Production who had to change the schedule frequently. It was a show that I frequently thought about quitting, but I made it through all the way to the end because I had such a great crew working with me.

"Wardrobe is the hand that rocks the set. They are the one department that seems to know what's going on before anybody else."
Chad Darnell, Extras Casting Director

Janet Stirner Ingram
Key Costumer
(HANNAH MONTANA, CRANK, S.W.A.T., BOOGIE NIGHTS)

The Heart's Filthy Lesson

I always thought I wanted to be a journalist writing about the movies so I got a degree in film studies from London University. When I graduated all my friends got jobs in various aspects of the business. At that time in London there was a lot of money going into film and there was some really interesting companies cropping up. One of my close friends went to work for Title Films and suggested I come work there. It seemed intriguing to me so I took the job. It was my first real experience working in production. When I came to LA, the first job I got her was working as a Production Secretary on SE7EN. I very quickly came to the conclusion that it's a pretty thankless job. It did have its benefits though because every department came through the production office at some point. So I got a really good feel for what the departments were like and it started me thinking what aspect of filmmaking I would prefer doing.

Dream A Little Dream

I had always dreamt of doing costumes but assumed that I couldn't possibly do that because I didn't have a design or fine arts background. But after talking with people from the Costume Department I realized it wasn't the case. They told me that in order to succeed in any of the departments, I just needed to have a good eye and work hard. That was all I needed to hear. Through the contacts I made on SE7EN, I was able to get a job as an Office P.A. on NIXON, getting breakfast, making coffee and getting office supplies. When I was on that show, I submitted to the Costume Department and they were able to see how serious I was and how hard I would work to get ahead. They ultimately helped me get a job at a costume house where I worked for awhile. Because of that I was able to get into the Union and land my first job as a Costumer on a low budget movie.

You Make A Better Door Then A Window

My first experience on a movie set was absolutely terrifying. I had no idea what I was supposed to be doing. I had a great teacher who was very clear about what needed to happen but all that seemed to escape me when I was in actually the thick of it. Working in a Production Office taught me some things, but it in no way prepared me for what the set was actually like. I would find myself constantly getting in other people's way and the D.P. always had to tell me to move because I was standing in the shot. Every once in a awhile, I'd just duck down behind a table and they'd yell, *"Action,"* and of course, I didn't realize that the camera was going to move, so I'd wind up in the shot again. I was so naïve that I didn't even know that I should be even more embarrassed then I actually was. Fortunately, it didn't freak me out and I learned a lot really quickly. I was lucky that the crew was great and very supportive.

The Dresser

You have to be respectful and businesslike in your relationship with the Actors. It's a tricky situation that can become very personal and complicated. Hair and Make-Up typically have different relationship with the Actors then Costumes because they're in their personal space a lot longer then we are. So they bond easier. Some Actors do have personal Dressers though, and these individuals make a lot more money then just an everyday Set Costumer. These positions are extremely coveted because of their financial rewards. I don't see a problem with Costumers attaining these types of positions with Actors as long as it comes from the right place. If you legitimately click with an Actor and develop a working friendship then more power to you. Unfortunately, I have met many Costumers over the years that want to do it just for the money, so they insinuate themselves into the Actor's personal space and try to manipulate the situation. It's not only ethically wrong, it's bad set etiquette.

"We help tell the story through the clothes."
Mary Jane Fort, Costume Designer

Monica Haynes-Nino
Costumer
(Benjamin Button, "Star Trek: DS9/Voyager/Enterprise" The Aviator)

Wise Advice

I'm going to tell you what a person that I truly respect and admire told me. The three most important things that he looks for in hiring a person are: One who shows up on time, one who has a smile on their face no matter what the situation is and one who will get stuff done. He also believes that if there's a problem, don't come to him with it unless it's something you can't figure out for yourself but have tried to find a solution. I've always remembered these things. They've always been a part of my work ethic and have worked well for me over the years.

Cool Threads, Dude!

Prior to working in the film industry, I worked in the vintage world as a manager of a clothing store. I collected vintage clothing starting in 1981 when I was in high school and it was popular to wear vintage. I soon began to learn a little bit more about the pieces of clothing I was collecting. After high school, I went to trade tech for a couple of years and learned more in depth about the industry that I was planning on going into. It was a complete departure from what I actually went to college for, so this was a change for me. While continuing to work in vintage clothing, I encountered a lot of Costumers who would come into the store and ask me to pull together things for them because many of them didn't have a lot of knowledge of period wardrobe.

Sew As You Go

Because I had been working with it a lot, I could direct them towards the pieces they were looking for and usually help pull together a look for them. I realized after this happened several times that these people were probably making a lot more money than me even though I had as many skills (if not more) in that area as they did. So I decided to go back to school and tone up on the other skills that I wasn't as proficient in, especially sewing. This paid off because it became very helpful in getting my first job. I started working as a "custom-made" person, sewing, working on clothing, putting it together, and the actual Wardrobe construction. I earned my thirty days in the industry and was able to apply for membership in the industry.

God Bless David Hasselhoff

I decided that I wanted to go ahead and go into finished work, which is what they call the covered work the Costumer does either in a costume house or on set. You're working with garments that are already completed, you're not actually building the garments. So I went to work for American Costume for two years. I started in the women's department and was soon running it. I left that job hoping to work on sets but wasn't able to procure work for about two years. This was a down point in my life. Because I wasn't able to get work, I lost my union status. (Once you become a rostered employee, which means you are on the Producer's roster to work on a union film, if you don't maintain a certain number of hours in a given period, you can actually lose your benefits and pension hours). It was like having to start from scratch. I had made a promise to myself that if I hadn't gotten costuming work by the end of a two-year period, I would leave the business. The last week, of the last month, of the second year I got a call from "BAYWATCH" and I went to go work for them. This one job got me back into the industry. I then continued to work on various projects until I landed my first feature DEVIL IN A BLUE DRESS. I was really interested in working on this show because I became known for pulling together period clothing from 1920-1970's. This lead to a fruitful career with most of the pictures I have worked on being period films from the '20's, 30's 40's.

To Boldly Sew...

There are some people, because of their expertise, that are always hired to go on location, or for military pictures, or who are very good with sports pictures. Word gets around in the industry. I'm one of those people who are known for period pieces. Ironically, I fell into "STAR TREK" purely by accident and ended up working on it for about six years. It was really one of my better experiences in costuming. In the end, I look at futuristic costuming as period in a sense...future period, of course.

Bloody Good Work

When I was working on SERENITY we were told that there was a particular pint of blood that the Director (Joss Whedon) wanted to use. Normally, this would be handled by the Make-Up or the Special Effects Department and it wasn't something that we carried in our own kits. Luckily, the Make-Up Department lent us a quantity of the requested blood. In this instance we had a one-of-a-kind shirt that the Actor gets shot in. It was already bloodied and tattered. Unfortunately, we now had to shoot the stunt prior to him getting shot. The challenge was having to sew up the shirt and take the blood away as much as we could for take one of the stunt and then, hopefully, not getting the shirt too bloody on the second take so we could reuse it again. Everything turned out fine, but it was a nightmare only having one piece of wardrobe.

"For some reason, people on the set have a hard time understanding exactly what we do. I could live with this if it wasn't for the fact that every time crew members rip something or spill something on their personal clothes, they seem to think it's our job to get it out. Like we are the people to see if you have a rip or a spill."

Andrea Weaver, Costumer

Patricia Zinn Etheridge
Set Costumer
("NED & STACY", "JUDGING AMY", GREASE, JAWS 2)

If The Shoe Fits

When I was 16, I wrote a letter to the head of the Universal Studios Costume Department, whose name I got from the credits at the end of my favorite television show. I told him I would very much like to work for him and that began a very long and happy story that led to my current 39 years as a film Costumer. I certainly did not know what work I wanted to do for him, but I have never been sorry for choosing this path. I worked my way up from the stock room at Universal's Costume Department, to working on sets assisting wonderful experienced Set Costumers, to having my own shows as a Set Costumer, to being a Key Costumer, then Costume Supervisor (and being nominated for an Emmy); and finally deciding the only work I really wanted to do was on the film set, and for the past 15-plus years I have worked as a Set Costumer.

Suit Up

The most important thing a Set Costumer must always keep in mind is that, every minute of the work day, you represent the Costume Department. You are the visible tip of the iceburg that consists of the

Designer, the Supervisor, the Key Costumer, as well as the Custom-Made Costumers, all of whom work collectively to produce the costumes for the film set you are working on. Those costumes are delivered to the Set Costumer after enormous work and collaboration with other Departments (this discussion alone is probably an entire chapter!) The Set Costumer serves the Costume department best by being a vigilant co-operative member of the film crew, and by helping create a supportive environment for the Actors.

On Being A Set Costumer

The responsibilities of the Set Costumer begin before they get to the set-in "trailer land." The Actors' dressing rooms are set up with the costume to be worn in the scene which is about to be filmed. (In a perfect world this costume has been selected, fitted and approved by Actors/Producers/Directors, and co-ordinated with other costumes for color, season, etc, and with other departments like Set Decoration. i.e. *Does she match the couch?*) This costume is worn to the set by the Actor and the Set Costumer becomes the guardian of it (and of all the costumes in their care on that set.)

During filming the costume is watched so that it is being worn as designed by the Designer, and watched for continuity. Matching the exact way a costume is worn is essential for the editing process. (How many buttons are open at the neck, how high are the sleeves rolled, is the jacket on or off, is the tie snug and does the knot match). Continuity is assured by careful set notes and photographs-sometimes polaroid, sometimes now digital.

Throughout the filming day the Set Costumer is responsible for making sure each costume is correct for each scene, and that the costume is worn so the continuity is a match. All these notes and photographs are kept in the set book (sometimes called "the bible"). The set book is used during production to be certain of costume continuity each day of filming; during post-production as a reference for inserts and added scenes or re-shoots; and weeks or months after production is complete for episodic storyline continuation, or film sequels.

Clothing Makes The Man

A major responsibility of the Set Costumer is to work with the Actor to create an environment that makes them confident and comfortable. (When an Actor steps out of the swimming pool scene it is great to have a warm dry terry cloth robe waiting when the Director says *"Cut;"* those 5" high-heels look fabulous, but its nice to have a comfortable slipper standing by to wear to lunch; if you're filming in the desert having a clean pressed double shirt for Take-2 makes the Actor look and feel "cool"-assuming that's right for the character and story, and the continuity of the scene)

The Whole "Kit" & Kaboodle

The "set kit" all Set Costumers have is as different as each of the Costumers themselves. The whole objective of that kit is to anticipate possible costume "snafus" and be able to fix them quickly to reduce those dreaded and costly "costume delays." (A term you never want to see appear on a production report!) Food & drink spills, lost buttons, broken jewelry, slipping straps, all can be corrected quickly with a good set kit in the hands of a calm experienced Set Costumer.

TALES FROM THE SET

It was a Costumer's first day on set and she noticed that something was wrong with the Lead Actor's wardrobe while they were in the middle of shooting a scene. She suddenly yelled, *"Cut"* to stop them shooting so she could fix it. The whole set went quiet and everyone just looked at her in stunned disbelief. It was awful. This poor young girl didn't have a clue. She thought she was doing the right thing. Fortunately, the Director had a good sense of humor about it and started laughing at how ludicrous it was. Within seconds, the entire crew was having a good laugh at the girl's expense. Needless to say, it was immediately explained to her that, as admirable as it was to want to save the shot, that's something you never do.

Janet Stirner, Key Costumer

On THE AVIATOR I was asked to work with some very expensive jewelry pieces as part of the wardrobe. This was something I hadn't previously done. I had to work with a guard and be responsible for the priceless vintage jewelry. There were a couple of instances where I would have a malfunction with one of those pieces. On one occasion there was a dress clip, which flew out of my hand and landed on the floor. When I went to retrieve it, I noticed that two of the diamonds had fallen out.

I had to get the Actress dressed and on the set but had to figure out how I could get this piece on her. It was a continuity piece that had already been shot on her and it had to match! So I found the diamonds and, having no other choice, I super-glued them into the clip. This isn't something I would recommend. I was horrified and didn't know what the ramifications of my actions would be. All I knew was that I had to have her dressed and in perfect condition as she had been seen previously, so they could shoot. I didn't think they would have appreciated me holding up camera for two diamonds. So we got her on set and it worked out well. After she was finished, I took the dress clip and went to my supervisor. Luckily, there is something in film called insurance. So the insurance company was able to cover it. Fortunately, I didn't do any damage to the diamonds or the

clip other then them having to be reset professionally. Remember, accidents do happen, and you have to be ready to rise to the occasion.
Monica Haynes, Costume Supervisor

I was working on a superhero movie where one of the Lead Actresses was wearing a white neoprene suit. We had built three of these suits: A hero, a back-up and a stunt. They had finished filming with the hero suit and needed to shoot a stunt sequence. We suited up the Stunt Woman and handed her off to the Stunt Department to be rigged in the flying harness. Anybody who has ever worked in stunts knows that most of their gear is aluminum. So the metal and oils tend to rub onto things especially your hands. Needless to say, they weren't exactly taking too much care with keeping the suit clean while they were hooking her up and wound up man-handling it with their dirty hands. This, of course, was transferred to this pristine white suit that needed to be that way for the shot. It wound up turning into a crisis because when they were ready to shoot, they realized that the suit was dirty and they looked to me to fix it.

I ultimately had to do my best to bleach out the stains so they didn't lose their day. Meanwhile, we had to have new suits manufactured back at the shop for future shooting because that one was now trashed. Mind you, these suits are extremely expensive and take time to make. This all could have been avoided if the Stunt Crew had just worn rubber gloves when they were handling the suit.
Jerry Constantine, Make-Up FX Artist

One of the earlier movies I worked on was a made for TV movie and I was the third or forth Costumer who was asked to work with the Lead Actress. There was a piece of wardrobe that was supposed to be worn in a particular scene for her, and not having been on the show the whole time, I didn't know the status of the wardrobe. It was brought to me around lunchtime and I was told to sew some frogs on it (frogs being the closures that are usually looped, you see them a lot on Chinese garments). So I was doing this and it was getting closer and closer to the time when she was supposed to be getting dressed.

I took the garment to her on set, and put it on her, at which time she noticed that the frogs were not the way that they were supposed to have been. Evidently, the garment hadn't been completed. I was the last person that she saw, the one that brought it to her, so I was the one who caught the heat.

Being a set person, you have to trust your Department Supervisor to bring you the finished garment in the state that it's supposed to be when the Actor puts it on. Certain things happen, sometimes last minute, but this was not the case. This was a garment that was supposed to be completed well before she received it. So, in taking the heat for my department, one of the questions I should have asked when I received it was has the Actress had this garment on before and is she aware that this is the way its supposed to be? Being young and inexperienced, I didn't think of these things. And once the incident occurred, it caused an immediate breakdown in trust between the Actress and myself, which had at that point been hard earned. There's a lot of responsibility there. I should have had more information and that taught me to ask more questions, especially when working with high profile Actors. You must listen to the Actor's needs and see if you can help them.

Monica Haynes, Costume Supervisor

I was shooting a period film outside of Santa Fe, New Mexico and an Actor that we had fit months ago in Los Angeles was arriving. He didn't have a big part, so we did his fittings six weeks early. Unbeknownst to us, during those six weeks he quit smoking. When he showed up he was literally 30-40 lbs heavier. To make matters worse, he arrived at night-time the day before his scene. Because this was a period film we had nothing for him because his wardrobe no longer fit. I remember driving to Walmart late at night and buying basic flat front khaki's and several shirts and spending all night sewing them together.

Mary Jane Fort, Costume Designer

CHAPTER NINE

"What part of <u>Hot Set</u> didn't you understand?"

THE
<u>ART</u>
DEPARTMENT

A BRIEF OVERVIEW

How a film looks can be just as important as how it's written or directed. The Art Department's sole job is to bring a unique vision to the visual style of a production.

The Production Designer is the key personnel of this department. They are typically one of the first people brought onto a film, usually at the very beginning of pre-production. Using the script and concepts from the Director as a springboard, they create works of art, mock-ups and/or sculptures to demonstrate a possible feel for the film.

Movies are a visual medium and the audience relies on clues to establish the type of film they're watching and the art direction dictates the mood and feel. For example, a horror movie will typically have dark and claustrophobic sets designed to cast ominous shadows when lit, while a musical might have bright and cheery sets to accentuate the fun and energy. It's not to say that these are always the case, it's just to demonstrate how the look can inform the story.

Once this look has been established, the Art Department's team of highly trained Artists turns the drawings into workable sets and set pieces. Studio space and stages are rented and carpenters are hired to erect the sets on the stages according to a predetermined format designed to ease filming.

After the sets are in place, Scenic Artists get to work painting them and decorating the interiors to make them look like real environments. Sometimes it is necessary for exterior locations to be created indoors. In these cases, Greenspeople are brought in to load up the area with real and/or fake trees and plants to fool the audience that the location really exists outdoors.

The difference between a well designed film and a poorly designed film is astronomical. Like great art, a richly crafted look tends to draw the eye and make an indelible impression in the minds of the audience.

THE PLAYERS

Production Designer: Works with the Director in creating the overall artistic look of the film in every aspect. The head of the Art Department.

Art Director: Responsible for physically bringing the Production Designer's vision into reality.

Set Decorator: a.k.a. Leadperson or Swing Gang. Acquires all the items to dress a set or a location. Supervises painting, furniture, upholstery, floor coverings, etc.

Set Dresser: Works under the Set Decorator making sure that the sets are maintained during the shoot.

Construction Coordinator: a.k.a. Construction Foreman. Guided by the Art Director, he/she builds all the sets necessary for filming.

Carpenters: Crew members that work with wood to physically build the sets, furniture, props and camera tracks.

Scenic Artist: Paints the sets and graphics that appear on the sets.

On-Set Painter: Crew member that stands by on the set in case any last minute touch ups are required.

Greensperson: Handle live and artificial plants needed for a shot.

TERMS YOU SHOULD KNOW

cove
a.k.a. ground row. A lighted baseboard on a piece of background scenery

dutchman
Painted canvas strip attached between flats to cover cracks.

four-walled set
Set constructed with four walls that allows for continuous 360° shooting. Usually one or more of the walls are wild.

hot set
Set that is totally prepared to be shot that has everything in its exact location. Moved items would destroy the continuity between shots.

limbo set
Set or location with no defining characteristics.

lot
The entire area of a studio both exterior and interior where production takes place and the sets are constructed.

mottling
Process of texturing a flat surface in order to give it a three-dimensional appearance.

practical set
Describes a set that is a pre-existing location or utilizes elements of an existing location.

"redress"
To change the looks of a set to suggest the passage of time or to make it look like an entirely new location.

scenery
The background of a shot that either exists in an exterior location or has been manufactured on a stage.

scenery dock
Storage area on a lot that maintains the various set pieces such as flats, foliage, etc.

"scrub"
a.k.a. "strike." To remove a set or elements of a set when it is not in use or completely wrapped from filming.

set dressing
All the Art Department elements (i.e. furnishings, draperies, decorations, etc.) that are utilized to give a certain feel to a set or location.

sike/backdrop
An enormous painted scene or enlarged photographs that hangs from the ceiling behind a set that is only usually perceived through windows or doors.

sound stage
Soundproof building located on a lot where sets are constructed and interior filming takes place.

stage brace
a.k.a. strut. A brace usually made of metal or wood that fastens to the back of a set piece or scenery piece and attaches to the floor in order to stabilize it.

standing set
A set that is completely constructed and assembled.

swinger
a.k.a. flapper. Hinged flat that can be swung out of the way to make room for the camera or for better ease in utilizing space for lighting or personnel.

three-walled set

A set that contains two side walls and a back with no front.

unit set

A set containing various parts that can be reassembled in order to create different looks.

wild wall

a.k.a. floating wall. A part of the set or a flat that can be removed with relative ease to make room for the camera.

THE RULES OF SETIQUETTE

• Get to know how the set works, such as how pieces fit together, what walls are wild, what works and what is non-functional. In the long run, it will make your job that much easier.

• Mind the sets when you're on them. Many people labored long days to construct and ready them for filming. They wouldn't appreciate you chipping off the paint or otherwise damaging the set just because you're bored.

• A "Hot Set" means a "Hot Set." Stay out and don't touch!

• Throw out your personal garbage while working on a set. Sometimes refuse can be misconstrued as a prop or set dressing and not be removed prior to shooting. This, of course, will cause continuity errors.

• Don't attempt to open doors or windows on a set, because they might be solid and non-functional. Forcing them to open obviously will cause damage.

• Make sure before you open a door on a set that it's clear. Because stages are usually cramped, every corner is utilized by either personnel or equipment.

• Only sit on a chair that is designated by Production. Most chairs are part of the set and the Art Department is responsible for. Worse case scenario is that a chair is a breakaway and more than likely won't hold your weight.

• Keep in mind that a practical set is someone's personal property. Treat it like you would treat your own home...unless you're a slob.

• Many films utilize logos or graphics specifically designed for the movie. These will frequently appear as stickers to be adhered to props or set pieces. They are not available for your "cool" decorations or a memento to stick on your personal effects. i.e. Don't bug the Art Department for them.

ADVICE FROM THE EXPERTS

Patrick Tatopoulos
Production Designer
(TOTAL RECALL, LIVE FREE OR DIE HARD, INDEPENDENCE DAY)

Signature Style

Very often people look at the Production Designer as the man who creates the look of the movie but in reality it is his job to establish the look of the Director's vision. Creatively the ultimate vision for the film comes from the Director, not the Production Designer. A great example of this is Tim Burton. No matter what Designer is brought on board, the movie will still look like a Tim Burton movie. This is a man that's got a signature style that's so strong that even though these incredibly talented Designers he works with bring a lot to the table, at the end of the day it's his brain that creates the world. And working within the Director's vision doesn't take credit away from what we create because an accomplished Designer opens up the world for the Director allowing it to be fully realized in three dimensions.

Baby Steps

I came to the States about 20 years ago because I wanted to work in Creature FX as a Sculptor. I was fortunate to get a low-level position at one of the makeup effect labs. They soon noticed that I had an eye for design and I very quickly started working as an Art Director at the shops, designing, sculpting and painting the creatures. A few years later I was working on BEASTMASTER 2 and the Director asked me if I could help with the sets. They had a great Production Designer but he didn't draw and they wanted to know if I would come onboard as the Art Director. So I stepped into this world and realized, *"You know what? It makes total sense. You design a creature that has to fit in a world, so why not design the world as well?"* This job didn't exactly put me on the map, but it gave me my first step to something else.

Independent Thinking

I had an architectural background back in France and I started to get excited about drawing sets. But I still liked to do creatures as well. I decided why not do both. So I started to establish myself as a guy that can do creatures and worlds. Roland Emmerich was the first to really buy into what I was doing. He gave me my first shot at opening my creature shop for STARGATE to design and create the warriors, helmets, and surfaces. After the movie wrapped Roland told me that what I had created really defined the look of the movie because they ended up using some of my helmet patterns as inspiration for the sets. Inadvertently, my style had become a big trademark of the film and he said, *"Next movie we do together, you're designing it."* Well, Roland's next movie was INDEPENDENCE DAY and as promised I was hired to work as a Production Designer focusing on the alien world. I designed the alien first, and without thinking about it I started designing the spacecraft and then one day I looked at them and realized that the top view of the alien's head was an exact match of the spacecraft. Did I think about it? No. But somehow, there was some sort of an organic way of melding those two things together: the characters that fit that particular world. From that point on it became what I pushed for on future projects, to be the one that would handle all these aspects of the design.

City Lights

As a Production Designer you should always be on very good terms with the D.P. My advice is to start building a friendly relationship with the D.P. early on at the conceptual level of the movie because at the end of the day you could design the most incredible set imaginable but if it's not lit properly, it will look terrible. One such example that is always going to stay in my mind is when I worked on Alex Proyas' DARK CITY. I did some very rough marker and pencil design work and created a look that Alex Proyas liked very much. Dariusz Wolski came on board as the D.P. and took a look at this rough design and said, *"You know what, I love the look of this concept. I'm going to make this work."* So Dariusz and I sat down together to discuss how we could achieve this and he came up with the idea of using industrial lighting instead of typical movie lights. Instead of re-interpreting the concept, he chose to embrace it. As the Designer I supported him in every way I could and that to me is an optimal, top of the line relationship with the D.P. Ultimately we all got a movie that we're very proud of. This was a big deal for me because it made me understand early on that we all need to work together to achieve greatness. It pays off in the end big time.

Sydney J. Bartholomew
Production Designer
(SHALLOW HAL, THERE'S SOMETHING ABOUT MARY, "PEE-WEE'S PLAYHOUSE")

Practical Advice

- Keep your mouth shut.
- Look what other people are doing and stay out of their way.
- Look what other people are doing, for you may learn something.
- If the situation arises, ask questions and make friends.
- Make sure it's a good Caterer.

Pointing The Finger

Blame only wastes time. I look at a set like a boat. If there is a hole in the hull and you're taking on water, discuss the ways of removing that water so you don't lose the ship. Blame is like guilt and it doesn't help. You can go over what someone did wrong till you're blue in the face, but the key is to make sure that it doesn't happen again.

On Attitude

If you are cool and you instill that calmness and coolness with everybody else on the set, it goes up and down the line, to people above you and people below you. It shows that you've got the confidence to live. In many cases, my job is to sustain that confidence.

Communication Skills

I have to coordinate with every Department to make sure that their stuff works with my design. So we're not building a *Tower of Babel*. It's bad etiquette and bad movie making if there's no communication between Departments. The only people above me that I have to answer to are the Director and the Producers. Laterally, it's the D.P. Other than that, the only other person that I have to answer to is myself and my own sense of pride about what I have to get done.

On Being A Production Designer

Everything you see on the screen has either been designed by me or has passed through my hands or my eyes. It involves the methods it takes to make it to the screen: How it's built, how big, how little, what color, what shape. Basically, without a Production Designer you don't have a Production. I end up being the largest Department on a set and, because everything revolves around what I design, I can't be a day late or a dollar short or I'm screwed.

"The Art Department is the hardest working Department on a set. They're always setting something up, changing something during the shoot, or striking something when it's done. I have a lot of admiration for them."

D. J. Ritchie, Sound Mixer

Cynthia Kay Charette
Production Designer
(IN THE MIX, NORMA JEAN & MARILYN, NEW NIGHTMARE, PUMPKINHEAD)

The Magic Hour

I'm a dreamer and I love the film business because it allows me the ability create new worlds. As far back as I can remember, I was always trying to create things. When I was 6 years old, I would get up in the middle of the night, move the furniture around and do my thing until the elves came (at least that's what I told my mother). I was the artist in high school, voted most creative. I knew that I didn't want to sit behind a desk my whole life.

So when I went to college, I majored in theater design. What I love about theater is that the audience goes into a dark room, then the curtain goes up and there's magic. That's the same feeling I get when I'm in a movie theater: that blackness that becomes another world.

Dreams On A Budget

I spent some time in London then eventually came to New York. At that time I was going to do theater but soon discovered that it was very difficult to make a living. Even the Tony Award winning Designer's salaries weren't that great compared to what could be earned doing film. One day a USC friend of mine called and offered me a job on a low budget movie he was directing. At the time, I had a full time job as well as many other commitments. I called my Mother and she said I should take it. I couldn't believe I was going to give up everything I had worked hard for to go work on this $250,000 budget film. On this film I wound up working Production, Costume, Art Department and just about everything else you could do on a set. My crew consisted of three kids from high school.

This film was an anthology and in it there were four episodes, one was Civil War, the others were 1930s, 1950s, and 1970s and I was to create all of this. I had women working for free making the Civil War costumes while I was painting the 1930s carnival sets. The film came out pretty good and I was hooked. I got the film bug big time. I moved to Hollywood with this one film under my belt and struggled to get whatever jobs I could. I finally got another film and that lead to the next one and so forth. I did non-union work for about ten years and at that time I thought I was the horror queen because I did a lot of horror movies. I really wanted to break into comedy and eventually did, and now I am trying my best to get into drama, which is just a whole other thing.

Giving Props…"Props"

I really depend on the Property Department because depending on the size of the film, I find that I'm not able to be on set all the time. I typically have to move ahead and get ready for the next day so I really have to depend on someone to take care of my sets and keep me informed of what's going on. I generally tell them what's important to me, what to look for, and what not to let happen. So I've had Prop Masters call me when I was on another set and tell me to take a look at something, because it didn't look right. So they look out for me.

Freddy vs. Pumkinhead?

One of the movies I've done that always elicits enthusiasm is Stan Winston's PUMPKINHEAD. I really enjoyed working on that film because I was creating a whole new world and I got to be imaginative beyond what the written word was. Horror films get into your psyche and I love that aspect. I love researching histories and myths and using them subliminally in my design. It might just be something small in the background, but I include it because it brings certain realism to the scene, even if the audience never sees it up close.

On WES CRAVEN'S NEW NIGHTMARE, we made a conscious effort not to do the same old thing. We've seen Freddy in his boiler room, so let's show something new and exciting and find the real roots of evil. With horror films there is so much more that you can do so I studied Dante's inferno and made a labyrinth of the seven deadly sins with multiple levels. Mind you, all of this was before SE7EN came out.

A Funny Idea

Comedy is completely different. You are playing off of people's joy and light. So what is that? To me, comedy is colorful and playful. It's more jumpy and rhythmic with swirls and things that slide. You are playing off of humorous ideas and words to create these sets. Ultimately you get to create a new world no matter how mundane or fantastical it might be and there is true magic in that.

A Little Love Goes A Long Way

If you want to be an Artist, go paint in a room by yourself, in the film you are nothing without your crew. If you don't have a crew you can trust then you might as well give up. This is why it's absolutely necessary to know how to treat them. You want to be able to get the most out of them and make sure that they will be there for you when you are standing in a tornado because it happens a lot. I try really hard to treat my crew with respect by knowing their names, offering kindness, and saying *"good morning"* every day. These kinds of things are so important.

"My job entails a lot of pulling my hair out and babysitting."
Joe Del Monte, Construction Coordinator

Thomas T. Taylor
Art Director
(VALKYRIE, "HEROES", "SIX FEET UNDER", THE FUGITIVE)

All The World's A Stage...

Growing up I had a strong interest in theater, which I adopted from my mother and brothers. So I did some performing in high school and in college before making the transition to behind the scenes work. As much as I enjoyed Acting, I felt way more comfortable with having a portfolio in hand with my artwork than going to cold auditions to try to land a part in a play. It was more tangible to have a body of work and I really enjoyed sketching and drawing and was rather good at it as well. The more work I did, the better I got and the better I got, the more jobs I was getting doing it. I easily fell into this path that ultimately led me to becoming a Designer for theater.

Fame...I'm Gonna Learn How To Fly!

I did my undergraduate work in California where I got my degree in Theater with a focus on design. I was accepted to the graduate program at Carnegie Mellon where I got a really good training for designing for the stage. This naturally led me to New York to further my theater education. I went to Julliard for a year as a painter and soon passed the Union exam. It was pretty tough. There were over 100 applicants and they only accepted 4. I passed the second time I took it. That experience dropped me into a world of learning as well as finding employment painting on some huge Broadway productions. After sticking with that for a number of years, I got an opportunity to work for TV and began working more as a Designer. I still had the painting in my back pocket, which afforded me the ability to go back in between bigger jobs when I didn't have anything else going on. It made it possible to make ends meet. That might have been one of the keys to pursuing my design career. As a painter, I could also be available for jobs that the other Designers were not available for. Their commitments kept them from being able to take jobs that came up on short notice. I could easily drop my brush at a moment's notice if an opportunity came up and take the job.

Paging Dr. Taylor

I worked for many years in daytime TV, that was a great training ground for designing for three camera shows. Having to do a one-hour show every day was pretty demanding and rigorous. I learned about compromise, because I didn't have the time or money to do what I would typically be able to do in a feature film. I learned the tricks of the trade of how to get the best bang for my buck and where to efficiently spend my money. I ultimately become a well-oiled machine. Eventually, I got opportunities to do TV movies and did a number of them before coming out to Los Angeles. I got hired onto "GENERAL HOSPITAL" which was perfect to make the transition from New York to Hollywood and to get established. I then freelanced until I got the opportunity to work in film. I started as an Assistant Art Director then I continued to work the next 12-14 years on feature films as Art Director.

The One-Armed Man

THE FUGITIVE was the first feature I worked on and it was new and different working on something that big. I was working on location and hadn't ever done that before. It's different living out of a hotel room and having your work and social life so concentrated around your job. You are totally immersed in your work. It was exciting but it was also crazy as well. It was also my first exposure to the inefficacies of working in the film environment, which made my job more complex and difficult. What had been routine for me in TV, was completely different from the chaotic world of film where things change unpredictably and rapidly. There were constant rewrites, they changed the ending, and there was a lot of involvement from other people and departments. There was also the pressure of time like in TV, but I had less control as to what I could do, given the restraints of the production.

The Philippines Missile Crisis

The most challenging film I've worked on was THIRTEEN DAYS. I was taken to the Philippines where I was in charge of simulating a Cuban missile base and recreating U.S. Air Force base. It was challenging working in a different culture and not being in touch with all the resources that I had here in the US. I was working with people who were not used to the requirements of our industry, especially in regards to delivery of supplies and time management. Yet I found that the work I did was really successful and ultimately I had a great time because my crew became very competent and resourceful in a short period of time.

"There are a lot of politics involved on sets. Besides doing a good, competent job, you also have to properly deal with people who can make or break you."

Jeb Adams, Commercial Production Designer

Maggie Martin
Set Decorator
(THE TOWN, RED EYE, OUT OF SIGHT, "THE BEN STILLER SHOW")

There Is No "i" In "Set Decorator"

Not all Set Decorators are created equal. There are ones who want to do their own thing and others that work more as a part of the Art Department. There are also different approaches to the job. I am less autonomous than others because I like to be collaborative. We get input from a number of sources. The Production Designer, Director of Photography and Director are all sources of inspiration. Though ultimately, I like to get as much inspiration from the script itself, if possible.

The Art Of Design

I found over the years that most Set Decorators are more visually driven than me. I have a theater background and because of that, my perspective on decorating is much more driven by character and story. My degree is in Art not Film; in fact I hardly have an interest in film at all. I barely go to movies but I like stories, so I read a lot instead. My inspiration is typically not from design or fashion which some sets require. I'm just not really interested in that. It's fun to do, but I prefer to do things that are weird and gritty. Since film is a visual medium, the goal is ultimately to create an interesting look, but not necessarily beautiful or fashionable. What it comes down to is just working your butt off because no matter what, it's always going to be a challenge to find just the right stuff. It's not just what you want, it's what's right for the story, the Director, The Production Designer, the Actors, etc.., not to mention time and the budget.

Do I Know You?

If you really want to have the filmmaking experience on set, decorating is not the way to go. Set Decorators are rarely on the set. I typically open the set and make sure everything is all right and then am usually off working on the next set to be used. If I've done my job well, I'm almost never there. I spend most of my time shopping, surfing the net, doing budgeting or having meetings. However, I will come back if there's a set that has developed over the course of time to make alterations. For instance if I need to show the passage of time, or something happens like a fight and I have to change it to reflect this. Other than that my appearance during the shooting is pretty minimal and most of the crew hasn't a clue who I am. I think it's pretty humorous at wrap parties when people constantly ask whose wife I am.

The Rabbit Out Of The Hat Routine

When I first started out as a Set Decorator, the Directors were more prepared. They had spent the time to have a clear vision of how they wanted to shoot things. Unfortunately, the style of directing has changed a lot in recent years and the newer Directors are more off the cuff, so they don't talk as much with me about their vision. I think they prefer a more spontaneous approach, which can be magical at times, but usually it means that we have to stay on our toes and constantly alter things to obtain these sudden inspirations.

Come on Baby, Light My Fire...

Working on LADDER 49 had some unique challenges because we had a great deal of research to do. It's not very often that I have to worry that people will get injured if I make a mistake on what I chose to decorate the set with. Sofas typically don't injure people but on a set with fire, you have to give what the sofa is made from much more thought. We had to find materials that wouldn't burn or would burn for a while but then stop. We also had to be sure that none of them would emit toxic fumes, other than basic smoke. We wound up using a lot natural fibers because they were the safest. I discovered that silk is a bad thing to burn, because it emits a toxic fume when it's burned. If it wasn't for the research I did, I never would have known that. So kids, do your homework.

"When things go wrong there are no such things as problems, there are only solutions."
Sydney J. Bartholomew, Production Designer

Joe Del Monte
Construction Coordinator
("CSI: Miami", "Las Vegas", The Majestic, Flipper)

Rock On!

I was going to school back east and my sister was living in Los Angeles with her boyfriend who was an Art Director. It was the '80s and most of his work consisted of working on Music Videos for MTV. He encouraged me to come out to work for him. Being in my early '20s at the time, it sounded like a great opportunity. Little did I know that I would be working crazy hours for low pay. My first job was working on the David Lee Roth "Just a Gigolo" video. I worked for 4 days straight with no sleep for a flat rate of $75.00 a day. I was young and foolish but I certainly learned quickly about working on sets because they had me doing every job you could imagine.

I Love The '80s

After working for some time on music videos I almost became a Grip and I got offered the chance to go on tour with Iron Maiden as a Rigger, but at the last minute I lost out on the job to a British guy (go figure!). I was a little burnt out at that point so I tried a number of non-industry jobs after that, but soon discovered that the hours were just as crazy. I realized that because the hours for Set Construction were more contained, I could work and still have a social life. So I jumped back into the industry and started at the bottom in working solely in the Art Department. I built sets, painted them and drove the trucks. Things were pretty lax in the '80s and I typically got paid in cash. In the '90s OSHA and the IRS cracked down on our department and it became much more regulated with people relegated to specific jobs. From there, I worked my way up, eventually becoming a Coordinator with my first feature being FLIPPER, which shot in the Bahamas. No complaints there.

On Being A Construction Coordinator

I'm the liaison between the Producers and the Production Designer. I need to create the vision in the Designer's head while at the same time deliver the sets to the production within the time and budget. It's a constant balancing act between the creative and the administrative. I have to manage the logistics of scheduling as well as interacting with all the other Department Heads by attending the production meetings so everyone can stay on the same page.

The Art Department Style

This is a very image conscious business, so even though I work in construction, I still need to carry myself in a professional and set savvy way. I try to instill that onto my crew as well, because a lot of times I have to send them to the set to help and they need to realize that they are representing the Art Department so how they act or carry themselves on the set reflects directly on the department as a whole. So when I hire people, I'm looking for that "all-around" guy who not only can build quick and accurately, but who has a good attitude and can carry themselves well with the rest of the Production.

You really become immersed in whatever job you're working on. If it's something you haven't dealt with before it can be a little tricky until you get well versed in the specifics. I'm always looking for new materials to build sets with. Researching them and hunting them down is a big part of my job. In other words, if I'm doing a science-fiction movie, the materials are going to be a lot different than the ones I would use to create a fishing village in the Bahamas. Knowing where to find things is a big challenge, but after a while you build up a knowledge base so you know you can go to this one place if you're doing a western, and get the proper nails or hardware of the time or you know where to go if you need to manufacture something to match the time period. Another big challenge in my job is when I'm on location in an area I've never been to before. Not only do I generally have to work with a local crew and get to know them, but I need to figure out the local places where I can most efficiently get the supplies I need.

TALES FROM THE SET

We were setting up camera angles and blocking Actors for a scene that involved a young man in pajamas confronting a devilish woman with horns and a leather skirt. The scene called for the man to pick up a cell phone and pretend to call the police. Unfortunately, since we didn't disconnect the phone, the man practiced his method acting a bit too much and called 911. The call was traced to the house and five minutes later a policeman showed up at the door. Thank god I was able to tell him it was just a movie before he came onto the set and saw a man in his PJ's and a leather-clad woman.

Michael Jung, Director

The first time I shot a movie in Italy, one of the crew members started hammering while we were shooting. I went over to him to ask him to stop and he was surprised because up until recently they would never shoot with sound. He told me that Fellini never asked him to stop. I told him I wasn't Fellini and he said *"That's for sure."*

Stuart Gordon, Director/Writer

I had a problem this year with a Production Designer and I was forced to call the Union not once, but twice! The Designer was being lazy, and having me do things that I'm not supposed to. This is a team effort but teams only work well when everyone's doing their job and when someone's not pulling their weight, they can bring the whole ship down. As much as we all work together, we all have our own jobs and responsibilities in our individual departments and just because there are crossovers, especially with Props, doesn't mean we should be taken advantage of. I had to stand up for myself and the Union came through for me and got the Producer involved. Ultimately we had to explain to the Designer what he needed to be doing and if he didn't comply he was not going to work again.

Bruce Mink, Prop Master

I was working the night crew on a show and we ran out of spackle while we were finishing up the set walls. There was nothing open that late at night (this was before 24 hour building supply stores) so we got the bright idea to raid the Craft Service refrigerator for their tubs of cream cheese. It worked great and we were able to finish the set for the next day. Fortunately, that particular set was only being used for half the day's shoot and lucky for us, the Craft Service guy had a good sense of humor about it. To show our appreciation, we made sure we replaced the cream cheese first thing in the morning so the crew could enjoy their bagels.

Joe Del Monte, Construction Coordinator

For those who don't know, Jaguars are preordered and paid for before they are manufactured and shipped over from the UK. There were a number of custom ordered Jaguars (that were absolutely beautiful) that were on their way to their new owners. Some genius had the idea that they should take these cars before they were delivered and film a commercial with them in Northern California. So they took them out to the countryside where a Stonehenge Set had been built. They were going to film the cars by the stones as the sun rose behind them. So the cars had to be positioned the night before and they were meticulously covered up, and taken care of. Well, as you might expect, in the night a storm came up and blew the stones onto the cars completely taking them all out. The point is, don't ever let a film crew borrow anything of personal value no matter how cool you think it would be. It's the movie business, not real life and there are real things that are precious to people and those things have no place on a film set because inevitably they're going to get ruined.

Maggie Martin, Set Decorator

CHAPTER TEN

"These are props, not Craft Service!"

THE
PROPERTY
DEPARTMENT

A BRIEF OVERVIEW

A prop is any object that the Actor comes in contact with that is not a costume or part of the set. This can range from anything from a pencil to a chair and everything in between. The production hires a Property Master whose job is to determine down to the smallest detail, every prop item needed for the movie.

They start by going through the script and listing everything mentioned in the screenplay. A good Property Master will also anticipate the other items needed, as well. For instance, if at a dinner party the script only mentions a certain character's salad fork, they must assume that they'll also need entire table settings for all the dinner guests.

They must also determine if there are items that need to be specifically manufactured for the show. Obviously, props in a futuristic science-fiction film can't be purchased at a store. So they need to be not only made, but designed as well.

The Property Department stores all their gear in a large truck or trailer that usually also contains a lot of generic props as well. Most will carry different varieties of certain items just in case the Director changes his mind or if a prop isn't working out. They also stock various tools and supplies that can be used to alter or change an existing prop if necessary.

The crew consists of members who work solely on the set and Propmakers who work back at their shop building the items. The crew might also include a Food Stylist who deals only with food items on the set.

Another task that falls under this department is handguns. Not only do they provide realistic, non-working guns and stunt versions, but they also supply guns capable of firing blanks. These members of the department are highly trained. Guns are dangerous, even if they're only firing blanks and strict safety guidelines and procedures are followed when they are used.

THE PLAYERS

Property Master: In charge of all items that an Actor can pick up or use in a scene. Responsible for obtaining, altering or building items that will be needed during the course of filming.

Set Props: Responsible for making sure that props are on the set and in the correct position for filming. They are also responsible for continuity on set.

Propmaker: Skilled individuals or companies hired by the Prop Master to construct or alter the props needed for filming.

Food Stylist: Prepares and maintains food items used as props on the set. Includes edible as well as inedible food items.

Armorer: A federally licensed weapons handler who is responsible for the use and safety of all firearms on the set.

TERMS YOU SHOULD KNOW

aging
a.k.a. weathering. Process of making an object look old and used.

blank round
a load of ammunition that creates a muzzle flash but fires no bullet

breakaway
An item that can be safely broken with limited force. (i.e. sugar glass for real glass).

"Clear & safe"
Called out after a scene is finished to alert the crew that a working gun has no more rounds and is safe.

cleared item
A trademarked product that a manufacturing company has given a movie production the right to use in their film.

director's chair
Wood and canvas chairs designated for specific cast and crew members. Names usually appear embroidered on the backs along with the movie title.

double
A safety back-up for a hero prop in case it is damaged or otherwise unfit for use.

dressed
The prop is located in the correct position for filming.

dummy round
A load that has the appearance of a real working bullet but is incapable of being fired because it doesn't contain gun powder.

gak

Random items strewn around a set in order to dress it more realistically.

greek

To modify and/or obscure an existing label so not to be recognizable. Derived from the fact that text is changed to look like greek lettering.

"Gun is hot"

Called out when an Actor has a gun in his hand with a live blank round. For safety reasons, cameras should roll at this point.

gun loads

There are three types of gun loads: Full Load-Very loud. Used for semi and full automatic guns. 1/2 Load and 1/4 Load-Quieter and safer. Used for revolvers and shotguns.

hero

Best quality version of a prop.

"Misfire"

Called out when a working gun containing blank loads is triggered but nothing happens. Can be potentially very dangerous because technically the gun is still hot.

N/A beer

Non-alcoholic beer used for food and bar scenes so Actors don't become drunk after multiple takes.

ND

(Non-descript) Generic or non-specific items unrecognizable as a real trademarked or copyrighted product.

non-gun

Working gun specifically designed to fire electronic blanks. Considerably safer than firing blank loads.

personals

Refers to items worn on the Actor's body such as rings, watches, jewelry, eyeglasses, etc.

product placement

Using a brand name item as a prop. The manufacturer pays a fee to the production to display their product in the film. This provides extra money to the production and allows the manufacturer to better market their product.

prop box

A large-wheeled container that typically has many drawers and is used to house the smaller props used for the days filming.

property sheet

List of all the props to be utilized during the production. Usually separated by each scheduled shoot day.

prop plot

Layout that shows where all the props are placed in a specific scene.

replica gun

Gun incapable of firing. Sometimes made of urethane foam or lightweight metal.

rigged

When a prop is modified to work a certain way that may be easier for the Actor or more camera friendly. (i.e. "rigged" handcuffs are incapable of locking).

rubber/foam/stunt prop

Doubled version of a prop that is typically cast in rubber or foam and painted to match. Used to protect the Actor or set from harm.

Streaks & Tips

Water-based spray paint designed for hair that is utilized to age or color a prop. Comes in a multitude of colors and is easily removable.

THE RULES OF SETIQUETTE

• Never handle props on a set without permission. Items are costly to repair or replace if they get damaged or lost.

• Props are either owned by Production or rented for the duration of the shoot. They are not sold or given away at the end of production so don't ask.

• Never sit in or move a director's chair that is not designated for you. They are meant for the Actors or for key personnel who have a right to expect that their chair is waiting for them when they want to sit. Movie sets are stressful enough and having a place to sit and cool down is important.

• Food on a standing set is not for eating - it has been placed there to appear in the scene. Food for the crew is found at Craft Service or provided by the Caterers.

• Never, ever handle a working gun on a set unless instructed by an authorized member of the Prop Department. Too many accidents and deaths over the years have been caused by careless use of supposed harmless firearms. Blank rounds can kill!

• Breakaway glass can still be dangerous. Don't play around with used or discarded pieces. The shards are not sharp but they are capable of impaling.

ADVICE FROM THE EXPERTS

Scott Maginnis
Property Master
(THE GIRL WITH THE DRAGOON TATTOO, INCEPTION, 12 MONKEYS)

Having Had

It is extremely important to show up on time. On most film sets, the crew will be standing on the set ready to work at call time, so if any member of the crew is late, that means that the rest of the crew has to pick up the slack and do extra work. This does not sit well with most people, especially at the beginning of the day. When you look at a call sheet sometimes you'll see *"having had"* and what that means is, let's say your call time is *"7am having had"* that means: having had your breakfast, totally prepared and standing on set ready at 7 am. I suggest that people get there early so if you want to eat at catering before call it won't make you late for work.

Touchy-Feely

Be nice to people. When working on a film for 12 hours a day, you will be spending more time with the people you work with than you do with your family, so it's very important to get along with them. At the end of the day, your colleagues are going to remember your work but they're also going to remember you as an individual. When they're crewing up for the next job, if you're somebody they get along with, you're going to be forefront in their mind to get that first call on that next job. Trust me, 90% of jobs are gotten through word of mouth, so the more people who had a good experience with you, the better chance you have of getting the call for the next job.

Cross-Dressing

Within the confines of the movie, the character would essentially pick out the clothes they're going to wear, the bag they're going to carry, the glasses and watch they put on. All those things cross over with props and costume design. For instance, on most movies I'll do the watches and rings, but sometimes if there's a specialty ring, the Costume Designer might do that. A necklace is also a grey area.

Sometimes the Costume Designer will want to make that, but there are other times too when I will make that. And extreme example was on THE GIRL WITH THE DRAGON TATTOO. Daniel Craig is suspended in this harness rig that Mechanical Effects made but I provided all the harnesses, the chains, the bag that went over his head, the restraints and the tethers. However, Wardrobe was involved in the look because it was something that was going on the Actor's body, so they got involved creatively with the look of it. We also had to work heavily with the Stunt Departments because they were the ones actually rigging the Actor up in the air. So ultimately no matter what we all did, it had to be safe as well as comfortable knowing that David Fincher wanted to do 2 full days of takes.

Give Me Some Props!

You can pretty much trace every job I've ever had back to my first job. A friend of mine was working on a TV show for Castle Rock that Rob Reiner was producing. What started off as a call to do a three-day job as an On-Set Dresser, quickly extended to a three-week gig, which lead to a five-month job. That same company then hired me for their next show. It all went from there. Now the On-Set Dresser works a lot with props and because I was working hand in hand with the Prop Master, I ended up doing a little bit of work with him. I realized that I had a knack for props so I then started doing lower budget movies as a Prop Master myself. And then little by little, I started getting a little bit of everything: Set Decorating, Art Directing and even Production Design work. I always showed up on time, did my best and was nice to people and for better or for worse it turned into a career.

Ex-ception

I'd say probably, one of the most difficult films I did was INCEPTION. There was never a dull moment. When Christopher Nolan notices you have a SECOND of free or idle time, he figures out something for you to do and pushes you a little bit further. Not in a bad way, but just to get as much out of you as he can. It just made for an absolutely exhausting 10 months. You have to go in thinking *"I'm going to do the best I can, that's all I can ever give."* And if you make a mistake, don't dwell on it, just move beyond it, because everybody's going to make mistakes. There were a couple of times where I had to go up to Chris and say *"Okay I screwed this up. Here's what I messed up and here's my solution."* And he was always really grateful that I just walked up to him and told him that. Because then he knows everybody makes mistakes, nobody's perfect, and we're all out there killing ourselves trying to make a good movie. And I think a lot of times you look back and you think, boy was that sheer determination that got me through this. And sometimes it is!

"Working on films, you really live the experience. I lived BIRDMAN OF ALCATRAZ and really felt part of the story."

Richard H. Kline, Cinematographer

David L. Glazer
Property Master
("Melissa & Joey", "Boy Meets World", Made, When Harry Met Sally...)

"Familiar" Problems

I have a problem with people that have too much familiarity. New crewmembers to the set, no matter how experienced they are, shouldn't just walk right in and decide they can talk to the Director or they can talk to the 1st A.D. about something that I should be handling.

If my Assistant gets overly familiar or gets too physically close to video village, I'll come up and say *"Hey, listen...don't stand so close to video village."* Or if it's egregious, I'll just say *"Look, please don't talk to the Director or the A.D. on this set because I prefer to maintain the chain of command."* I try to be polite with my new Assistants and most of them get it the first time. I say something because they are usually operating out of a desire to be doing a good job.

But there are people that walk on to a set and just immediately assume *"Okay, I'm here doing props for the day, what I say goes."* Then they'll start bossing around the Extras or start bossing around the DGA Trainee and I don't like to see that stuff. I won't stand for somebody coming in to work with me who in starts trying to take over the department.

Arts & Crafts For Grown Ups

I don't think anybody grows up as a child and says *"I'm gonna be a Prop Master"* unless maybe their dad is a Prop Master. I started out as a P.A. and whenever I got sent out to do errands, I always seemed to be the guy that could find anything needed. Word got around about me and pretty soon the Prop Department was asking me to help them out and eventually they asked me to work as the their official P.A. and then as an On-Set Prop Assistant.

What I discovered was that working in props was fun. It's arts and crafts for grown ups. I already decided early in my career that I wasn't going to be a big-time Director and I didn't have the chops to be an Actor and props was an interesting road to follow. So I followed it. And as in all things when you're working and you've got bills to pay, you get a job and all of a sudden you look up one day and 10 years have gone by. That's what happened to me.

Props To The Actors

I've learned some interesting things over the years working with Actors. First off is that when Actors get on the set you've got to give them time to walk on set and get settled. I've worked with a lot of moody people over the years and the last thing you want to do is jump on them immediately to hand them their watch or their wedding ring or to say *"Okay, in this scene you're gonna yada, yada, yada."* I've learned to observe them from afar for like 5 minutes to gauge their mood before I walk up. I found this has helped me to maintain a good working relationship with the Actors over the years. The other important thing that I tell my Assistants is to never take your eyes off the set. Other departments can sit there and read or do the crossword puzzle but I don't allow my Assistants to do that on the set. I know EVERYBODY is texting or on Facebook but I tell my

Assistants to keep that to an extreme minimum because it's not the Actor's responsibility to keep track of their props and they are constantly setting their props down absent-mindedly at Craft Service or in other random places. And when Production is ready to roll and they don't have "the prop," they're not going to yell at the Actor, they're going to yell at you.

ADD - Assistant Director Disorder

The A.D. department can be your best friend or your worst enemy. The best A.D.s will understand what you do and keep you informed about the changes in the schedule. They also know that if you accidently forget something or you've got to run for something, to vamp for you for a minute instead of doing that horrible thing most A.D.'s do which is to say *"Waiting on props."* Which is hands down the worst thing a prop person can hear on set.

The important thing is that they know that you're not an enemy. But unfortunately there are some A.D.'s that immediately think everybody on the crew is their enemy and that's a problem. Some even deny you the chance to set your props. They'll say *"We're lighting now! Don't step on the set!"* They'll keep yelling at you to get off the set saying *"You'll get your time! You'll get your time!"* but by the time you get *"your time"* all of a sudden, they bring the Actors on set and they're ready to roll even though you never got the opportunity to walk in and set your props properly.

Yes, We Have No Bananas…We Have No Bananas today!

In 2000, I did a show called "STATE OF GRACE" for The Family Channel. It was a period piece set in North Carolina in 1965 about two little girls who were best friends - one was Jewish, one was Catholic. When I interviewed, the UPM gave me the usual spiel that it was a SUPER low-budget production and they had no money. Of course this didn't keep the Writers from writing elaborate scripts and the Directors wanting the moon.

One day I had to run out because they wanted bananas for a scene. The UPM came storming into my little wooden-box-of-an-office and started yelling at me for buying the bananas because they weren't in my budget! Mind you, bananas were like $0.30 a POUND!!!

And that was just the beginning. Almost every day they hounded me about one purchase or another. I don't LIKE to be a dick, especially because it's hard to get hired again but, I was so ready to quit, I didn't care. So I did my own "tough love" on them.

I had a form made up so every time there was a request or an addition that wasn't in the initial budget, they had to check off an APPROVE or DISAPPROVE box. For example I'd scribble on my form *"the Actor wants to eat apples in this scene and it's not in the script."* I'd then march up to the UPM's office and interrupt him and say *"I need this signed right away."* I quickly became such a pest, but I said, *"Hey, I'm not gonna get yelled at by you anymore."*

One particular instance, I had to make a period 1965 girls' school bag. So, I got the UPM to approve because it was a lot of money and had to be manufactured at History for Hire. When the bill finally came for approvals, the Line Producer lost his mind. He was yelling at me, *"How dare you spend this amount of money, this, that and the other."* I simply reached over into my file, held up the form and said *"Here, your UPM approved this."* I didn't make any friends on that show but I survived to the end and that's all that really mattered.

"One of the cardinal mistakes a lot of departments make is they build what THEY need to build without understanding how it integrates with all of these other departments."

Greg Nicotero, Make-Up FX Artist

Bruce Mink
Property Master
(Austin Powers, Bill & Ted's Excellent Adventure, The Mask)

Fits Like A Glove

I went to film school at Ithaca College and wanted to work in the movies but wasn't quite sure doing what. I fell into propping because I'm generally more art and design oriented and in one's life, *"the glove's got to fit."* If it doesn't fit then you probably aren't going to do it for long and you're really not going to be that productive at it. Fortunately it fit for me.

I lived in San Francisco for three years and while I was there I built up a portfolio by working first on non-paying gigs and then moving on to industrial, marketing, and educational jobs. The advantage to these smaller productions is that you can hone your skills and take photos of what you've done, because in order to convince someone to hire you, you need to show them something. You can't just say *"Hi, I can do this. Hire me please."* That typically doesn't fly very well. I interviewed a lot until I finally met a Prop Master who took me under his wing. I worked with him for several years and he was the one who brought me to Los Angeles.

Search And Destroy

A major part of my job is to break down the script to determine what I'm going to have to provide for the show. I call it "search and destroy." I need to figure out what I need to rent, build or buy. Propping is ultimately about sourcing, which is knowing where you can find this, or have that made, or who can build this or who can point me in another direction where I can rent it. Without having sources you are scrambling and not getting the best quality prop that you could get. The other part of the job is running the props which is making sure the props are where they need to be on the set when they need to be there. Continuity is vital, especially with props, so we constantly photograph the set to make sure that we know where everything goes from scene to scene.

Show & Tell

One lesson that I learned is that you need to show your Props to the Director as early as possible. Especially before they're to be used on the set. It's one thing for me to interpret the props, but it's another to compile them for the director's interpretation. Because things change and schedule's shift, you may need to change your props, and you can't be just *"I Dream Of Jeannie"* and blink your eyes and have them change in front of you.

Comedy Is Hard

I generally like working on comedies, but ironically they are typically hard shoots. THE MASK was very challenging but at the end of the day, very rewarding because even though the Director (Chuck Russell) was very demanding, he, after a long, rough, day actually thanked me for doing a good job. That went a long way because there was an appreciation. He earned my respect and made me want to work that much harder for him. AUSTIN POWERS was also extremely challenging. This time it was a demanding comic Actor (Mike Myers) with a demanding comic movie, but again I felt appreciated for my hard work and it wound up being fun despite the hard shoot.

"Shooting is easy. Prepping the show correctly is the hard part."

Scott Bauer, Prop Master

Maureen Farley
Property Master
(Moneyball, The Mist, The Notebook, The Green Mile)

All-Around Girl

I got my Bachelor's Degree in Film & Television from Montana State University. When I first came out to Los Angeles I thought I would work in the Camera Department but I wasn't able to crack into that and soon fell into assisting a Prop Master. On one of the shows I was working on they didn't have a Set Dresser so I was asked to do that job. Within two years I found myself jumping back and forth among various positions in the Art Department and ultimately becoming a key within that short time. I found that this was an easy fit because as long as I had a good work ethic and good common sense, I did a good job no matter what they threw at me. It certainly also helped having a film education because I understood the role of all the other departments on the set.

Kids, Don't Try This At Home

BLOW had some interesting challenges especially in regards to researching the different types of drugs and determining what we would use to simulate them. I would talk with people and read High Times magazines to understand what I would need. Then there was a lot of shopping. I'd go to Chinatown to find herbs that could be substituted for Pot. I found a great plant that only required a light dusting with spray paint to double for the cannabis plants. When an Actor has to snort cocaine we generally use lactose powder, which is powdered milk. I used a saline solution to rinse out their nose if they had to do a lot of this so they didn't become too irritated. I could also use the crystal form of Vitamin B. It's safe to use, but it can tend to burn the Actor's nose.

The Executioner's Song

I love doing period movies. At one point I had done six in a row. Doing the research and providing to the production more than what is scripted is very important to me. You are constantly learning new things and that's an amazing aspect of my job. I like to know what I'm doing on a set, not just what the script dictates. While working on THE GREEN MILE I got in touch with this gentleman at the Louisiana University who specialized in the death penalty. He was extremely helpful in making sure that everything I was building or buying was a technically correct as possible. The Director will decide how he wants to ultimately present it, but it's my job at the very least to present him with what is correct and historically accurate.

This Section Sponsored By...

There are a lot of companies that represent products for product placement in film. You basically submit the script to them with a list of products that you think might work for the movie. Some of the products want exclusive deals, but if you're doing a bar scene, you don't want everyone drinking the same type of beer; it's just not realistic. I prefer to have real-world products in the movie I prop. So if the companies like the script or feel it's a worthwhile venture they will provide the product for the shoot.

Clear This!

Clearance of products has become a real issue on sets. It's gotten so out of control that you have be careful that you're catching everything down to the refrigerator magnets. If a product is being used in the manner it was intended and it's sold in the store, my opinion is that you should be able to use it without having to clear it. I can understand if it was being used in an inappropriate manner or in a way that might harm its image, but when I have to spend important time making sure that every book, periodical, or poster that may or may not be seen is cleared, it can get rather over the top. We wind up using a lot of generic stuff that ultimately doesn't serve the character or the movie as a whole.

Take A Seat And Listen

As much as dealing with the Director's chairs is truly a pain, we put up with it because it gives us the leverage to maintain an extra individual in our Department for the duration of the shoot. Whenever I get into an argument with Production about having an extra member of my team, I just tell them if they get rid of him then who's going to move the chairs. That usually puts a stop to it. It winds up being our ace in the hole.

"Trust me, my job isn't just gluing sesame seeds onto hamburger buns."

Jean Hodges, Food Stylist

Mark Richardson
Property Master
(HALLOWEEN(2007), THE PRESTIGE, THE DEVIL'S REJECTS, "POWER RANGERS")

"Hey Rocky, Watch Me Pull A Rabbit Out Of My Ass"

Doing props is like doing a magic trick. Whatever props you have on set make sure you have doubles and if you're bringing it to the Director for the first time have different choices (yes, even if it was discussed in the meeting.). You must constantly try to read between the lines because when you're in the desert and the 1st A.D., Script Supervisor, or the P.A. says to the Director *"Hey, wouldn't it be funny if she was playing with a slinky"* you better have it in your kit. But if you don't, here are some comebacks that won't work but will help you sleep a little better at night.

• *"It wasn't in the script."*
• *"It wasn't on the call sheet."*
• *"It's not in the budget."*
• *"We'll definitely need a Slinky Wrangler."*
• *"That's weird. I just had one in the prop truck because we did the same gag on the last show I worked on but the last time I saw it, it was going down the stairs without a care."*

Time Paradox

If they had a time machine, every Prop person I know would not go back in time to kill Hitler or invest in Starbuck. They would take out that Bastard who said *"I'll take care of your chairs on set."* There's nothing worse than showing a nervous Actress how to hold a Glock when a day player comes crying to you because his chair has no saddle bag and the star's chair does. Chairs are the crosses Props must bear (Okay, most of the time we make the P.A.s do it).

On Being Prepared

Anything the Actor touches, holds or eats is a prop. If you're in with the Art Director, The Art Department will help with the set dressing and hook you up with plates, glasses medical tools, etc. Props should have the hero items while The Art Department will have the rest (you hope). You should always have a huge toolkit packed with spray paints, fullers earth, dirt, blood, and Hudson sprayers, just to name a few. Props should be able to help out Production with flashlights, umbrellas, dust mask and even small fans and heaters. In other words, if you got it, stick it in the truck. It's better to be safe than sorry.

Practical Advice

Props is the red-headed stepchild of the Art Department. NEVER badmouth the art design of the show. I repeat NEVER. Also keep in mind, P.A.'s are going to be helping you so always treat them with respect and be cool to all the other departments as well, especially the A.D. staff. If you don't work well with the 1st A.D. you won't work with that production ever again. He has the ear of the show. So under no circumstances be a "dick" on set. If you feel the need to bitch about something, go to Craft Service, eat a donut and try to make light of it. THEN LET IT GO!

"My first time on set was really exciting. I particularly liked the free food."

Maureen Farley, Prop Master

Jean Hodges
Food Stylist
(Argo, Moneyball, Dreamgirls, The Last Samurai, Pulp Fiction)

The Next Food Network Star

I was born and raised in Los Angeles and both my parents worked in the industry. When I graduated high school I decided to go to a culinary school in New York. One of the classes that was offered during the summer program was a food styling course. I thought it sounded interesting, like maybe I would eventually do stuff for Gourmet Magazine. After I finished school, I moved back to Los Angeles and discovered that a lot of my friends were working in the industry.

They asked me to make food for the movies or TV shows they were working on. I wound up working on a lot of Roger Corman movies as well as other low-budget films and that's how I got started. As time went on my friends started moving up the ladder and started working on the big budget shows and they took me a long with them.

Chew On This

On features and TV, a Food Stylist is responsible for any and all food seen in a shot. This is not typically the featured element. In other words, unlike a commercial where the food item is the main attraction, this food is just part of the set design to enhance the realism for the Actors and the overall look of the scene. When you are doing commercials or print ads about the food, the responsibilities are completely different, because it becomes all about creating the perfect specific product as opposed to creating the perfect atmosphere.

Bottom Of The Barrel

The best way to break into my field is to get a job as an Assistant to a Food Stylist because we are always looking for help. People think my job is glamorous, but it's the farthest thing from that. It's actually quite difficult. It's more expensive and stressful than catering, which is considered the bottom of the totem pole of the food service industry. You have to prepare all the food in your own kitchen, load it into coolers, pack up and load all your equipment (microwave, refrigerator, stove, tables, etc…) and drag it all to the stage and set it all up.

The shoot usually requires multiples of the items and you are there sometimes before call and leave way after wrap. Then you have to pack it all up and get home to clean all your own dishes. My job is also very transitory; even if I'm on a film it typically won't be for the entire shoot. It may only be a couple of days here and there. I have to constantly be doing other shows in order to stay busy. I might even do multiple jobs in the same day. I could be doing two TV series and a feature at the same time. This requires me to have a staff of people that I can send to various sets to represent me.

Eat Your Veggies

There are a lot of different techniques for maintaining the look and quality of the food depending on the requirements of the shot. When you're dealing with background foods the plates become about color, height and style because that's the only way you're going to see them. One of the common things we do is to barely cook the food. The longer you cook something the more of the color and vibrancy is lost. For instance if you just quickly blanch broccoli the colors will brighten up and it can sit for an entire day. If I cooked it to the point where you could eat it, it wouldn't last an hour under the hot movie lights. We don't utilize a lot of fake foods, though we will use other foods to substitute the real thing. For instance we sometimes use mashed potatoes for ice cream.

Pass The *"Facon,"* Please

Not only do we have to deal with the requirements of the scene, but also sometimes have to deal with the specific requirements of the Actors. A lot of Actors have specific diets or allergies, so sometimes food has to be altered to work around these. I've had Actors who were strict vegetarians that had to eat steak in a scene. We have to make the steak out of tofu but still make it as realistic as humanly possible.

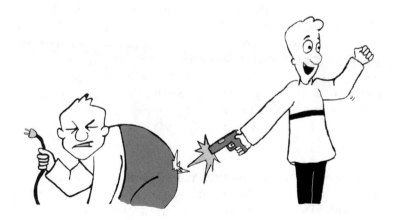

TALES FROM THE SET

When I first got started in the Prop Department I learned a lesson about the director's chairs the hard way. I was working on a movie and had to set up a fairly extensive video village. Because there were more chairs then usual, I was working at a rushed pace. I evidently didn't set the hinges properly on one of the chairs. Of course, who comes to sit down in that seat but the Producer. He fell through the seat bottom and landed in the hinges. Fortunately, he was pretty cool about it and chalked it up to my inexperience because I was so new. But he could have been humiliated or hurt so I now always check the seat bottoms to make sure that the chair is set up properly.

Scott Bauer, Prop Master

The devil is in the details and this is a lesson that I learned the hard way. We had a "product" in the movie we were making that during the course of the story gets lost (which is an integral plot point). After we wrapped the entire film, we were going through the contracts and to our horror, discovered that there's a clause in this company's contract for their product saying, *"In your movies, you cannot damage, slander or lose our products."* Of course, we'd already shot the movie and we certainly didn't have money to reshoot it…But this is a VERY powerful company. It turned out that the Producer responsible for all the things that I would normally be on top of if I hadn't also been acting in the film had not properly read the contract. As the Producer of the film, there's no excuses and ultimately it's my responsibility and problem to solve. My "brilliant" solution was: Screw it. Keep it in the movie. What are they going to do? Sue the movie? I'll of course let you know how it all turns out after the movie's released. D'oh.

Noel Clarke, Actor/Writer/Producer/Director

I once worked with an old-time Prop man named Jackie Ackerman who was in his '70s at the time. He was a beloved old Prop Master who claimed to be the guy who *"wagged the cowardly lion's tail."* I don't know WHY or HOW, but he was assigned to work with me on SCROOGED. We were working on the scene where Bill Murray sees a waiter catch on fire and we're setting the table. As Jackie walks away somehow the tablecloth got caught in his belt but he kept on going. He pulled the entire tablecloth with ALL the food and ALL the plates on to the floor - There was this real stunned silence. Fortunately we had a great first A.D. named Chris Soldo and he just said *"Ladies and Gentlemen....Jackie Ackerman."* And then everybody applauded and there was friendly laughter. We cleaned up and reset the table. Chris Soldo is an example of a guy that was so classy. He could have been such a jerk. But instead of embarrassing the man or making a big deal, he made a joke out of it and earned a lot of respect doing it.

David Glazer, Propmaster

On SCARY MOVIE 2, we had a dinner scene where Chris Elliot was to wheel in a turkey and before he cuts into it, he does some fairly disgusting things to it. In order to make turkeys look good and plump for camera we barely cook them. You typically just stick them in a really hot oven until the skin gets really crispy looking. You then paint it. Most of the turkeys you see in ads are raw because a fully cooked turkey doesn't look that great. So everything is going fine on set, we've done multiple takes and we're getting through the scene. All of a sudden, Chris sticks his fake "gimpy" hand into the turkey's cavity and lifts it off the tray. You can immediately see that the bottom of the turkey is as white as a ghost. He then proceeds to lick the turkey. I had a principle Actor licking a raw turkey and I just got so worried. As a Food Stylist, I'm responsible for the safety and health of the Actors that I provide food for. If this had ever been discussed that he might lick the turkey than I would have fully cooked it. Sometimes things just happen on set that you have no control over. Fortunately, he didn't get sick and it was funny and ultimately got used in the finished film.

Jean Hodges, Food Stylist

I was working on a film in the jungles of Hawaii and I was supposed to bring these certain water jugs that were established earlier in the filming when we were shooting in Los Angeles. The jugs were French made and had been purchased in Tahiti so they were very unique to say the least. The Director decided to do a pick up shot that wasn't on the schedule that might show the jugs. Unfortunately my trailer was still on its way to Hawaii by boat so there was no way to get them. Having found something reasonably close, I went to the Actor and told him what was up. He told me not to worry about it and convinced me that the shot was above the props and wouldn't be seen.

Sure enough, we get on set and the Director wants to know where the jugs are. The Actor told the Director that you wouldn't see them in the shot. This infuriated the Director and asked the Actor how he knows what will or won't be seen. He's the Director, he knows what will be in frame. The Director than offered the Actor to look through the lens to prove his point. The two of them switched places as the Actor looked into the lens while the Director got on his mark. Unbeknownst to the Director, the Actor while looking through the lens, reframed the shot so it was tighter. He then turned to the Director and told him that the jugs were out of frame like he thought they would be. The Director stormed back to the camera and looked through the lens, immediately realizing that the shot had been changed. He turned to the Actor and said *"You reframed the shot."* The Actor calmly replied *"And that's the shot we're going to do."*

The Director was so embarrassed that at lunchtime he called me into his trailer. He told me to sit down at his table with him that has a big plate of food on it. He proceeded to chew me a new one while slamming his hand down on the table. But as he did it, the food flew in the air and splattered his clothes. Needless to say, this only added insult to injury.

Anonymous Prop Master

I was working on a show where a window blind needed to be fixed right before a bar room brawl. Someone immediately popped up and said they'd fix it. He ran towards the window and before anybody could say anything, he stepped up on the nearest chair to reach it. It was a breakaway chair, and his foot went right through it. There went $350.00 in a flash. The lesson here is, if you have to fix something, get a ladder and stay off the set furniture.

Maureen Farley, Prop Master

CHAPTER ELEVEN

"Does it look like a toy?"

THE
SPFX & STUNTS
DEPARTMENT

A BRIEF OVERVIEW

How cool are Special Effects! You know you love them. Ever since the dawn of filmmaking there have been effects and it's for a fairly simple reason: People love spectacle, and that's what this department is all about.

Special Effects are broken down into different groups. Some are hired as members of the crew while others are subcontracted shops that manufacture the effects and operate them on set. However, there is usually a Supervisor or Producer who oversees all the effects and make sure that all the different departments coordinate their efforts while on set.

Mechanical/Physical Effects, Pyrotechnics and Stunts are typically part of the crew. Because they are used so frequently it makes sense to have them as an integral part of the process. It is very common to have to rig items or sets even for dramas and comedies and even these films require stunts and fire gags as well.

Now Make-Up and Creature Effects are a whole different animal. Most FX companies are privately owned and handle both aspects. They bid for the jobs and are hired by Production to build, provide, and maintain specific items. These can range from a specialty superhero costume (i.e. IRON MAN) to an animatronic dinosaur (i.e. JURASSIC PARK).

Even though most Visual Effects take shape in post-production it is still necessary for the Visual FX Technicians to be on set to make sure they get the raw material they need to ply their trade. Because real Actors interact with computer generated characters, the live action parts have to be believable or the illusion doesn't work.

More frequently than not, a sequence will involve a gag that could be done by more than one department. A good Supervisor will know each department's strengths and weaknesses and determine what method is not only the most cost effective, but will give the most bang for the buck.

THE PLAYERS

SPFX Coordinator: a.k.a. SPFX Supervisor a.k.a. Visual FX Producer. Responsible for all the special effects in a film and works as a liaison between the effects shops and production

Mechanical / Physical Effects: Deal with on-set rigs that have moving elements and natural phenomena like rain, snow and storms.

Make-Up Effects: Utilizes prosthetic appliances to alter or transform an Actor's appearance.

Creature Effects: Creates monsters, aliens, animals etc, which utilize animatronics or Puppeteers to bring the character to life.

Visual Effects: Help create sequences on-set and in post-production that aren't budgetary feasible or physically impossible by using blue/green screens, miniatures, rear projection, motion control and/or CGI.

Stunt Coordinator: Heads the Stunt Department and choreographs and controls all the stunts in the film. Also in charge of hiring the Stuntmen and making sure that safety guidelines are being followed on set.

Stuntman: Highly trained SAG-AFTRA performer used to double an Actor for scenes that are physically dangerous or require a certain skill to achieve.

Pyrotechnician: Licensed Technician that controls all fire elements on a set that range from squib hits to enormous explosions.

TERMS YOU SHOULD KNOW

Animatronics
Refers to the use of rods, cables or radio controlled servo motors to bring an object or an inanimate character to life.

blue/green screen
A process that allows an Actor or set to be shot against a blue or green background that can be removed and replaced with a different element in post-production.

CGI
(Computer Generated Imagery) Refers to the use of a computer to create characters, items and/or sets that may be too expensive or impossible to create in the physical world.

clunker box
Device used to initiate a sequence of explosions or pyrotechnics.

composite shot
An image derived from more than one element combined into one shot. i.e. Models, matte paintings, CGI, blue screen, etc.

cracker smoke
A type of smoke that can be used safely on set that is derived from heating mineral or baby oil.

flame bars
Metal tube with holes that gas can be pumped through and ignited to create a controllable fire. Sometimes placed in the foreground to create the illusion of a character being surrounded by fire.

foggers
Propane or electric device that burns glycol or oil based smoke to create a large amount of smoke at once.

jerk harness
Cable controlled rig that attaches to a Stuntman's back that forcibly yanks them backwards during a stunt sequence.

lifter
Hand-made black powder "bomb" designed in one ounce increments. Range from 1oz. to 8oz. in size.

matte painting
An incredibly detailed painting done on glass that is used in combination with live action and/or CGI elements to create an object or environment to cost prohibitive.

motion control
Computer controlled system that allows the camera to move in precisely the same manner every time allowing for greater ease in compositing in post-production.

plate shot
Clean take of a set or element used for compositing in post-production.

prosthetics
Foam or silicone pieces molded from an Actor's face that are glued onto their skin in order to distort the features or to create an entirely new look like a creature or animal.

rain tower
10 to 20 ft. long aluminum pipes on stands with sprinkler heads used to produce large amounts of artificial rain.

rear projection
Process in which a live or still image is projected onto the rear of a translucent screen while live elements are shot in front.

servo motor
Motor that can be manipulated by radio control. Ideal for animatronic creatures because of their size and strength as well as the fact that a Puppeteer can operate off screen.

squib
Small explosive attached to a metal plate that can attach to an Actor's body to simulate a bullet hit. Sometimes used with a blood-filled condom to heighten the effect.

THE RULES OF SETIQUETTE

• Don't touch the prosthetics on an Actor's face. Not only is it rude but the oils on your fingers could lift the edges of the appliance that a Make-Up Artist took hours to blend down and conceal.

• Animatronic puppets are not toys. As cool as they are, you should never touch one unless authorized. If something should break it may take hours if not days to repair.

• Don't tell a Creature Effects Artist that they must be *"great during Halloween."* They hear this all the time and it gets old.

• Just because someone is dressed like a monster doesn't mean they should be treated like one. So don't poke and prod someone in a creature suit, they're uncomfortable as it is.

• F/X items are either owned by Production or by the individual F/X companies. These extremely costly properties are not just thrown out or given away to random crew members so don't ask.

• Don't ever touch a locked off camera for a plate shot. It is crucial that they replicate the sequence exactly. Even the slightest movement could destroy the take.

• It is important to keep a blue/green screen clean. Any dirt or debris will be detected by the camera and time and money will have to be spent to digitally remove the imperfections.

• It is vitally important to act as professionally as possible during stunt sequences. Trained Stuntmen are risking their lives to achieve a shot and it is deadly serious business. Never mess with their gear and don't needlessly distract a Stuntman before a shot.

• Avoid stepping on or touching any wire associated with a pyrotechnic effect. Needless to say, an explosion that happens before it is designed to, could cause loss of time and money as well as injury or loss of life.

ADVICE FROM THE EXPERTS

Patrick Tantalo
Special Effects Supervisor
(STEP UP 2, ACE VENTURA: PET DETECTIVE, "CSI: MIAMI")

Let's Get Physical
You need to have the drive to want to do this. It's not a 9 to 5 job, it's a constant. You're always working hard and you have to come in like a dry sponge to soak up all this knowledge. Everybody you work with will teach you something. Even the bad people you work with have something to teach you. If you keep your mind open you can learn from everybody. It's important to listen and watch what people do. If you have a good attitude you'll notice that most people will help and encourage you to learn. If you come in with an attitude that you know it all or just limit yourself, people will put up a wall in front of you and you'll find it a lot harder to get into this business.

The Adventure Of A Lifetime
Every job is a new adventure. You are dealing with creative egos and you must be open to new expressions and ideas. Some problems have arisen from encounters with newcomers or personalities that overstep their boundaries. When Producers or other Department Heads try to IN DETAIL tell you how to do your job. People must have respect for each other's positions on a movie set. They should worry about their own jobs and leave the skilled department members to carry on with their work.

One Hell Of A Producer
I was prepping some effects gags for a show and I went to Costume to get the clothing required for it. Out of nowhere, the Producer ran over to me and grabbed the wardrobe from my hand. I told him I was prepping the gag for the next day's work and he informed me *"He was going to do the gag because he felt He was more qualified."* I calmly told him that was *"fine"* then walked onto the set and informed the 1st A.D. that since the Producer was more qualified to do the Special FX, he should finish the show. I quit and left. As it

turned out several other Department Heads were told the same thing by this pompous ass and walked off the show as well.

Old Man River

For Hallmark Pictures "THE OLD MAN" we had to recreate the 1927 flood of the Mississippi River. Instead of working in an existing bayou or river we built our own lake. We found a location and built a 2-acre lake, using bulldozers to dig out the area. We installed rigs to make it look exactly like the real Mississippi River including rapids and dump tanks to show the levee break. We also plumed rain in the tress. We completed this all in one week with only 16 people. In the end, it wound up being more cost effective because the company could be based at the actual location where we were shooting other scenes as well and we could also avoid the dangerous possibilities of real locations such as alligators and diseases.

On Safety

When it comes to any big stunts or explosions, the Effects Coordinator takes control of the set in order to maintain the highest level of safety. There are cases where people do get hurt, but it's usually caused by inexperienced crew members or inexperienced Producers breathing down your neck and trying to rush you. That happens more than you think. On big effects you're typically prepping most of the day and usually by the time they get to shooting it, it's the end of the day and everybody's in a big rush to get it over with. They don't want to take the time to let you do your work and make sure it's absolutely safe. This is when accidents can happen. If I can't do something safely, I just won't do it, no matter what the personal consequence.

"These days there are no limits to what stunts you can ask somebody to do. Everything can be photographed in some way, especially with the advent of computers."

Roy Clark, Stunt Coordinator

Greg Nicotero
Emmy Award™ Winning Make-Up F/X Artist
("THE WALKING DEAD", INGLORIOUS BASTERDS, TRANSFORMERS)

Out Of This World Inspiration

There was a wealth of inspiration in the late '60s and early '70s that fueled my imagination. Back then, science fiction was compelling and visually stimulating. I talk very often about Castle Films. They came out in the mid '70s and they were these 8-minute digest versions of all the great Universal monster movies, as well as the GODZILLA and Harryhausen films. So at a young age, I literally spent 8 minutes at a time watching the highlights of CREATURE FROM THE BLACK LAGOON, JASON AND THE ARGONAUTS or THE SEVENTH VOYAGE OF SINBAD. And by doing that it allowed me to cut my teeth on special effects.

What captivated me about all those movies was they showed me something that I had never seen before and it kept me guessing as to how they did it. You look at PLANET OF THE APES and you're like, *"Okay, that's amazing, how'd they do that?"* You look at JAWS and there was a real sense of wonder and a sense of awe about, *"Oh yeah, they must have got a real shark and put a stunt guy in a real shark's mouth!"* It was that sense of wonder that got me watching the great science fiction movies like WAR OF THE WORLDS and THE TIME MACHINE and marveling at the special effects aspect of them.

This Story Is CRAZIES!!!

Having the opportunity to grow up in Pittsburgh, and work with George Romero and Tom Savini was a complete fluke. My uncle had been an Actor in THE CRAZIES, and so when I met George, my opening line to him was, *"My uncle Sam was in THE CRAZIES!"* And that was it, we just started talking, and he was like *"Hey kid, we're doing CREEPSHOW, do you want a job working on the movie?"* And I'm like, *"Oh I can't because I'm in school and I'm studying to be a doctor."* A few years later they were about to start making DAY OF THE DEAD and George once again asked me to work on it. And I thought, okay, I turned down a job on CREEPSHOW and I'm not going to make that same mistake twice.

I had also become friends with Tom Savini, because we had traded videotapes. So it was as simple as calling Tom up and saying, *"Hey I just got hired on* DAY OF THE DEAD, *I want to be your Assistant and Coordinator."* That job didn't actually exist until I had sort of made it up. From a production standpoint, Romero and Rubenstein loved the idea because it allowed Tom to be free to come up with the gags and be creative while I managed the department, hired the crew people, bought the supplies and broke down the shooting schedule. I had no training about special effects or movies other than what I had read in magazines and what I had known from being a fan but I was able to actually create that job for me and succeed at it.

Really Gross Anatomy

My dad's a retired physician, so when I was growing up becoming a doctor made the most sense. The irony of all of it was, when we were on set for DAY OF THE DEAD, I became the default Medical Advisor. There's a scene when Lori Cardille cuts off Tim DeLeo's arm, after he's been bitten by a zombie. And I got a phone call saying *"Nicotero, we need you on set!"* and I go up to set and George is like, *"So, do we need to cauterize this wound or can we just tie it off?"* And I said, *"No. No, you need to cauterize it, otherwise you'd bleed to death whether you tie it off or not."* He's like *"Okay Good."*

Soon after Howard Berger, Robert Kurtzman and I started KNB FX, we got called to talk about doing effects for a movie called GROSS ANATOMY about medical school students that were going through gross anatomy class and dissecting cadavers. The Producer was Deborah Hill and she says, *"Oh, so I hear from George Romero that you were pre-med."* And that was critical in us getting that job because they loved the fact that I had studied anatomy. I was also an art minor and a biology major in college, so that made complete sense to them.

We did GROSS ANATOMY and then Kevin Costner saw the cadavers we did and hired us to do the buffalo in DANCES WITH WOLVES. So within two years we went from a no-name company to a company that had provided effects for DANCES WITH WOLVES, which was the biggest film of 1990.

"Frank"-ly My Dear, I Do Give A Damn.

I had done a short film and had directed second unit on THE MIST and Frank Darabont came to me one day during prep for the 2nd Season of "THE WALKING DEAD" and said *"You're going to direct an episode this season."* There wasn't even a thought in his mind, he just said, this is what you're gonna do. He then asked if I wanted a zombie-heavy episode or a zombie-light episode?"

Now I've previously directed zombie action for George Romero, and I've shot effects stuff. So what I really wanted was to be able to show people that I can work with drama, I can work with Actors and characters. The episode that I got is literally like 12 ANGRY MEN. It's a bunch of people pleading their cases about whether they're going to murder someone or not!

There was even a 12-page scene with every Actor in the show. And understanding and knowing editing and coverage and what I needed to do, who I needed to cover, where the camera goes, where the master shot is, where we set up, where we establish everything. All those things came really naturally to me. And I hadn't anticipated that.

I still got a little nervous because I'm was going to have all these Actors standing in a room going *"Okay, where do you want me to stand, what do you want me to do?"* The fact that I knew the Actors and I knew these characters immediately established a certain trust and when they had an idea or a question or something that they wanted to do, I knew the answer because I knew the characters as much as they did. It was an absolutely amazing experience to be able to work with that cast and it all happened because of Frank.

Time To Upgrade Your Modem

I had the best film school training on the planet, because I was able to stand on set next to Frank Darabont, Robert Rodriguez, Steven Spielberg, Quentin Tarantino and Martin Scorsese. As a film technician, you have to interface with all these different people. One thing I find that's tremendously helpful is to listen to not just the Director, but to listen to every department and share information from your department.

Nowadays everybody preps movies via the internet. There are movies I've done where I was never in the same room as the Director. The Director was in Louisiana or in Prague, and you have to think like a Director and certainly listen to what other departments have to say.

For example, you have a scene where a guy gets attacked by a pack of dogs. Well, we need to interface with the Stunt Coordinator to find out how much the Actor can do. You have to interface with the Animal Wranglers to find out how safe it is and how much realism you can get out of a dog so it doesn't look like they're just licking and playing with him but like they're actually attacking him. Art department has to interface to make sure there's nothing inside the fake body parts that would be detrimental to the dog. Then you got to think about the wardrobe. If the fabric is loose and the dogs grab it, they're going to rip the shirt off in the first take. As a Director you have to think about, how many takes am I going to be able to do this? So you have to first and foremost, understand filmmaking from every departments point of view.

"In regards to Special Effects and Stunts...I want to maintain my 100% safety record."

Gale Anne Hurd, Producer

Joel Harlow
Emmy Award™ Winning Make-Up F/X Artist
(INCEPTION, STAR TREK, WAR OF THE WORLDS, "THE STAND")

R-E-S-P-E-C-T

Always be respectful no matter what the other person's position is on the crew. A Production Assistant may be low on the totem pole as far as the set hierarchy but they'll be indispensable in getting your job done. They're the conduits that you communicate through. So, if you make their lives miserable, it can come around and bite you in the ass. Be friendly, because most people would rather work with someone who is friendly than someone who is talented. Given the choice most people opt for the pleasant experience.

Half The Job

Lighting a make-up is half if not more of how it's going to ultimately look on film. If you light a rubber make-up flat it's going to look fake. If you light it well it's going to look real. In my opinion the Director of Photography does half of the make-up job.

Being Objective

Sometimes you are so close to something that you can't see if it looks right. It always helps to have another Make-Up Artist's eye for an objective view of your work. That is of course if you are open to that, which every good artist should be.

Touchy Feely

Because a lot of people aren't around Special Make-Up Effects a lot, when they see something unusual, they like to look with their hands or make obnoxious comments: *"It looks like my wife"* or *"It looks like my ex-girlfriend," "you must be a lot of fun at Halloween."* It's particularly bad when we've got prosthetic bodies lying around. Crew members like to put them in poses with no regard for the fact that it's a piece of art. When you're on set you're supposed to act professional and respect other Department's property...sometimes it just doesn't seem to apply to our stuff.

On Being A Make-Up Artist

I arrive on set in the wee hours of the morning to apply a make-up on an Actor that could take anywhere from 2-5 hours. In doing this I have to put the Actor at ease. It's important that I do a good job with the make-up but it's equally important that I make sure the Actor is comfortable. In essence I become a baby sitter for that Actor for the rest of the day making sure that he has water if he needs it, making sure he's comfortable, and even watching him while he eats so he doesn't mess up the make-up beyond repair.

"We have to make the impossible, possible."
Patrick Tantalo, Special Effects Supervisor

Loni Peristere
Emmy Award™ Winning Visual Effects Supervisor
(SERENITY, "BATTLESTAR GALACTICA","FIREFLY", "BUFFY, THE VAMPIRE SLAYER")

Is It Cold In Here?

Visual effects personnel are not always the most welcomed members on a set because we take time away from the regular everyday production schedule. So It's important to look, listen and observe for at least five minutes upon arrival on the set. You never know where the Production is in their day, how their scenes are going, whether or not there's a performance that's in progress, or whether they're ready to see or talk with you. It's vitally important to read the temperature of the set for those first five minutes before you make yourself known and state your case.

On Being A Visual Effects Supervisor

A visual effect is a useful tool for telling a portion of the story, usually an action or scene, that can't be told through principal photography. Most of my responsibility is determined prior to me arriving on a set. It has been discussed, formatted and executed in pre-production. When I arrive on the set, it's to supervise that portion which will later be incorporated into a post-generated character or action. Being on set allows me to watch the scene in rehearsal and find where the effect takes place in the action of the scene and record all the valuable information needed to complete the shot or scene in post-production.

Unsung Heroes

Having already spoken with the Writers, the Directors, the D.P.s and Production Designers in pre-production, when I walk onto a set, I find myself going to the 1st and 2nd A.D.s to discuss what the requirements of my shot are and where in the context of the scene the effect should take place then the Gaffer to talk about what lighting requirements I might have. I'll also discuss with the Script Supervisor what the measurements that I would like to record within the context of the script so those measurements can be recorded, copied and sent to post-production, production and Visual Effects so that we can accurately record camera information and translate it into 3D. What happens as a result of this dialogue with these departments is that often times we will come up with solutions, addendums and accents that ultimately will make the shot even better.

We Are Family...

Joss Whedon & Co. are a very intimate group of people. All of us have known and worked well together for almost seven years. So set life is like a group of friends getting together to work on their favorite thing in the whole world. We're full of excitement but also self-criticism and we never argue, but rather debate whose idea is cooler in the way friends do. At the same time, we are also professionals, so all the goofing and the excitement is contained in the fact that we realize that we have a budget and a schedule to maintain.

"Movies are a very complicated machine, and if you really look at the model of filmmaking, it defies all odds. It really shouldn't work."

Greg Nicotero, Make-Up FX Artist

Scott Beverly
Visual Effects Artist
(THE DARK KNIGHT RISES, INCEPTION, SPIDER-MAN 3)

Summer Lovin'

My mother worked for a number of videotape post-production houses in the '60s, '70s and '80s and even now continues to market syndicated programming to the European and Asian markets. So that combined with growing up in Hollywood got me interested in this industry. In junior high, my best friend's father was Gene Warren, a Special Effects Cinematographer and owner of Fantasy II Film Effects. During the summers I would work for Gene in his studio helping to produce shots for some of his earlier films. After I got out of high school I needed work and one day Gene offered me the opportunity to work for him on a freelance basis. Gene taught me most of what I have learned in the film industry including the fundamental concepts to achieve the best and most convincing end results possible. Eventually the gig turned into an every day thing and went on to last for over 25 years.

Doing It *"Old School"*

I was taught pretty much every aspect of film effects. I was forced to work the optical printers as well as develop the black-and-white prints for test comps. And it was very much what you would call "old school" effects. I didn't have the luxury of digital compositing at the time. I barely had the luxury of motion control, which was new when I started out in the industry. Repeating camera moves were done by hand, keeping track of the numbers and frames. Messing up a single frame or, say accidently kicking a light, would ruin an entire sequence and we'd have to start all over again.

D.P. Or Not D.P.? That Is The Question

The D.P. really has to have an understanding of what elements are going to be layered on an effect shot and is key in producing a quality effect shot. The way the scene is lit and composed is absolutely essential especially if you're generating an element that involves smoke, dust, fire or crashes. If certain key steps aren't taken into consideration, you'll have problems integrating the effect into the live footage. I have unfortunately worked with D.P.s who have the attitude of *"We'll fix it in post."* You can certainly get away with some things like if somebody leaves a ladder in the background and you couldn't afford to reshoot the scene, but for the most part having a D.P. that understands what you are trying to do as an end result considerably helps out the shot because there are a whole host of events that can happen that can really foul a plate element.

Just Because You Have It...

In modern filmmaking there is now a grab bag of CG tools available to Directors but you have to remember that that's what they are: Tools. If you don't know what the tool is used for it can be used the wrong way or just plain abused. Having a Director that has a clear understanding of what he can do with that particular tool is what really makes that tool brilliant. What you are unfortunately seeing more and more of today is that some of the upcoming filmmakers believe that CGI is the ONLY tool in their kit. And not having a clear understanding of what it can and cannot do really makes for shots that are just awful and audiences are savvy enough to know a poorly composed effect that has overused digital when they see it. One of my own personal theories behind this is that many filmmakers alot a considerable budget for a post facility that has the capability of CG, and just like in any business, that post facility is out to get all of that dollar. All too often I find that we are being brought in to rescue shots that have not quite "cut the mustard" with CG and we're tasked to produce additional components to help sweeten the shots. Unfortunately by the time that they figure out that the shot isn't quite working out or they can't get the shot to come together to everybody's liking, the money and the time has been spent. And that puts undo pressure on the people brought in to fix it and make it worthy of the film.

Panic Attack

The reason why I think I've been pretty successful is because I put a lot of pre-planning and pre-structuring into the effects I do. Having said that, there are times when I wake up with a cold chill and go, *"Oh my God, what about this? How am I going to deal with that?"* Of course that's reality in most any business. The difference is that in some cases the shot that I'm working on has been valued at well over a million dollars and it's going to be gone in a second.

Ironically, I've had Producers come up to me 5 minutes before pulling the trigger and say *"Scott! Isn't this the great part? You get to see your work come together!"* and my typical response is *"Oh my God. You don't seem to understand, this is the WORST part."* What they fail to realize is that this is the moment when everything has to work, because I'm looking at a million dollars a second and if something doesn't work properly, the egg is on my face.

So when I start ramping up to the shots and I'm thinking through the hundreds of events that have to happen to achieve the shot, it's a feeling of, *"I hope nobody stepped on that wire and broke that lead"* or *"I hope that the key components release when it's supposed to."* It may not look it at the time, but believe me, those emotions, feelings and thoughts all go through my mind all at that one moment.

"Thanks to DVD, a movie that you do will be around for a long, long time. I think that makes everybody intense because at the end of the day we're making something that, good or bad, could last till the end of time."

Andre Royo, Actor

John Medlen
Stunt & Fight Coordinator
(THIS MEANS WAR, SPIDER-MAN, "LOST", "ALIAS"
"BUFFY, THE VAMPIRE SLAYER")

Safety First

When there's action involved, I need to be alert, aware of the surroundings, who is on set and what's going on. Mainly, it's a safety issue. As a Stunt Coordinator, I'm 100% responsible for making sure that the people are safe on a set and if I give 100%, it makes it that much better and safer. It's wrong to kick back and carry on a casual conversation while people are risking their lives for you.

My Spidey Sense Is Tingling

Every day is a learning experience and every show is different. But I love that constant change. I even try to mix it up between features and television because they are so different. With features you go do it for a couple of months and then it's over, with television you're dealing with something that is more constant and repetitive and you sometimes have to wing it. A lot of times you have to come with the choreography on the day or if you're lucky the day before and normally there aren't any fancy techniques at your disposal.

Burning Like A Flame

When I worked on SPIDER-MAN, I did the reshoots for the end sequence in the burning room. I got a lot of prep and rehearsal time and time to talk with the Director. We only had so many days to do these fights and it worked out perfect. We actually sat down and reviewed tapes that I shot during the rehearsals. He decided which ones he liked and I went in and re-edited my shots to his specifications and he wound up using my videotapes when he had the sequence re-storyboarded to utilize those shots. That's exciting because you feel like you're getting your best use out of the choreography and the product.

The Hustler

Sometimes you get Stunt People that come to hustle the set. They approach the set Security Officer and tell him that I'm expecting them or that they have to drop off some equipment, so the security guy lets them on the set. I had an incident when a Stunt Person got upset when I told security that he was not allowed on the set. He voiced his opinion loudly about being thrown off the set and disrupted the shooting. The Producers came up to me and wanted to know what was going on and then told me that that person will never work on their show.

On Good Manners

I can't abide when a Stunt Person comes on set and is rude especially to Costume and Make-Up. They think that it's not going to get back to me or I'm not going to say anything about it. They think that they're protected by the Stunt Department and that they can have any attitude they want. These are the people that I will never bring back to work with me again because I feel the crew that I'm working with is my team. Stunt people coming in for the day are visitors to help do an episode. When they are rude, it reflects on my department and on me.

TALES FROM THE SET

On one of my early films, I had a female 1st A.D. and a cowboy-type Transportation Captain that were actively having an affair. Everyone on the set was aware that this illicit relationship was going on. One day we were out in the desert filming this big explosion, which used an enormous mortar to achieve the shot. While the Special Effect Artist was literally leaning over into the mouth of the mortar adjusting the charge, I was watching my 1st A.D. completely not paying attention to what was going on. I casually asked her if she was ready and suddenly she instinctively jumped up and yelled *"Action!"* The Special Effects Tech heard it and popped out of the mortar screaming *"No. no, God, no!"* Fortunately, nobody had their finger on the button. But that was the worst breach of professionalism and etiquette I've ever seen on a set.

Wes Craven, Writer/Producer/Director

One time while I was supervising a complex flying sequence for a TV Movie, the Leading Lady, a Famous Singer/Actress, showed up on the set after being seven hours late. Because she was in a hurry and couldn't be bothered with the technical aspects of the sequence, she rushed us through the prep and didn't pay adequate attention to the safety instructions we gave her. As a result she wound up bumping her head against a C-Stand and received a goose egg on her forehead the size of a golf ball. This also set the day back another several hours. Fortunately we were able to salvage some usable footage but had there been a level of respect and timeliness, not only would we have had more time to get the action for the shot that we needed, but she would have been prepared for what the requirements were for the shot and could have avoided injury.

Anonymous Visual Effects Supervisor

When I was shooting FROM BEYOND, we had a very elaborate make-up that covered most of the Actor's body. He had to have his arms curled up underneath the make-up. It took 7-8 hours to apply. He came to me and asked if we could work late and shoot all the scenes with him so he didn't have to get into the make-up ever again. I agreed. We started with the close ups and worked our way to the wide shots. Things were going along fine until we got towards the end of the day and he started having trouble with his lines. This was very strange because this was an Actor who was very precise and disciplined. As he continued to muff lines I all of a sudden realized that something was wrong. I told the FX Artists to take the make-up off immediately. We discovered that it was impairing his circulation. He wasn't getting enough blood to his brain and his arm had swollen up to about twice the size underneath the make-up. It was pretty scary.

Stuart Gordon, Director

It's important to respect the stunt equipment and listen to the Stunt Coordinator. One time I was on set doing an air ram sequence to propel a Stuntman in the air. When the Director yelled *"Cut"* some crew members immediately charged onto the set before it was safe. One of them stepped on the air ram and the thing went off and broke the person's leg.

Eddie Matthews, Stunt Coordinator

The Director, several other crew members and I were sitting at a lunch table having just prepped a squashing cockroach gag. There was an empty seat next to me and we all decided that whoever sat in the empty seat I would put the fake roach on their shoulder. We all waited with anticipation. when suddenly, who sits down next to me? The D.P.! Everyone went wide-eyed. I was going to call it off, but the Director looks at me and says *"you don't have the balls."* The challenge was on. I stealthily placed the rubber roach on the D.P'.s shoulder as everyone tried to play it cool. One of the others at the table yells out! *"Oh my god look at that roach on your shoulder!"* The D.P. leaped up screaming, trying to slap it off but it went down inside his shirt. After jumping around frantically screaming, he ran off. Everyone at the table just sat with their jaws hanging open. The Director was the first to speak. He said *"well, that didn't work out."* Everyone was silent. *"But, it was funny!"* and everyone gave a half-hearted laugh.

I said I would go and find him and apologize. The D.P. disappeared for over an hour and a half. When he finally showed up he had completely changed clothes and showered. I apologized and explained the whole plan. He told me under other circumstances it would have been hilarious, but he had a childhood phobia of roaches. Needless to say I kept the practical jokes to a minimum for the rest of that show.

Patrick Tantalo, Special Effects Supervisor

I once saw a well-known Stuntman, while discussing a car chase sequence with the Director, start telling him what should happen in the scene. He suggested in detail this whole big sequence. When the Stuntman was finished, the Director politely turned to him and said, "You know that's really nice. I'll tell you what, when you direct your next picture you should put that in." The lesson here is: if you overstep your boundaries, expect to get put in your place.

Roy Clark, Stunt Coordinator

CHAPTER TWELVE

"Pizza? But it's not even 2nd Meal!"

ALL THE REST...

A BRIEF OVERVIEW

Last, but certainly not least, are the remaining other Departments that round out the crew. These range from the Caterers to the members of the production office.

Let's start with the food, because the crew has got to eat. A well fed crew is a happy crew. Depending on the production, they'll either have a walk away lunch, which means that the crew is responsible for providing their own food or they'll have a Caterer which is a food service hired by production to feed the crew.

Fortunately, most hire a Caterer. Because production can stretch on for months, a good Caterer will not only provide the basics, but also add a little flair and, more importantly, variety. Even the best food in the world gets boring if it's always the same.

Moving on (pun intended), the Transportation Department handles anything dealing with trucks trailers, or cars. They coordinate crew parking, set up base camp, and can provide picture cars.

Many movies require the use of animals, whether it be an African elephant or just a plain ordinary house cat. Specially licensed and trained individuals provide and directly work with the animals during the shoot. All animal activity on a set is monitored by the Humane Society.

This brings us to the production office. Led by the Production Office Coordinator, the office staff schedules flights and hires cars to pick-up and drop-off Actors. They also deal with the massive amounts of paperwork required to keep a production going such as call sheets, production schedules and script changes.

And finally, without Production Accounting, no one would get paid which is usually the crew's top priority. This department handles crew payroll, issuing checks, petty cash and, if on location, per diem.

THE PLAYERS

Caterer: Provides hot meals for the entire crew for breakfast and First Meal.

Medic: Chief Medical Personnel on a set.

Location Manager: Secures practical locations for filming outside the studio. Arranges security, parking, traffic control and coordinates filming at these locations.

Transportation Coordinator: Hires and manages the Drivers, trucks and trailers for the production.

Transportation Captain: Oversees the daily schedule for transporting cast and key crew members as well as supervises all the Drivers.

Picture Car Coordinator: Locates the picture cars and supervises them on the set.

Animal Wrangler: Supervises live animals on set.

Animal Trainer: Teaches live animals to perform tasks required by the script.

Human Society Representative: Monitors animals on a set to ensure they are being treated properly.

Technical Advisor: Specialist in a field that works with the Production to provide information about portraying a profession or event accurately.

Production Office Coordinator (POC): Runs the Production Office and handles the multitude of paperwork and day to day arrangements.

Assistant Production Office Coordinator (APOC): POC's right hand. Deals with preparing, distributing and filing paperwork.

Production Secretary: Handles the phones and distributes printed material.

Office P.A.: Primarily assists the office staff but also various other departments as needed.

Publicist: Works with the press as a liaison to publicize the movie during and after principal photography.

Production Accountant: Issues checks and petty cash and processes payroll.

Post-Production Supervisor: Oversees the entire post-production of the film. In recent years it has become an on set position because they must constantly liaise with many different departments especially on FX heavy productions.

TERMS YOU SHOULD KNOW

(two / three) banger
Name for a room in a trailer. A "two-banger" has two separate rooms. A "three-banger" has three.

Base Camp
The main area where the Actors, Make-Up, Wardrobe and other production trailers are parked on a set or on location.

commissary
A restaurant located on a studio lot where Actors and crew members from various productions can eat during breaks.

First Meal (aka "Lunch")
A meal break that is required exactly six hours from the initial crew call time. Lateness to wrap actors and crew for first meal can result in "Meal Penalties" which is money paid to the cast and crew for the inconvenience.

green room
An area for the Actors to relax on or near a set if base camp is too far away.

honeywagon
A long production trailer containing the bathrooms and a number of small rooms.

location
Any exterior or interior area used for filming not located on a studio lot or in a sound stage.

NDB
(Non-Deductible Breakfast) A light meal provided at general crew call to sync cast and crew for timing of First Meal break.

picture car
A vehicle specifically used for filming. Sometimes rigged or modified to assist in filming.

scout
To actively search out a location and determine its viability for filming.

Second Meal
A meal break that is required exactly six hours after the end of first meal. Usually not as grand as first meal and at times relegated to a "walking meal" which means cast & crew continue to work as they eat.

shuttle
Vehicle on a set used solely for transportation of cast and crew to and from the set.

star wagon
A more elaborate trailer with various amenities to accommodate the needs of an Actor.

trailer
Vehicles specifically designed for the individual needs of each Department. (i.e. Costume trailer, Make-Up trailer, Hair trailer, etc.)

THE RULES OF SETIQUETTE

• The catering staff cooks for an average of 120 to 150 people on a daily basis. Treat them (and the Craft Service personnel) with the same respect as you would a waiter in a fine restaurant. Just because the food is free doesn't mean you have the right to criticize the quality.

• The set Medic is not a pharmacy. Only utilize the Medic for emergencies or set related illnesses. Don't expect them to provide you with your daily vitamins. It's not their job.

• Keep the honey wagons clean. The whole production needs to use the restrooms and it's irresponsible to make a mess and not clean up after yourself.

• Crew parking should be determined by the Location Manager and should be followed to the letter. Misplaced cars could slow down production by blocking routes or being in the way of production vehicles.

• Don't mess around or sit in the picture cars without permission. These cars are expensive and valuable. The Transportation Department is not your personal car dealership.

• Never approach or pet an animal without the Trainer's permission. It's very time consuming and difficult to properly train stage animals and distractions from you can make it that much harder for the animal to perform properly.

• Don't expect the Production Office or Production Accounting to respond to your needs immediately. Fill request forms (check, run, petty cash) out completely and have then approved in advance. Make sure that timecards are filled out completely and accurately.

• Don't pester the Publicist about obtaining publicity material on the film or for free posters. They are not responsible for marketing the film to you especially since you've already seen it.

ADVICE FROM THE EXPERTS

Kristi Frankenheimer
Location Manager
(Kiss, Kiss, Bang, Bang, Legally Blonde 2, Path To War)

On Being A Location Manager

As a Location Manager, I scout, obtain and arrange all the locations on a movie. Knowing where to go and being aware of certain periods and looks and then being able to combine those with the logistical needs of a movie production company is a major part of my job. What's great about this is that it combines all the different aspects that I enjoy doing whether it been dealing with the financial matters or creative issues. Over the years I tried numerous other positions on set but they all eventually bored me to tears. Even being a Line Producer didn't really do it for me so I eventually moved back into being a Location Manager even though my peers thought I was completely crazy.

Step Right Up, Folks

I explain my job to people like this: When you see a circus it's all put together. Everything that it took to get it set up, well, that's my Department. The Circus performs and then goes away. All that's left is that little tumbleweed rolling by and people marveling that it's like the Circus was never there. Well, that's my Department too.

S&M

It's only fun if you're a little bit masochistic and you have the need to solve crisis without recognition or money. It's a thankless job. The pay is the lowest of any Department Head on the set, the hours are long and you never get any sleep. There's also the added pressure that if we screw up on any given day, the production will not have anything to film. We have to be the head on the beast. If there is a complaint made against the production it goes directly to me. Anybody on the crew can affect my job negatively. If one crewmember in any department mouths off to a neighbor when you're on location, it can make my job hell. Ultimately, the only reason to do it is for self-gratification or if you're a little sick in the head like me.

Reverse Nepotism

I always find it hysterical when people spout out about nepotism to me because I worked as a Location Manager for 14 years before my Father (John Frankenheimer) finally hired me. When I asked him why it took him so long, he told me he first wanted to make sure I knew what I was doing.

Humble Beginnings

I started as a P.A. making phone calls on a film that my Father was directing as a favor to him. It was the first time I ever worked for him and he really needed my help making research calls for him trying to track down a steel mill for the Art Department. When they finally brought on the Location Manager, she had seen what I had done and was so impressed that she hired me to assist her. At the time she had no idea that I was the Director's daughter and three days later she found out and, in a panic, wanted to fire me. I fortunately convinced her to keep me on and we eventually became good friends.

Bikini-Bash

Many years ago we had to shut down a bridge in San Pedro because we had a car rigged to explode. We were told emphatically that we could not shut down the Port of San Pedro but we couldn't have boats passing underneath the bridge when we shot. So we hired a bunch of models in bikinis and along with me in my bikini, we jumped into a speedboat and passed out beers to the local fisherman to keep them busy while we filmed the scene.

"Some jobs are great and you hope they'll never end and some you'd just rather forget. The good news is at the end of the day, I still get to be with my favorite part of any job, the animals."

Stacy Gunderson, Animal Trainer

Phil Schriber
Transportation Coordinator
(G.I. JOE: RETALIATION, MISS CONGENIALITY, VARSITY BLUES)

Road To Somewhere

I originally worked in the RV industry renting vehicles and one of my first jobs was renting motor homes to the production of THE BEST LITTLE WHOREHOUSE IN TEXAS for the Actors. I got to know the Transportation Coordinators and they would use my RVs from time to time. After a while I got more and more involved and decided to sell the business and become a Driver. I then bought a Honeywagon and drove that for a number of years then from that grew into working in the Transportation Department full time. I ultimately became a Coordinator by paying attention to my job and approaching it as I was working for the project as opposed to just collecting a check.

At Your Service

What some people don't understand is that Transportation is a service part of the business. We are there to assist all the crafts on the set. We have one on one dealings with all the departments and we are responsible for making sure that all the cast & crew and equipment are in the right place at the right time. This gives you a real overview of the entire set and it is important to understand what all the departments do on a set or it's hard to service them.

Remember The Alamo...Again!

THE ALAMO was a particularly challenging show. In the 14 months of the shoot we changed Directors. It was the longest shoot ever in Texas. We had a 49-acre set which was at the time the largest free-standing set in the world. We had to supply fuel and power for all the departments. When we got to the ranch there was no water or electricity. We drilled wells and laid miles of cable. The Art Department actually built buildings that we could hide the trucks behind. On a normal size show we'll have between 30-35 Drivers. On THE ALAMO we topped off at over 100.

The Tooth Fairy

I was on a show many years ago where an Actress, who for reasons beyond my understanding, became very good friends with me. One time at three in the morning she refused to come out of her trailer. We discovered that she had knocked out her false tooth. Evidently, nobody on the production knew that she was missing a tooth and she wanted to keep it that way. Unfortunately, we were working in a small town of literally 8,000 people so we had to get the police to track down the local pharmacy to get it opened so we could get some tooth cement. We had to do this all without letting the Production catch on.

"If you're a frustrated artist and are good at math, the Accounting Department is the place to be if you want to be in the business and around creative people. It's not boring like corporate accounting."
Rachel Prentiss, Production Accountant

Stacy Gunderson
Animal Trainer
(GARFIELD, SECONDHAND LIONS, SNOW DOGS)

On Animal Etiquette

Never be afraid to ask questions. If you don't know ask. Things are always done for a reason, especially with animals. They are not your pets at home and the Trainers have gone to great lengths to train them a certain way. Sometimes you will be asked not to touch or talk to animals on set. This is not to be mean. It just means this animal is easily distracted or doesn't have much set experience. Sometimes, the Trainers will let everyone deal with the animals. This will only be with set savvy animals. So really it is up to the Trainer's discretion.

School's In Session

We are basically animal teachers. The Director tells us what he would like to see, then we break it down into achievable pieces for the animals to do. People should always remember that Actors act and animal react. Our job is to get the right reaction.

Here Kitty, Kitty!

Safety can not be practiced enough when these animals are on set. Never forget, a trained lion is still a lion and will still do natural lion things. Once they are trained, they do not become like a dog. That is probably people's biggest misconception. People want to come and make friends, take pictures with, and in general just hang out too close to dangerous animals. I understand it, I have it too, but it is never that easy. Trainers start out with these animals when they are babies and establish a relationship with them. They understand what the animal is thinking by watching the animal's body language or listening to their vocalizations. Just remember the Trainer is under more stress with a wild animal as opposed to a dog or house cat. The Trainer needs to keep the trusting relationship in a new environment and keep the entire crew safe at all times.

We take care of problems and don't talk about them.
Anonymous Transportation Captain

Rachel E. Prentiss
Production Accountant
(FAST FIVE, RUSH HOUR 3, WEDDING CRASHERS, PLEASANTVILLE)

A Place In This World

My Department has to be on set at least twice a week. I'll go at the beginning of the week and meet with the Production Manager and the Unit Manager for cost reporting, then my Payroll person will go out at the end of the week with the checks and per diem. When I go out on the set, it can be daunting, because I want to make sure that I'm not in anybody's way. I'm sometimes unsure of where exactly I should be standing on a set. So I usually try to go at lunch time when people are more relaxed. I found if I make my presence known, the people will usually come to me.

Gypsy Girl

I think anyone in this business has to have a little bit of Gypsy in them. I'm 43 years old and have been doing this since I graduated from college. It's still amazing to me that I set up and break down an office at least twice a year. You never really know where you're going to go or what's in store for you. There are times when you wonder why you're doing this and yet there's never been a film that I've been on, no matter how hard it is, that you don't get excited what the next project is going to be.

The most positive thing about this business is the opportunity to travel. To anyone young starting out, do as many location shoots as you can possibly do. It gets harder when you get older and have family. I've lived all over the United States and every place I've been is now a part of me. My life's an adventure.

One For The P.A.s

The one thing that I find disheartening in this business is the people who think they are somebody because their position and therefore that gives them the right to be a jerk. I think the hardest working group of people on a set are the P.A.s. Just because they are learning is not an excuse to yell and scream at them. They are people and deserve all the respect you can give them. A lot of people feel that they were yelled at as a P.A. so they're going to yell and scream at P.A.s working for them. I hate when I see people do it in front of other people. If you really have an issue with someone there are places to go to do it in private.

With A Friend Like Harry...

Because I deal with the money, a lot of people don't think my department is important but it's amazing how everything can stop if somebody doesn't get their money. I had a situation where a Director had brought in a friend from out of the country for a second unit five day shoot. He didn't inform anyone that this was happening. At the end of the week we get his friend's start-up paperwork and discover he's from Santa Domingo. I realize that I can't pay this person. He's not a U.S. citizen nor does he have a work permit. This goes round and round for weeks until ultimately the Director gets upset and refuses to work because we haven't paid his friend. We literally had to get the studio involved and fortunately they backed me. Ultimately we paid the Director an extra service fee and it was his responsibility to pay his friend.

"The Location Department is kind of like the Marines. They storm the beach and we come up right behind as the support."
Phil Schriber, Transportation Coordinator

Juli Nunn
Production Manager / Coordinator
("So You Think You Can Dance", "Top Gear USA", "Strictly Come Dancing: It Takes Two")

On Being A Production Coordinator

Being a Production Coordinator entails doing just about everything. My job and the Production Managers are two of the hardest working positions on a set because you're not only being asked to do things for the Executives, but also by every department. We help everybody with everything and make sure that it all gets done and that nothing falls through the cracks...Nothing!

Open Late

I am pretty much on call 24 hours a day. If somebody on the production needs something even if it's after wrap, they will call me. It might be something to do with work or it could be for personal reasons. It's part of the job, but sometimes it's a big challenge to just pick up the phone knowing that there could be any number of wacky requests on the other end. Since I'm the Coordinator I also get things passed down from the Production Manager. So, I'm pretty much getting it from all angles. It's important to maintain a clear head and not get frustrated when you need to juggle a lot of tasks and appease a great many people at one time.

Practical Advice

If you want to advance, you always have to make sure you are one step ahead. You should take the initiative, watch how things work and just jump in and do it without having to be told all the time. I don't like it when I see my Office P.A.'s sitting on the computer just screwing around because they've finished the task I've given them. They should be finding something else to do or coming to me to ask for something to do. In a Production Office there is always work to be done. Show initiative and learn as you do it.

On A Personal Note

Because we deal with a lot of problem solving and high stress situations, it's also vitally important not to take things personally. I've found that when I have screwed up that it's best to just accept it and move on. Dwelling on it only makes it worse. There's also times when you're going to get yelled at for things that aren't your fault and you also have to just take that too. Getting yelled at is unfortunately a big part of the job, because my department seems to be an easy target for the other departments to vent at.

The Babysitter's Club

On "DANCING WITH STARS" the crew generally went out to celebrate after the wrap of each show. One of those nights I went straight home after wrap because I was pretty wiped. At 3am the phone rang and it was one of the Producers. Evidently he was with a P.A. who had gotten completely blitzed and didn't know where he lived. The Producer wanted to know if I had the address. They were driving up and down Sunset Blvd looking for his apartment. As far as I knew, the P.A. lived in Santa Monica not Hollywood. Fortunately I had his address and they were able to get him home safely. That same night I had a P.A.'s boyfriend call me up trying to figure out where she was. At the end of the day, my job's a lot like babysitting.

"It's important to ingratiate yourself with everyone on the set, not just the people with the perceived power. The guy who sweeps the floors might have some great stories to tell. The more you know about what everyone else does on the set the better you will do in your job."

Ellen S. Pressman TV Director/Producer

Donald Bruce
Production Accountant
(BOBBY, BLACK DAHLIA, SIXTEEN BLOCKS, THE GREY ZONE)

The Man With The Money

The primary responsibility when a Production Accountant goes on set is to pay the crew. In addition to that there might be meetings with the Production Manager and/or Line Producer about the cost report, meetings with the 2nd or 2nd 2nd A.D. about the production reports, or meetings with Department Heads or crew if there are issues with payments, monies due, or operations of their particular department. I try to get to the set either during the lunch break or what's predicted to be the end of day so that I'm not disrupting the set because let's be honest, when the money shows up, everybody wants to get their check. As far as the rest of it is concerned, it becomes a matter of hurry up and wait. You may have to sit and wait until people are available. Etiquette says you don't go out and superimpose your needs upon the needs of the shooting set. It's that simple.

Don't Bank On Things Always Going The Way You Planned

I studied Arts Management when I was in college and the original intent was to work with a Theatrical Producer but for one reason or another, I veered away from that and had a couple of other careers. I did a stint in Promotion in the men's wear industry that sort of meshed in with my theater aspirations, but to get a steady paycheck I made a left turn in my career and went to work for a bank. The intent was to stay there for a year until I could get a nest egg but I ended up staying seven. Fortunately, I had re-established contact with an old friend of mine from my theater days who had made the transition into TV. She had become a Production Accountant on a Norman Lear showed called "SUNDAY DINNER" and was looking for an Assistant. She said, *"Come work for me, it'll be fun, it's a short-term gig."* That was 25 years ago.

Bank Of Columbia

Having worked at a bank, working for a company like Columbia Pictures (now Sony) was not that big of a transition. The first thing you got handed to you when you went to work on a Columbia show was their policies and procedures manual, which at the time was a 3" binder and now I've heard it's up to 5" and 6". It's every little thing you would be doing and how they want you to do it, which thankfully was very similar to how they do things in banking. It was just a matter of learning their accounting software and adjusting to the working hours, which tended to be fairly long days because Columbia expected their reporting to be done in a very specific fashion. The other adjustment was working on a movie lot and the excitement that comes with working around the kind of creativity that comes with television and movies.

Learning On The Job Is Not Always A Good Thing

Recently I worked for a pair of Producers, that didn't know the difference between a "cost" and a "budget." That became a real exercise in diplomacy because I couldn't tell these two that, *"Ok, you don't know what the hell you're doing. Shut up and go sit in the corner and let the people who know how to do this job, do this job."* That's not cool. So about a third of my time was spent teaching them what I did, so they had an understanding of what they were supposed to be doing. And that's always a challenge to an Accountant when they're dealing with inexperienced Producers.

The Name Is Bond...Completion Bond

One of the main things about keeping control over a show is proper communication between the Department Heads and the Production Office when they're ordering stuff so that the Accountants can anticipate costs and see where things fit into the budget. Movies can spin out of control if the Producers allow anybody on the set to order what they want and do what they want without alerting the Accountants. The loan for a film is based on distribution contracts that have a finite delivery date. The bank wants to make sure the project is finished and delivered within that time frame. So the production typically has to take out an insurance policy (called a completion bond) to make sure that things get done in the proper time frame. Having a Producer on the set tell a Department Head that they can go out and rent a $10,000 piece of equipment that wasn't originally budgeted causes problems on the backend especially if you've got the completion bond company breathing down your neck and you're trying to justify expenses that you don't know anything about.

"Making a movie is a collaborative effort and everybody should be helping each other. But like in everything, there's politics involved, so you've got to be nice to people and for the most part they're going to be nice back."

Scott Maginnis, Prop Master

Steve Demko
Post-Production Supervisor
(THE AVENGERS, CABIN IN THE WOODS, THE LINCOLN LAWYER)

Production-Production Supervisor

With the advent of the digital camera as a viable recording method for major motion pictures, the workflow for dailies is now handled on-set. This started early on with the Sony Genesis camera and now it's been spread on to HD formats. The newer cameras that are now able to shoot beyond 2K resolution (The Sony F65 is a true 8K camera) provide a ton of data that needs to get managed. So as soon as you open up that shutter and start capturing your very first frame, you're technically already in post-production. During the actual shooting of the movies, it's become a Post-Production Supervisor's role to acquire the captured footage and start to manage it.

Visual Effects

Visual effects are a prominent force in every motion picture. Even romantic comedies and dramas are loaded with visual effects these days. Whether it is beauty fixes to the Actors, removing signage that can't be cleared, a crewmember that might have fallen into a frame on a particular shot, or even a weird reflection in a character's sunglasses, you have to deal with all those using visual effects. On top of that, Visual Effects shots often need to get turned over quickly, especially if it's in a reshoot situation and there's a visual effects house that can't wait to start working on it in order to meet deadlines. I've done shots on some movies where I had to send out footage as it's shot. And in order to do that, I've got to be on the set.

Accept Nothing

I'd messed around with video cameras as a kid but this was in the 1980s where you basically get one take. You hit pause and then you try and get the next shot with no editing at all. The editing was done in the camera. Coming out of college I didn't know what I wanted to do. I just knew I wanted to be a part of movie making. My first opportunity was as an Art Department Production Assistant on a film called THICK AS THIEVES starring Alec Baldwin, Rebecca DeMornay and Andre Braugher. Being on a set where there's different departments and everything's got to work in a synergistic way in order to make your ambitious day, without going into OT and/or extending your budget was quite a wake-up call. The first thing I knew to do was to accept the fact that I knew nothing.

A Little Help From My Friends

You find that on set there are people that want to help you. They want to impart their knowledge and pass it on because they know it can only make the people around them better. Those are the people that you need to identify. And once you've done that, hopefully their personality matches with yours so you can get to know them on a personal level. From there you learn to discern the important factors of what your immediate job is. Sometimes there's a P.A. in your department who's done a lot of stuff before you, a really experienced P.A. close to moving up to becoming an Assistant Director, or someone who's been stuck in that position for a while. More than likely he knows a lot more than you and more often than not, he's willing to help you learn because he knows it's ultimately in his best interest.

Paging Dr. A.D.

I worked my way around many different positions on a set. I was a P.A., a Grip, a Cameraman and then after that I became an Assistant Director. I was interested in everything that everybody did and loved seeing it all come together. I soon discovered that Assistant Directors know everything about everyone. They know what each department needs and what each department has to do. They're the ones that schedule everything on the set. They're the ones who integrate themselves with Talent as well as with the Producers. They have their finger on everybody's pulse and know every part of what everybody's doing. Because of this it was very exciting to be a part of the Assistant Directors group. It's where I found myself to be most comfortable.

Synchronicity - Part 2

There are many people who just stay as Assistant Directors and often become Producers or get into directing. For me it was more about the producing side of things and I was savvy enough to get into production supervising on commercials and music videos for some large production companies. Something I discovered early on is that most Producers, once they're done shooting, just want to deliver the project and get on to the next thing. So as a Production Supervisor on staff at a commercials and music videos production company, I found myself doing a lot of post-production work simply because nobody cared about the project anymore. I'm suddenly the guy that they're entrusting to deliver this and make sure that it all gets taken care of so we can get our final payment. I became skilled at post-production out of necessity, learning about various deliveries and editing systems. It wasn't long before I developed a passion for post-production and its importance in the process of making movies.

One day I got a phone call from a film production company and they said they had some movies going they thought I might be good for. I soon found that except for the photochemical process for theatrical releases, film post-production is essentially the same process, it just takes a lot longer, there's a lot more of it and there's a lot more money involved. Deciding that this was my new career path, I worked my way back up the ranks there and soon started delivering big-budget blockbuster action pictures to major studios. Fortunately my years of on-set experience which taught me to synchronize various departments, made my transition to being a Post Supervisor that much easier for me.

"If you're not willing to work hard then don't take the job."

J. David Ahuna, Key Grip

TALES FROM THE SET

I was working a show with a number of young Actors and my crew literally had to wake them up every morning to get them to set on time. It got to the point where my Drivers were given the Actor's hotel room keys so they could wake them easier. It was like some kind of bizarre Boot Camp.

Phil Schriber, Transportation Coordinator

I was working on a period film and the picture car was a stick shift. No one bothered to ask the Actor whether he could drive one or not. Unfortunately for us, the situation worsened when we discovered that, not only could he not drive a stick shift, but he didn't know how to drive, period. He lived his whole life in New York City and never found the necessity to learn. We had to teach him on the spot.

Anonymous Producer

I was working on "GEORGE WALLACE" and we were shooting at the State Capital in Sacramento. We had to jump through so many hoops to get this location so Gary Sinise as George Wallace could stand up and give his *"Segregation now, segregation forever"* speech. After months of work we're at the location with over 500 extras in period costumes. Just as we are about to shoot the scene a van pulls around the corner and five guys jump out with huge 20 ft. banners and signs. They also have a bullhorn to yell out their religious rhetoric. As soon as I saw this, I tore off across the field towards the demonstrators to try to see if I could get them to go away (they have a 1st Amendment right to be there so I can't forcibly make them leave). But before I can get there one of the crewmembers stands up before them and starts yelling at them. This completely set the protestors off, so by the time I got to them I had to do some serious damage control. What made matters worse was that the demonstrators were in the frame so we couldn't shoot while they were there.

It took me almost 20 minutes to edge them back out of the frame and just as it was looking like I was going to clear it, the crew member came back and set them off again. I was immediately back to square one. This was shaping up to be the worst day of my life. Finally, a half hour later the demonstrators finally gave up and took off. The entire production applauded as they drove away. Unbeknownst to me the Still Photographer snapped off a shot of me standing there with the state capital in the background and me with my Diet Coke and cigarette (my staple diet at the time) sandwiched between the protestors on my right and the Producer laughing his ass off to my left. Every time I look at that picture, I'm reminded that it can't get much worse.

Kristi Frankenheimer, Location Manager

I was working on a low budget movie and we were fortunate to have a B+ type star. We didn't have the money for a Driver so we had one of our Set P.A.s pick her up for her first day of shooting. This particular P.A. had never worked on a movie before and was too afraid to speak up about what kind of car he has. It turned out he had the rattiest, oldest and clunkiest vehicle known to mankind. Not only does it not start in the morning making him 45 minutes late to picking her up but also the passenger side door doesn't open. So when he finally gets to the Actress's house she has to climb through his disgusting car in order to get to her seat. The window doesn't roll down so she has to deal with the funky smell and, of course, the car doesn't start when they attempt to leave for the set. Ultimately they were a couple of hours late for the first day of shooting. Luckily, the Actress had a good sense of humor about the incident but she did come and see us to insist upon a driver and a rented car for the rest of the show. We were happy to oblige.

Eric Miller, Transportation Coordinator

I was working on a show and we were filming in the flats of Los Angeles. For logistical reasons the next day of filming required a company move to the very top of Griffith Park. Because we had been working until late at night, I explained to the Producer that it was probably not in our best interest to attempt the company move until the light of the next morning. Griffith Park can be hazardous at night because when you're moving big trucks like that you don't have a lot of visibility. It's very dark up there and there are clearance issues because of the overhanging trees. Unfortunately, the Producer insisted it had to happen that night. We got into a huge argument about it but in the end I had no choice and had to obey his orders. As expected, the move was a complete nightmare and took four to five hours more than it should have. At this point it's sometime in the wee hours of the night and we pack it in and go home and get some sleep knowing we have to be back there before call (which is only a few hours away).

When I arrived on set in the morning it was only me and the Producer there and when we looked at the line of trucks, I swear to God, it looked like a war zone. Every truck and trailer, front and back and on both sides, had been scraped and scratched and many had flat or punctured tires. As a Transportation Coordinator you pride yourself on returning vehicles in the best condition possible. There was literally twenty years worth of damage done to these trucks in one night. I looked over at the Producer and he turned to me and said, *"Don't F-ing say it!"* and walked off. Needless to say, the damage bill was pretty massive.

Anonymous Transportation Coordinator

ON SET
"CHAIN OF COMMAND"
FLOWCHART

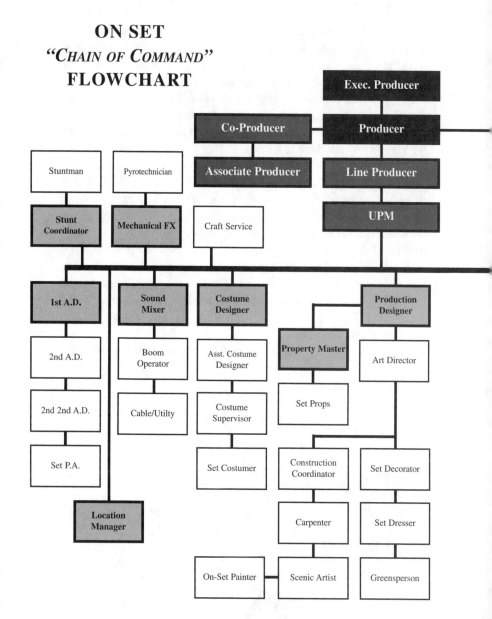

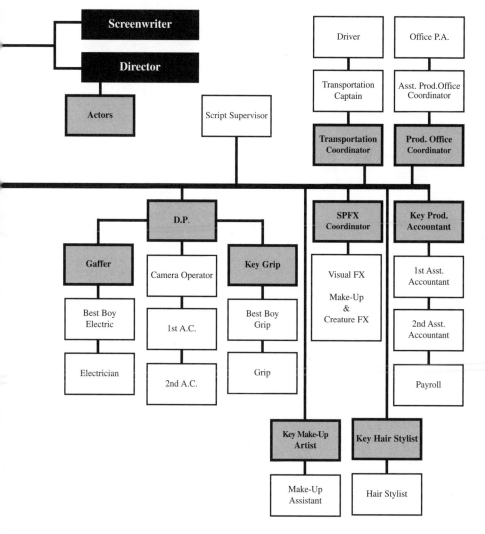

Screenwriter

Director

Actors

Script Supervisor

Driver

Office P.A.

Transportation Captain

Asst. Prod.Office Coordinator

Transportation Coordinator

Prod. Office Coordinator

D.P.

Gaffer

Camera Operator

Key Grip

SPFX Coordinator

Key Prod. Accountant

Best Boy Electric

1st A.C.

Best Boy Grip

Visual FX

Make-Up & Creature FX

1st Asst. Accountant

Electrician

2nd A.C.

Grip

2nd Asst. Accountant

Payroll

Key Make-Up Artist

Key Hair Stylist

Make-Up Assistant

Hair Stylist

** This FLOWCHART represents the basic managerial (not creative) aspect of a film set and it should be noted that many sets vary in regards to this layout.

A

Abby Singer   18
accessories   180
Acting Coach   54
"Action"   18
Actor/Actress   53
actual sound   106
ADR   106
Agent   54
aging   180, 222
ambient light   126
ambient sound   106
ammeter   126
Animal Trainer   219
Animal Wrangler   219
Animatronics   246
apple box   144
arc lamp   126
Armorer   221
Art Director   199
Assistant   54
Asst. Costume Designer   179
Asst. Prod. Office Coordinator   219
Atmosphere   53
audition   54

B

baby   126
baby wipes   180
back end   54
baffle   144
(two / three) banger   268
barn doors   126
"Barney"   82
Base Camp   268
Best Boy Electric   125
Best Boy Grip   143
bible   180
blank round   222

blue/green screen   246
Body Double   53
body   82
Body Make-Up Artist   161
body mike   106
boom   106
Boom Operator   105
bounce card   144
breakaway   222
broad   126
brute   126

C

Cable / Utility   105
call back   54
call sheet   18
"Camera reloads"   18
Camera Operator   81
cape   162
Carpenters   199
Casting Director   53
Caterer   267
C47   144
CGI   246
"Check the gate"   82
cherry picker   82
circled takes   18
"Clear & safe"   222
cleared item   222
clunker box   246
commissary   268
composite shot   246
comtech   106
Construction Coordinator   199
continuity   18
continuity sheet   180
cookie   144
Costume Designer   179
costume house   180
Costume Supervisor   179

ABOUT THE AUTHOR

Raised on a healthy diet of science fiction and horror from the age of five, **Paul J. Salamoff** has been working in the Entertainment Industry for over 22 years and has worked in Film, TV and Commercials as a Writer, Producer, Executive, Comic Creator and originally as a Make-Up FX Artist.

He is also the Co-Author (with Chris Gore) of THE COMPLETE DVD BOOK and the writer of the acclaimed graphic novels DISCORD, TALES OF DISCORD: THE COMPLETE SERIES, LOGAN'S RUN: LAST DAY and LOGAN'S RUN: AFTERMATH.

Paul currently lives in Burbank, California with his wife Melissa, daughter Samantha, son Ethan, cat Banshee and a Dalek.